ACCOUNTANCY

First edition 1990
Third edition January 1993

ISBN 0 7517 1997 8 (previous edition 0 86277 573 6)

British Library Cataloguing-in-Publication Data

A catalogue record for this book is
available from the British Library

Published by

BPP Publishing Limited
Aldine House, Aldine Place
London W12 8AW

**Printed in England by
DACOSTA PRINT
35/37 Queensland Road
London N7 7AH
(071) 700 1000**

We are grateful to the Chartered Institute of Bankers, the Association of Accounting Technicians and the Chartered Association of Certified Accountants for permission to reproduce past examination questions. The suggested solutions have been prepared by BPP Publishing Limited.

BPP Publishing Limited

©

1993

CONTENTS

	Page
Preface	1
Syllabus	2
The examination paper	4
Study notes	8
Updating notes	22
Test your knowledge: questions	23
Test your knowledge: answers	26
Table of discount factors	29
Practice and revision checklist	30
Index to questions and suggested solutions	31
Questions	37
Suggested solutions	93
Test paper: October 1992 examination	187
Test paper: October 1992 examination suggested solutions	197
Further reading	215

PREFACE

The examinations of the Chartered Institute of Bankers are a demanding test of students' ability to master the wide range of knowledge and skills required of the modern professional. The Institute's rapid response to the pace of change is shown both in the content of the syllabuses and in the style of examination questions set.

BPP Practice & Revision Kits are designed to supplement BPP's Study Texts with study material for practice and revision tailored to accommodate any recent changes in the style and format of the examination.

The 1993 edition of the CIB Accountancy Kit includes the following features.

(a) The syllabus
(b) An analysis of recent examination papers, plus summaries of examiners' comments on the exams
(c) Study notes to jog your memory of each area of the syllabus
(d) A test your knowledge quiz
(e) A checklist for you to plan your study and keep tabs on your progress
(f) A question bank divided into topic areas containing:

   (i) a total of 19 tutorial questions to warm you up on key techniques before starting the examination standard questions;

   (ii) a total of 32 examination standard questions, most of which come from past examinations, including all examination questions set in the five examinations up to and including May 1992

(g) A full test paper consisting of the October 1992 examination

All questions are provided with full suggested solutions plus tutorial notes prepared by BPP. The tutorial notes to past examination questions contain detailed summaries of the examiner's comments where relevant.

If you attempt all the examination standard questions in the Kit, together with the test paper, you will have written answers equivalent to 9 examinations. So if you write good answers to all of them, you should be well prepared for anything you meet in the examination itself. Good luck!

BPP Publishing
January 1993

If you want more practice on objective questions, an order form for the relevant Text in BPP's Password series of objective test question books can be found on page 215. Should you wish to send in your comments on this Kit, please turn to page 216.

SYLLABUS

Students will benefit from studying this subject before attempting: Branch banking - lending and marketing; Banking operations - regulation, market practice and treasury management; Multinational corporate banking, finance and investment.

Aim

To provide an appreciation of the uses and limitations of accounting information as a basis for understanding the financial affairs of bank customers.

To meet this aim, the question paper will be designed to test the ability of students both to prepare and interpret accounting data. Particular emphasis is given to the nature, scope and limitations of management accounting information and the interpretation of accounts as identified in syllabus entries (a) and (f)-(h).

Question paper

The paper is divided into three sections.

Section A contains a compulsory 30 mark question on the interpretation of accounts.
Section B contains two 30 mark questions of which *one* is to be attempted.
Section C contains three 20 mark questions of which *two* are to be attempted.

In the examination, candidates will be allowed 15 minutes reading time before the start of the three hour period. During the reading time candidates may mark the question paper but may not write in the answer book.

Candidates may use silent *non-programmable* calculators in this examination.

Syllabus

(a) The nature and interrelationships of balance sheets, profit statements and funds flow statements; distinctions between working capital flows, cash flows and profit flows.

(b) The accounting requirements contained in selected SSAPs (Numbers 1, 2, 6, 9, 12, 13, 14, 17, 18, 22 and 23), FRS 1 *Cash flow statements* and in the Companies Acts 1985-89 (Note 1). The calculation of distributable profits.

(c) The preparation of group accounts: main principles for consolidating subsidiary and associated companies. Students will be expected to be able to make the main consolidation adjustments under the acquisition and merger methods, namely distributable profits, minority interest, goodwill (acquisition method only) and merger reserve (merger method only). (Notes 2 and 3)

(d) The nature and limitations of standard and conventional accounting procedures, including certain basic features of current cost accounting. (Note 4)

(e) Capital reduction, reorganisation and reconstruction, and the ranking of claims on liquidation (Note 5). Share and business valuations on the liquidation basis and on the basis of the 'going concern'; historical cost; replacement cost; dividend yield; earnings yield; price/earnings ratio; cash flows. Majority and minority interests.

SYLLABUS

(f) Business performance assessment; accounting ratios and rates of return; the statement of funds. Analysis of capital structure; long-term financing; overtrading; the risk implications of gearing; working capital requirements.

(g) Costs and 'internal' accounting information for resource allocation decisions: cash budgets and other forecasts; the impact of corporation tax and value added tax on accounting statements; the cash operating cycle; fixed and variable costs; marginal and sunk costs; break-even analysis; limiting factors.

(h) The appraisal of simple capital projects using payback, accounting rate of return and discounted cash flow. Cost of capital in 'money' and 'real' terms. (Tax implications ignored). (Note 3)

Notes

1. Emphasis will be on the calculation of figures for inclusion in the accounts rather than methods of presentation. Questions requiring the use of specimen formats will not be asked, but candidates will be expected to present their answers in good form. Students will be expected to be familiar with the nature of value added tax, advanced corporation tax, mainstream corporation tax and deferred taxation, but will not be expected to possess a detailed knowledge of the provisions of SSAP 5, SSAP 8 and SSAP 15.

2. Students will be expected to be familiar with, but not to make calculations which take account of, such matters as inter-company loans, transfers of goods, unrealised profit, and dividends paid out of pre-acquisition profits. (Students must be able to compute the balance of profit for inclusion in the balance sheet but will not be asked to prepare a consolidated profit and loss account or to present the consolidated balance sheet in a form suitable for publication, though they may choose to do so.) Questions involving sub-subsidiary companies will not be asked.

3. Questions on these syllabus areas will be confined to Section C of the question paper.

4. Questions on current cost accounting will be confined to Section C of the examination paper and will deal with the main principles. Students will be expected to be able to make adjustments in the profit and loss account to reflect the increased cost of replacing tangible assets (stock and fixed assets) and carry these adjustments through to the balance sheet. A knowledge of the arguments for and against introducing a system of current cost accounting is also required, as is an appreciation of the limitations of historical cost based accounting statements as the basis for business decisions during a period of rising prices.

5. Questions on capital reduction will not deal with the complications which arise when shares redeemed or purchased were initially issued at a premium

THE EXAMINATION PAPER

Paper format

The paper is divided into three sections.

Section A contains a compulsory 30 mark question on the interpretation of accounts.
Section B contains two 30 mark questions of which *one* is to be attempted.
Section C contains three 20 mark questions of which *two* are to be attempted.

In the examination, candidates will be allowed 15 minutes reading time before the start of the three hour period. During the reading time candidates may mark the question paper but may not write in the answer book. Candidates may use silent non-programmable calculaters in this examination.

The pass mark for the exam is 51%. In marking, the examiner takes into account handwriting and spelling, as well as the content and general style of the answers.

Analysis of past papers

A brief analysis of the topics covered in the specimen paper and recent papers is given below. All the questions in the specimen paper for the new syllabus were set under the old syllabus and were not amended for inclusion in the specimen paper.

New syllabus

Autumn 1992

Section A
1   Interpretation of accounts

Section B
2   Compare rescue scheme with liquidation
3   Cash and profit forecast

Section C
4   Stock and work in progress
5   Breakeven analysis
6   Analysis of decline in cash balance

This paper forms the test paper at the end of the kit, so only an outline of its contents is given here.

		Question number in this Kit
Spring 1992		
Section A		
1	Funds flow and interpretation of accounts	41
Section B		
2	Alternative treatment of various items in accounts	18
3	Operating statement and breakeven analysis	46
Section C		
4	Consolidated balance sheet; merger method	22
5	Lease or buy decision plus finance	47
6	Redemption of shares	28

THE EXAMINATION PAPER

> *Examiner's comments*
>
> The standard of performance was higher than previous years, with a pass rate of 39%. The compulsory question was well answered. Question 2 was more popular than question 3, but the questions in Section C were equally popular.

	Question number in this Kit
Autumn 1991	
Section A	
1 Interpretation of accounts	36
Section B	
2 Final accounts; legal restrictions on distribution	16
3 Forecast cashflow, profit and ratios	52
Section C	
4 Contribution and limiting factors	45
5 NPV and DCF yield calculations	49
6 Share valuation	30

> *Examiner's comments*
>
> The general standard had improved, with a pass rate of 38%. In particular, presentation had improved and the examiner stressed the importance of presentation in reporting information. Irrelevant material was often included in the answers, which tends to waste time and therefore loses marks for the candidate.

Spring 1991	
Section A	
1 Interpretation of accounts	34
Section B	
2 Asset valuation, prepare balance sheet	15
3 Budgeted profit and loss account, effect on working capital	35
Section C	
4 Current cost accounts	24
5 Compare rescue scheme with liquidation for bank customer	27
6 Evaluate effect on profit, working capital and gearing of six courses of action	16

> *Examiner's comments*
>
> This was the first paper set under the new syllabus. The pass rate was 36%, much in line with the old syllabus pass rate. The examiner felt that candidates did not cope well with the new compulsory interpretation of accounts question and he particularly emphasised the importance of presenting information succinctly. In general, students tended to omit analysis and concentrate on calculations.

THE EXAMINATION PAPER

	Question number in this Kit
Specimen paper	
Section A	
1 Funds flow and ratio analysis	–
Section B	
2 Cash budget and forecast accounts	–
3 Redraft accounts in accordance with SSAPs	–
Section C	
4 Breakeven analysis	–
5 Investment appraisal: payback and DCF	–
6 Calculations of profit, goodwill and minority interest for consolidation	21

Note. The specimen paper re-used questions, most of which appear in other papers.

Old syllabus

Autumn 1990

1	Cash and profit forecast	51
2	Reconstruction of profit and loss account assuming different accounting policies; discuss effect of different permissible methods of asset valuation	14
3	Budgeted profit and breakeven analysis	44
4	Ratio analysis: return on equity and gearing	32
5	Ratio analysis: profitability, liquidity and gearing	33
6	Consolidated balance sheet using acquisition and merger methods	20

> *Examiner's comments*
>
> The pass rate for this paper was quite high (46%) with the best performance on questions 1 and 3. Question 6 was unpopular and answers were either excellent or poor. The examiner commented that students' basic accounting technique was often weak and that thorough revision and practice of this area should be undertaken throughout the year.

Spring 1990

1	Cash budget and profit forecast	50
2	Funds statement and comparison of ratios	39
3	Companies Act formats	*
4	Project appraisal: ARR and DCF	48
5	Long-term contract work in progress	13
6	Report on effects of four possible changes in manufacturing policy	43

* not on the current syllabus

THE EXAMINATION PAPER

> *Examiner's comments*
>
> Pass rate 30%. Students failed to answer the question asked or wasted time providing unnecessary information, such as additional ratios for question 2 or reasons for the revision of SSAP 9.

Autumn 1989

Question number in this Kit

1	Investment appraisal: ratio analysis and funds statement	-
2	Working capital funds statement and accounts preparation	-
3	Treatment of items in accordance with SSAPs	-
4	Share valuation under different methods	-
5	Cash budget and profit calculation	-
6	Breakeven analysis	-

> *Examiner's comments*
>
> Pass rate 34%. As in his Autumn 1990 report, the examiner commented on students' lack of basic accounting technique which was particularly apparent in answers to question 2. As in his Spring 1991 report, he also stressed the need to *plan* answers to interpretation of accounts questions, particularly considering how to present solutions clearly and logically. Question 4 was poorly answered, question 5 and question 6 much better answered.

Spring 1989

1	Cash forecast and reconciliation of cash to profit	40
2	Ratio analysis and forecast working capital	-
3	Redraft accounts in accordance with SSAPs	-
4	Scheme of reconstruction	26
5	Revised balance sheet under two financing schemes	-
6	Calculations of profit, goodwill and minority interest for consolidation	21

> *Examiner's comments*
>
> Pass rate 36%. The examiner stressed the importance of providing full workings and of proper allocation of time between questions. Question 2 was answered well on the whole. Question 5 was well tackled by students who had taken the trouble to read a Signpost article on off balance sheet finance in October 1988's *Banking World*.

STUDY NOTES

Introduction

In your work for the Accountancy paper there are a number of points you should bear in mind.

(a) Study each topic carefully before attempting the related questions. Answering questions is a test of what you have learnt and also a means of practising so that you develop skill in presenting your answers. To attempt them before you are ready is not a fair test of your proficiency and the result may discourage you.

(b) In some areas, such as cash budgets, business valuations, discounted cash flow, group accounts and published accounts, it is useful to consolidate your knowledge by attempting a perfect solution to one question. Take as much time as you need and in the last resort refer to your study text. Then study the suggested solution carefully and be sure to identify any incompleteness or inaccuracy in your own attempt.

(c) Once you are confident of your grasp of a topic, attempt as many further questions as you have time for, this time under examination conditions. Unless time is very short, write full-length answers rather than notes or an outline. Avoid the temptation to skimp on the discussion part of questions. The examiner is testing your ability to take practical banking decisions; he is looking less for mechanical facility in computation than for evidence of sound reasoning based on a thorough grasp of principles.

(d) It is a common failing to rush into writing an answer which you hope displays what you know. This is not sufficient unless it is also what the examiner has asked for. No credit is given for irrelevant material, however correct it may be. You are allowed fifteen minutes before the exam begins to read through the paper. Use the time well to ensure you are quite clear about what the questions require. In particular study the discussion or interpretative part of each question and decide how to lay out the computations so that the figures you will require for comment are clearly derived.

The questions in this kit are designed to provide a wide coverage of the syllabus. By working through the questions, you should therefore be going over all the topics you ought to learn, and assessing your ability to answer examination-style questions well.

A few notes on specific syllabus areas are given below, to help you to see the wood from the trees if your studies so far have left you overwhelmed by the wide range of the syllabus.

How to use this Kit

To use this Kit properly, you should prepare your own answers to questions first, and then compare them with ours. Look to see how many points of similarity and difference there are between them.

Most of our solutions are lengthy, and deliberately so. Given the time pressures in an examination, there is a limit to the amount that candidates can write. However, we take the view that if you are using the kit as a study aid, we would be doing you a disservice by giving you the bare minimum of a solution. You will find, therefore, that our answers go into detail that you might find useful for study or revision: after all, an examination question that you eventually face might tackle the same topic from a slightly different angle, and so you need to learn the topic well.

(a) If you have omitted some points that we include, think about how significant your omissions are, and make a note of the points you ignored for future reference.

STUDY NOTES

(b) If your solution includes points that we omit, think about whether your own answer is fully relevant to the question. (A tutorial note might make a comment on points that would be irrelevant.)

(c) If the question calls for a numerical solution, the workings that we provide should be sufficient to establish where your solution differs. (There may be an error, or a difference in the assumptions used.)

Questions that call for a written answer are difficult to revise with, because it is human nature to be easily bored by writing out lengthy solutions. This is what we would suggest as a possible remedy for this problem.

(a) You should attempt a full written solution to one or two questions, in order to gain experience and familiarity with the task of producing solutions within the timescale allowed in the examination itself.

(b) For other questions you should prepare an *answer plan*. This is a list of the points that you would put into your solution, preferably in the order that you would make them. The Institute encourages answer plans to be prepared in the examination itself, because it helps the examiner to gauge the ability (and intentions) of a candidate.

(c) You should then read our solution; and

   (i) make a note of points that are new to you and that you think you should learn (for example by underlining certain sentences in the solution for future reference);

   (ii) *prepare an answer plan from our own solution*, to make sure that you understand the relevance to the question of the points we raise. This useful discipline will ensure that you absorb the points in our solution more thoroughly. (We deliberately exclude answer plans to give you the chance to do this.)

Use the Practice and Revision checklist in the kit to record your progress and to ensure that you have covered all areas.

Your own solutions in the examination

Your own solutions to questions in the examination should take heed of the advice given by the Institute.

(a) Prepare an answer plan.

(b) Be concise (remember, our own solutions are deliberately lengthy, in order to provide suitable study material).

(c) Use tabulation where appropriate: present your answer as a series of points. This saves time, and helps to provide a well-structured answer.

(d) Show all workings for numerical calculations.

The main causes of examination failure

The Institute also explains the main reasons why candidates fail an examination. These are as follows.

STUDY NOTES

(a) Failure to prepare, taking the forms of:

    (i) inadequate depth of knowledge;
    (ii) failure to keep up-to-date;
    (iii) misconceptions.

This can be countered by reading *Banking World*, especially the *Signpost* articles written by examiners. You are particularly referred to the March 1992, September 1991, January 1991, June 1990, October 1989 and February 1989 articles on (respectively) the treatment of fixed assets; the new syllabus; marginal costs, sunk costs and limiting factors; interpretation of accounts; breakeven analysis; and SSAP 9 and long-term contracts.

It is also extremely important to use a recent textbook as in this subject there are frequent significant changes in accounting regulations and standards. The new BPP *Accountancy* Study Text will be published in February/March 1993 and will be completely up to date.

(b) Failure to answer the question set.

    (i) Candidates waffle too much, perhaps because they have nothing better to write or cannot see the point of the question.

    (ii) Candidates fail to read the question properly. Make sure you answer every part of the question, and look for key words in a question that might help you to recognise what it is all about.

(c) Failure to complete the paper.

    (i) Candidates make inadequate use of time.

    (ii) Candidates indulge in 'question spotting', revising only a limited number of topics by guessing what might be in the paper. When the guesses turn out wrong, the question spotters find themselves unable to answer enough questions.

Examiner's reports

A few extracts from recent examiner's reports on the old syllabus paper illustrate similar reasons for examination failure.

> 'Accountancy is not a subject which lends itself to last minute cramming in the hope that the right questions will come up, and it is therefore important that students work steadily throughout the months available for study prior to the examination.'

> 'A matter drawn to my attention by a number of the assistant examiners, and something which was also clearly evident to me when marking scripts, was the lack of knowledge displayed by candidates of basic accounting techniques.... Clearly, candidates are 'forgetting' some of the techniques learned at an earlier stage in their studies.'

> '... the standard of analysis and discussion was disappointing. Answers were, in the main, long-winded, irrelevant and covered only a minority of the matters which needed consideration. Candidates must develop a precise analytical style which focuses on the crucial issues and excludes background discussion.'

> 'A further weakness was the failure to present information, particularly financial statements, in a clear and concise manner.'

STUDY NOTES

'Many of the students who fail this examination do so because of what might be broadly described as poor examination technique. In the recent examination a noticeable weakness was the absence of sufficient care taken when reading the questions.'

'... students expecting success ... must show themselves capable of displaying a reasonable level of competence over the full range of topics contained in the syllabus.'

The nature and use of accounting statements

This section of the kit contains questions designed to help you revise and improve your basic accounting skills and your knowledge of the classes and needs of users of accounting information. The questions are either much simpler than examination standard questions or approach a topic from an unusual perspective which should help you to get to grips with the underlying principles.

Regulatory requirements

Time and time again, the examiner reports that candidates give a poor showing in the examination when it comes to preparing a profit and loss account and/or balance sheet under the various rules which apply to these statements. Accounting standards represent the main problem. There is no denying that the content of standards is both dry and voluminous. But unfortunately there is no way around them - they simply have to be learned. Before sitting the examination you should be able to list the standards (by name and number) which are examinable according to the syllabus; make brief notes on the contents of each one; and, most important of all understand the problem which each addresses. If you do not understand the purpose of a standard, how can you possibly apply it to a particular set of figures presented to you in an examination question?

Here are some brief notes on the SSAPs and FRSs whose accounting requirements are examinable.

1   SSAP 2 *Disclosure of accounting policies*

    (a)   This requires companies to disclose their accounting policies in the notes to the financial statements. This ensures *comparability* and *consistency* between companies and accounting periods.

    (b)   *Accounting policies* (for example use of FIFO rather than average cost for stock valuation) are chosen from acceptable *accounting bases*.

    (c)   Accounts must be prepared in accordance with four *fundamental accounting concepts:*

        (i)   going concern;
        (ii)   consistency;
        (iii) prudence;
        (iv) accruals.

       Where the prudence and accruals concept clash, prudence should prevail.

Questions to try: 1 to 9 Tutorial questions; 10 Shepparton.

STUDY NOTES

2 SSAP 6 *Extraordinary items and prior year adjustments*

(a) This standard defines *extraordinary items* and *exceptional items*. It requires that exceptional items should be included in profit or loss on ordinary activities for the year (but separately disclosed in the notes) whereas extraordinary items are shown after profit or loss on ordinary activities and before dividends. The practical importance of this distinction is that earnings per share (EPS), an important investors' ratio, is calculated on ordinary activities and so an extraordinary loss does not reduce EPS but an exceptional loss does (and *vice versa* for extraordinary and exceptional profits).

(b) *Prior year adjustments* as defined by SSAP 6 arise from fundamental errors or charges in accounting policy and are used to restate profits or losses brought forward rather than to reduce or increase profit for the year. The aim of SSAP 6 here is to minimise *reserve accounting* and to ensure that all *realised* profits and losses are reflected in the result for the year as far as possible.

(c) SSAP 6 has now been superseded by FRS 3 *Reporting financial performance*. Although this change has not yet been reflected in your syllabus, you should be aware of the main implications of the new standard.

FRS 3 applies to all company accounts with a year end on or after 22 June 1993. The definition of prior year adjustments has remained fundamentally the same. The definition of extraordinary items, however, has now been restricted to material items possessing a high degree of abnormality which arise from events or transactions that fall outside the ordinary activities of the reporting entity and which are not expected to recur. Exceptional items must not be aggregated under the heading of exceptional items on the face of the profit and loss account, but each should be included within its natural statutory format heading.

The main effect of the FRS 3 changes is that extraordinary items will now become extremely rare. Profits or losses associated with the sale or closure of a major part of the business, for example, will no longer be classed as extraordinary as such events are considered to fall within the normal course of business and they may recur. Where FRS 3 affects any of the questions in the Kit, a note has been made in our solution.

Question to try: 11 Tutorial question: Horngren.

3 SSAP 17 *Accounting for post balance sheet events*
   SSAP 18 *Accounting for contingencies*

These standards aim to ensure that transactions are allocated to the correct periods and that contingencies are accounted for prudently. You should know the definitions of adjusting and non-adjusting post balance sheet events and contingencies. These standards are straightforward and uncontroversial.

Question to try: 11 Tutorial question: Horngren.

4 SSAP 9 *Stocks and long-term contracts*

(a) This standard lays down rules on the valuation of stocks and the special case of long-term contracts. You should read the Chief Examiner's *Signpost* article on this subject in *Banking World* February 1989 as it is a good summary.

STUDY NOTES

(b) The key points to learn on SSAP 9 are:

  (i) the definitions of *cost* (including *costs of conversion*) and *net realisable value*;
  (ii) the mechanics of FIFO, LIFO and average cost valuation;
  (iii) the effect of stock valuation on profit;
  (iv) the method of calculating and disclosing attributable profit, turnover and cost of sales on long-term contracts and the related balance sheet entries.

Questions to try: 12 Tutorial question: Barents; 13 Barber.

5 SSAP 12 *Accounting for depreciation*

You should be able to calculate depreciation on historical cost and revalued amounts and also the profit or loss on disposal of fixed assets. You should know how to account for a surplus on revaluation (namely, to credit it to the revaluation reserve). You should also know which items SSAP 12 and the Companies Act 1985 require to be disclosed in the accounts. All these topics are frequently examined.

Question to try: 4 Tutorial question: Trend

6 SSAP 13 *Accounting for research and development*

(a) This standard lays down the criteria which must be met if *development costs* are to be capitalised (or deferred). You must know the definitions of research and development and its disclosure requirements as well as the criteria.

(b) Remember that *research costs* can never be capitalised but must always be written off.

Question to try: 14 Poynton.

7 *Accounting for tax in company accounts*

(a) A detailed knowledge of SSAPs 5, 8 and 15 is not required but an outline knowledge of the significance of tax balances is required, as is an ability to carry out simple calculations and to make the appropriate adjustments to published accounts for the corporation tax change, advance corporation tax and dividends.

(b) Remember that *deferred tax* is a *provision* for corporation tax which may become payable in the future on accounting profits not yet taxable under the laws on calculation of corporation tax. For example, if the government gives higher allowances on capital investment in plant than the accounts show as depreciation, the corporation tax charge on profits in the year when the allowance is claimed will be calculated on taxable profits which are lower than the accounting profits. Since the difference will eventually iron itself out and the total capital allowance will not exceed the cost written off in the accounts by depreciation, a deferred tax adjustment is made to increase or decrease the tax charge in the accounts as necessary to smooth out the *timing differences* and ensure that profits after tax are not unduly increased or decreased by differences in the timing of tax flows.

STUDY NOTES

8   SSAP 22 *Accounting for goodwill*

   (a) This SSAP defines goodwill as 'the difference between the value of a business as a whole and the aggregate fair values of its separable net assets'. It can be either *purchased* or *inherent* and may be *negative* (that is, a business might be worth less than the sum of its parts).

   (b) This SSAP is under review but currently it requires that positive purchased goodwill should either be capitalised and amortised over its estimated useful economic life or (the preferred option) it should be written off against (deducted from) reserves.

   (c) Negative goodwill (also known as a capital reserve arising on consolidation) should be credited (added) to reserves.

   (d) Goodwill usually arises when one company purchases another. It would not be shown separately on the parent company's balance sheet which simply shows the cost or valuation of the investment. However, in consolidated accounts this investment is eliminated against its underlying components, that is, the subsidiary's fixed assets, current assets and so on and the parent's share of its post-acquisition profits. In cancelling off the parent's investment against the net assets acquired, goodwill emerges as a balancing figure.

9   SSAP 1 *Accounting for associated companies*
    SSAP 14 *Group accounts*
    SSAP 23 *Accounting for acquisitions and mergers*

   (a) These have been under review because the Companies Act 1985 has been amended by the Companies Act 1989 and much of the legal terminology used in the rules of group accounts has changed. However, the underlying principles are unchanged.

   (i) An investment in under 20% of a company's shares, where the investing company has no *significant influence* over the other company, is a *trade investment* and is not consolidated or treated in any way differently from any other investment.

   (ii) A 20% + investment (or a smaller one where there *is* significant influence) is treated as an investment in an *associated company*. (A 20% + investment is presumed to give significant influence but if it can be shown that this does not exist then the investment is a trade investment).

   (iii) An investment in >50% of another company's shares usually results in control of that company, which makes it a *subsidiary*.

   (iv) Associated companies are not consolidated. The investment is shown in the balance sheet at cost plus the investing company's share of post-acquisition retained profit. This is analysed in the notes as follows.

	£'000
Group share of net assets	X
Premium paid on acquisition (= goodwill)	X
Value of investment under equity accounting	X

   Equity accounting is the name for this treatment.

   (v) Subsidiaries are consolidated. There are two ways of doing this, the *acquisition method* and the *merger method*.

STUDY NOTES

(vi) **The acquisition method is much more common as few business combinations qualify for the *option* of consolidation under the merger method.**

The only way to learn how to prepare consolidated accounts is repeated practice.

(b) You should note that SSAP 14 has now been superseded by FRS 2 *Subsidiary undertakings* for accounting periods ending on or after 23 December 1992. This is no real cause for concern as the FRS merely updates SSAP 14 for the changes introduced by the 1989 Act. A summary of these changes had previously been published in the ASB's *Interim statement on consolidated accounts*. The principles outlined above are therefore still in force.

Questions to try: 14 Poynton; 19 Tutorial question: Hakluyt; 21 Grimshaw; 22 Hagg.

Questions to try which cover a variety of accounting treatment areas: 15 Harden; 16 Rowland; 17 Ashmole; 18 Attercliffe.

Limitations of published accounts

An important, but difficult, point to grasp here is the concept of capital maintenance. The preparation of a balance sheet requires that values should be attributed to assets and liabilities outstanding at the end of an accounting period. The amount of an enterprise's net assets (or capital) will depend on the method adopted for calculating these values. Ignoring any capital injected or withdrawn during an accounting period, the profit earned for the period will be the difference between the value of capital at the beginning and the value of capital at the end of the period. Another way of stating this is to say that a company must maintain the value of its capital in order to break even; anything achieved in excess of this represents profit.

There are many systems of attributing values. In conventional historical cost accounting (HCA) assets are valued at historical cost less any amounts provided for or written off in respect of depreciation or diminution in value. A company maintains its capital if the net book value of its net assets remains constant, or increases (making an historical cost profit) over an accounting period.

In current cost accounting (CCA) assets are valued at their 'value to the business'. The underlying capital maintenance concept is that of maintaining the 'operating capability' of the business, ie its ability to provide the same amount of goods and services with its existing resources. CCA provides a measure of how well the business is maintaining its capital against the effects of *specific* inflation.

This important topic is now attracting increased attention in the accountancy profession as inflation rises.

Questions to try: 23 Tutorial question: Gnomes; 24 Price.

Capital reduction, reorganisation and reconstruction

These questions usually focus on companies in trouble which are either 'cleaning out' the balance sheet or are starting again with a new company. You must know the ranking of claims on liquidation and the rules on purchase and redemption of shares, as well as the techniques of preparing accounts after a reconstruction.

Questions to try: 25 Tutorial question: Purchase of own shares; 26 Harbour; 27 Clayton; 28 Duke.

STUDY NOTES

Share and business valuations

There is no substitute here for question practice and common sense. Pay particular attention to preparation for the written parts of such questions which usually ask you either to comment on the uses of each valuation basis; or to advise an investor on the most appropriate basis in his circumstances; or to do both.

Questions to try: 29 Tutorial question: Business valuation methods; 30 Falkus.

Interpretation of accounts

The examiners are concerned, not so much with the standard of *calculating* ratios, but with the standard of *interpreting* them. A question on ratio analysis will invariably ask for some discussion based on the ratios you have calculated, so it is essential for you to know what each one signifies. Remember that you have to tackle a compulsory 30 mark question on this area.

As a first step, think about which ratios are needed in order to answer the question. There is no point in doing more work than necessary, and the examiner will not be impressed by the calculation of irrelevant ratios. When you have picked out which ratios you need, calculate them and set them out in a table, where they can easily be referred to during the discussion part of the question.

Your examiner has provided a useful description of the approach to an interpretation of accounts question.

> 'Candidates should take care when planning their answer to this kind of question. Accountancy is a device for communicating information for decision making and it might help the candidate to see himself/herself in the position of the supplier of the report and the examiner as the recipient who is seeking advice. In other words, it is the job of the candidate to produce a convincing and comprehensible report. If this objective is to be achieved, it will help a great deal to divide the report into appropriate sections and to set out relevant calculations in an appendix to the report. The appropriate sections will depend on the nature of the investigation, but the following provide a reasonable framework:
>
> - Identify recipient of report
> - Introduction
> - Financial developments
> - Liquidity and gearing
> - Asset turnover
> - Profitability
> - Conclusion
>
> Within each of these sections comments should be made about the significance of the information contained in the statement of funds (if any) and an examination of the company's ratios compared with [the norm].'

The *main* ratios to remember (the list below is not exhaustive) are as follows.

1 *Profitability ratios*

   Profit on ordinary activities *before* taxation is generally thought to be a better figure to use than profit after taxation, because there might be unusual variations in the tax charge from year to year which would not affect the underlying profitability of the company's operations.

STUDY NOTES

Another profit figure that should be calculated is PBIT (profit before interest and tax):

(a) the profit on ordinary activities before taxation; *plus*
(b) interest charges on long term loan capital.

It is impossible to assess profits or profit growth properly without relating them to the amount of funds (capital) that were employed in making the profits. The most important profitability ratio is therefore *return on capital employed* (ROCE), which states the profit as a percentage of the amount of capital employed.

$$\text{ROCE} = \frac{\text{Profit on ordinary activities before interest and taxation (PBIT)}}{\text{Capital employed}}$$

Capital employed = Shareholders' funds plus 'creditors: amounts falling due after more than one year' plus any long term provisions for liabilities and charges

A common variant is *return on equity* which measures profit after interest (and usually after tax) as a percentage of ordinary share capital and reserves.

Profit margin and asset turnover together explain the ROCE, and if the ROCE is the primary profitability ratio, these other two are the secondary ratios. The relationship between the three ratios can be shown mathematically.

Profit margin × Asset turnover = ROCE; or

$$\frac{\text{PBIT}}{\text{Sales}} \times \frac{\text{Sales}}{\text{Capital employed}} = \frac{\text{PBIT}}{\text{Capital employed}}$$

It might be tempting to think that a high profit margin is good, and a low asset turnover means sluggish trading. In broad terms, this is so. But there is a trade-off between profit margin and asset turnover, and you cannot look at one without allowing for the other.

(a) A high profit margin means a high profit per £1 of sales, but if this also means that sales prices are high, there is a strong possibility that sales turnover will be depressed, and so asset turnover lower.

(b) A high asset turnover means that the company is generating a lot of sales, but to do this, it might have to keep its prices down and so accept a low profit margin per £1 of sales.

2 *Debt and gearing ratios*

Debt ratios are concerned with how much the company owes in relation to its size, whether it is getting into heavier debt or improving its situation, and whether its debt burden seems heavy or light. When a company is earning only a modest profit before interest and tax, and has a heavy debt burden, there will be very little profit left over for shareholders after the interest charges have been paid. And so if interest rates were to go up (on bank overdrafts and so on) or the company were to borrow even more, it might soon be incurring interest charges in excess of PBIT. This might eventually lead to the liquidation of the company.

The *debt ratio* is the ratio of a company's total debts to its total assets.

(a) Assets consist of fixed assets at their balance sheet value, plus current assets.

STUDY NOTES

(b) Debts consist of all creditors, whether amounts falling due within one year or after more than one year. You can ignore long-term provisions and liabilities, such as deferred taxation. There is also a view that a bank overdraft, although shown as a current liability in the balance sheet, is often a permanent feature of a company's debt structure and so is as good as long term debt. If this view is taken, the bank overdraft should also be included as debt together with any other short-term loans which are likely to be replaced when they mature with a new longer-term loan.

There is no absolute guide to the maximum safe debt ratio, but as a very general guide, you might regard 50% as a safe limit to debt. In practice, many companies operate successfully with a higher debt ratio than this, but 50% is nonetheless a helpful benchmark. Many companies *are* high geared, but if a high geared company is becoming increasingly higher geared, it is likely to have difficulty in the future when it wants to borrow even more, unless it can also boost its shareholders' capital, either with retained profits or a new share issue.

A similar ratio to the gearing ratio is the *debt/equity ratio*, which is the ratio of:

$$\frac{\text{long-term debt}}{\text{ordinary share capital and reserves}}$$

This gives us the same sort of information as the gearing ratio, and a ratio of 100% or more would indicate high gearing.

The significance of the gearing ratios is that:

(a) the more highly geared the company, the greater the risk that little (if anything) will be available to distribute by way of dividend to the ordinary shareholders; and

(b) a high geared company has a large amount of interest to pay annually (assuming that the debt is external borrowing rather than preference shares). If those borrowings are 'secured' in any way (and debentures in particular are secured), then the holders of the debt are perfectly entitled to force the company to realise assets to pay their interest if funds are not available from other sources. Clearly, the more highly geared a company the more likely this is to occur when and if profits fall.

3 *Working capital liquidity ratios*

The 'standard' test of liquidity is the *current ratio*. It can be obtained from the balance sheet, and is the ratio of:

$$\frac{\text{current assets}}{\text{current liabilities}}$$

In practice, a ratio comfortably in excess of 1 should be expected, but what is 'comfortable' varies between different types of businesses.

Companies are not able to convert all their current assets into cash very quickly. In particular, some manufacturing companies might hold large quantities of raw material stocks, which must be used in production to create finished goods stocks. Finished goods stocks might be warehoused for a long time, or sold on lengthy credit. In such businesses, where stock turnover is slow, most stocks are not very 'liquid' assets, because the cash cycle is so long. For these reasons, we calculate an additional liquidity ratio, known as the quick ratio or acid test ratio.

The *quick ratio*, or *acid test ratio*, is $\dfrac{\text{current assets less stocks}}{\text{current liabilities}}$

STUDY NOTES

This ratio should ideally be at least 1 for companies with a slow stock turnover. For companies with a fast stock turnover, a quick ratio can be comfortably less than 1 without suggesting that the company should be in cash flow trouble.

Both the current ratio and the quick ratio offer an indication of the company's liquidity position, but the absolute figures should not be interpreted too literally. What is important is the trend of these ratios. From this, one can easily ascertain whether liquidity is improving or deteriorating.

Don't forget the other side of the coin either. A current ratio and a quick ratio can get bigger than they need to be. A company that has large volumes of stocks and debtors might be over-investing in working capital, and so tying up more funds in the business than it needs to. This would suggest poor management of debtors (credit) or stocks by the company.

4   *Working capital turnover ratios*

A rough measure of the average length of time it takes for a company's debtors to pay what they owe is the *'debtor days' ratio*, or average debtors' payment period:

$$\frac{\text{trade debtors}}{\text{sales}} \times 365 \text{ days}$$

The *trend* of the collection period (debtor days) over time is probably the best guide. If debtor days are increasing year on year, this is indicative of a poorly managed credit control function (and potentially therefore a poorly managed company!)

The number of stock days is calculated as: $\dfrac{\text{stock}}{\text{cost of sales}} \times 365$

The reciprocal of the fraction, $\dfrac{\text{cost of sales}}{\text{stock}}$

is termed the stock turnover, and is another measure of how vigorously a business is trading. A lengthening stock turnover period from one year to the next indicates:

(a) a slowdown in trading; or
(b) a build-up in stock levels, perhaps suggesting that the investment in stocks is becoming excessive.

Questions to try: 31 Tutorial question: Ritt; 32 to 36.

FRS 1 Cash flow statements (and funds flow statements)

In September 1991 the Accounting Standards Board (ASB) published FRS 1 *Cash flow statements*. The provisions of FRS 1 apply to accounting periods ending on or after 23 March 1992. It supersedes SSAP 10 *Statements of source and application of funds*. The FRS sets out the structure of a cash flow statement and it also sets the minimum level of disclosure.

The most obvious change from SSAP 10 is that the FRS requires reporting entities to report cash flows rather than accrual based funds flows and the basic structure of the cash flow statement is prescribed. In addition, SSAP 10 allowed exemption from preparing a funds statement only to those entities with turnover or gross income of less than £25,000. The small company exemption is far more generous in the FRS, leading to a much higher proportion of exemptions.

STUDY NOTES

The publication of FRS 1 has been welcomed because many analysts believe that the funds flow statement does not provide any information additional to that given in the rest of the accounts but merely shows the link between the balance sheet and the P & L account. 'Funds' has never been satisfactorily defined and so many different formats for the funds flow statement have been used. The cash flow statement, on the other hand, provides new information and its purpose is easier to understand. It is much more difficult to hide a company's liquidity problems when a cash flow statement is published because the format highlights the recurring cash flow which can be expected from routine operations and then shows to what extent investments have been funded from trading surpluses or from new finance. Especially in a recession, a company whose cash resources are declining is much more at risk of insolvency, even when profits are increasing or simply holding steady, than a company with good cash management.

Questions on funds statements are still relevant and make useful comparisons with cash flow statements. Also, although SSAP 10 has been removed from the syllabus, funds flow is still examinable.

Questions to try: 37 Tutorial question: Cash flow statements; 39 Notley; 40 Whaley.

Business decision making

There are two types of question in this category, both frequently examined. These are:

(a) breakeven analysis (short run decision making);
(b) investment appraisal (long run decision making).

(a) *Breakeven analysis*

You must know the techniques of calculating:

(i) breakeven sales;
(ii) the margin of safety;
(iii) level of sales to achieve a target profit;
(iv) maximum contribution per unit of limiting factor.

The only way to attain fluency here is question practice.

Questions to try: 41 Tutorial question: George; 42 to 46.

(b) *Investment appraisal*

Here you must master:

(i) accounting rate of return;
(ii) payback;
(iii) DCF, including both internal rate of return and net present value methods.

It's not just technique that's important here. You must know the pros and cons of each method.

Questions to try: 47 Landore; 48 Bucknall.

STUDY NOTES

Forecasts and budgets

This is one area of the syllabus where it is essential to be able to distinguish cash flows from profit flows. You are usually given details of sales, purchases and other expenses, and capital expenditure or other non-revenue cash flows (for example, share issues), along with related timings. You then have to allocate each cash flow to the right month or, less commonly, quarter. The aim is to work out what the business's bank balance or overdraft will be at the end of each period, which is obviously of central importance to a lending banker in assessing whether an overdraft is adequately secured and whether a business can generate sufficient cash to meet interest and capital repayments on loans.

Layout is very important in such questions and the only way to master the techniques and presentation involved is to practise several questions. Such practice will pay dividends as a question of this type comes up on virtually every paper, almost invariably in conjunction with a requirement to prepare a profit forecast. Do not neglect the written parts of such questions!

Questions to try: 49 Kaplan; 50 Rowan; 51 Hobhouse.

UPDATING NOTES

This section outlines the most up to date changes affecting the Accountancy paper. You should be aware by now that the standard setting regime changed quite significantly in 1990, creating a new Accounting Standards Board (ASB) to replace the old Accounting Standards Committee (ASC). The ASB will produce Financial Reporting Standards (FRSs) which will gradually replace the SSAPs.

1   FRS 1 *Cash flow statements*

   This FRS is on your syllabus, and so you should know the formats and disclosure requirements (which replace the provisions of SSAP 10 *Statements of source and application of funds*). The FRS applies to accounting periods ending on or after 23 March 1992 (see Study Notes for further details).

2   FRS 2 *Subsidiary undertakings*

   This FRS replaces SSAP 14 *Group accounts* and those parts of the ASB's *Interim statement on consolidated accounts* which relates to subsidiaries. It does not introduce any new rules, but merely consolidates those rules introduced by the Companies Act 1989 which are already in current use.

3   FRS 3 *Reporting financial performance*

   This FRS is far more wide ranging than the previous two. It institutes an extended format to the profit and loss account and a variety of new compulsory notes to the accounts. It replaces SSAP 6 and it amends a variety of other accounting standards (which are not on your syllabus). FRS 3 is not yet on the syllabus for this paper (see Study Notes for the effect on SSAP 6).

All these standards are covered in detail in the new BPP *Accountancy* Study Text, published February/March 1993.

TEST YOUR KNOWLEDGE: QUESTIONS

1 List seven categories of users of accounts.

2 What is the basic valuation rule for stocks and work in progress?

3 What is franked investment income?

4 Name four components of the year's taxation charge you would expect to find disclosed in a note to the profit and loss account.

5 In what circumstances may research costs be shown as an asset in a company's balance sheet?

6 What is segmental reporting?

7 Explain the general rule restricting the amount which a private company may distribute by way of dividend (s 263 CA 1985).

8 Distinguish between an accounting basis and an accounting policy.

9 What is an extraordinary item?

10 How are exceptional items disclosed in a company's profit and loss account?

11 Describe the accounting treatment of unrealised stock profits in preparing a consolidated balance sheet.

12 What accounting treatment does SSAP 22 prescribe in respect of goodwill arising on consolidation?

13 What is an associated company?

14 Define the additional depreciation adjustment in the context of current cost accounts.

15 Give the formulae for:

(a) debtors' collection period; and
(b) finished goods turnover period.

16 Give the formula for breakeven volume of sales.

17 Where would the following items appear in a statement of source and application of funds:

(a) profit on disposal of fixed assets?
(b) premium received on a new issue of shares?
(c) profit and loss charge for taxation?

18 Arrange the following liabilities according to their order of priority in a liquidation.

    Preferential creditors
    Secured creditors with a fixed charge
    Secured creditors with a floating charge
    Liquidation expenses

19 A company has regular annual equity earnings of £100,000. There are 500,000 50p ordinary shares in issue. Similar companies have price earnings ratios of 5. What value would you place on the company's shares using the price/earnings ratio as your valuation basis?

TEST YOUR KNOWLEDGE: QUESTIONS

20 Name three methods of evaluating a capital investment project.

Multiple choice questions

Ring the correct answer from the four options given.

21 In a statement of source and application of funds, which one of the items shown below might appear as an application of funds?

    A   Loss on disposal of fixed assets
    B   Decrease in bank overdraft
    C   Provision for doubtful debts
    D   Payment of dividends

22 What is the purpose of charging depreciation in accounts?

    A   To comply with the prudence concept
    B   To adjust book values to market values
    C   To allocate the cost of fixed assets to the periods expected to benefit from their use
    D   To set aside funds for replacement of assets

23 Which of the following is the odd one out?

    A   Scrip issue
    B   Rights issue
    C   Capitalisation issue
    D   Bonus issue

24 Consider the following group structure.

        X Ltd
        | 80%
        Y Ltd
        | 60%
        Z Ltd

What proportion of Z Ltd will be treated in X Ltd's accounts as a minority interest?

    A   Nil
    B   20%
    C   40%
    D   52%

25 A plc has two equity investments. It holds 20% of the ordinary share capital of B Ltd but has no voting rights; and it holds 18% of C Ltd's ordinary shares but controls its board of directors. Are B Ltd and C Ltd associated companies of A plc under SSAP 1?

	B Ltd	*C Ltd*
A	Yes	No
B	Yes	Yes
C	No	Yes
D	No	No

TEST YOUR KNOWLEDGE: QUESTIONS

26 Brown Ltd manufactures the Green. Raw materials per Green cost £9. Labour input is £2.50 and distribution costs are £3.50. Production overhead attributable to each unit is £6.

What is the 'cost' for stock valuation purposes of each Green, under SSAP 9?

    A   £17.50
    B   £15.00
    C   £11.50
    D   £9.00

27 In 19X9, Yellow plc received UK dividends of £15,000 (net) and proposed a dividend of £7,500. Assuming an ACT rate of ⅓, what should be shown in its financial statements in respect of these items?

	Investment income £	Dividends payable £
A	15,000	7,500
B	20,000	7,500
C	15,000	10,000
D	20,000	10,000

28 Holly Ltd's draft accounts show turnover of £1 million and cost of sales of £600,000. The final adjustments to the accounts are to write off a bad debt of £10,000 and to decrease the closing stock valuation by £50,000. What is Holly Ltd's gross profit margin for the year, based on the final accounts?

    A   34%
    B   35%
    C   44%
    D   45%

29 If a company's share price increases, what happens to its P/E ratio and dividend yield?

	P/E ratio	Dividend yield
A	Rise	Rise
B	Rise	Fall
C	Fall	Rise
D	Fall	Fall

30 Is stock of finished goods included in the quick ratio (or acid test ratio) and the current ratio?

	Quick ratio	Current ratio
A	Yes	Yes
B	Yes	No
C	No	Yes
D	No	No

TEST YOUR KNOWLEDGE: ANSWERS

1. Managers; shareholders; trade contacts; providers of finance; Inland Revenue; employees; financial analysts.

2. Stocks and work in progress should be valued at the lower of cost and net realisable value.

3. Franked investment income is dividends received (plus the associated tax credit) by a UK company from its shareholding in another UK company.

4. The following components of the year's taxation charge are commonly disclosed by note:

   (a) the charge for UK corporation tax on profits for the year;
   (b) the transfer to or from the deferred taxation account;
   (c) tax attributable to dividends received;
   (d) any underprovision or overprovision of tax in the previous year;
   (e) unrelieved overseas taxation.

5. Neither SSAP 13 nor statute permits research costs to be shown as an asset in any circumstances. *Development* costs, however, may be shown as an asset in circumstances defined by SSAP 13, principally relating to the project's feasibility and commercial viability.

6. Segmental reporting involves analysing profit, turnover and net assets between operating divisions of a group or company and between geographical markets and locations of divisions. It gives users of accounts useful information enabling them to make comparisons of the risk of and return on each activity of a business enterprise. Both the Companies Act 1985 and SSAP 25 require some segmental reporting but the latter only applies to public and larger private companies.

7. A company may only pay a dividend out of its accumulated *realised* profits (less realised losses) so far as these have not already been paid out as dividends.

8. An accounting basis is one of the detailed methods available for applying an accounting concept. An accounting policy is an accounting basis selected and consistently applied by management as being most appropriate to the circumstances of the business. For example, the straight line method and reducing balance method are both possible *bases* on which depreciation may be accounted for. Whichever method management chooses becomes the accounting *policy* of the business.

9. SSAP 6 defines extraordinary items as 'material items which derive from events or transactions that fall outside the ordinary activities of the company and which are therefore expected not to recur frequently or regularly'. *Note.* A new definition has been introduced by FRS 3 (see Study Notes).

10. Exceptional items are charged in arriving at the 'profit or loss on ordinary activities before taxation'. They are usually disclosed by way of note. They are stated gross, and any related taxation is included in the tax charge for the year. *Note.* A new definition and treatment has been introduced by FRS 3 (see Study Notes).

11. Intra-group profits on goods remaining in group stocks at the balance sheet date are:

    (a) deducted from the value of group stocks; and
    (b) deducted from group reserves.

    Any proportion of such profits which is attributable to minority interests may optionally be deducted from minority interests rather than from group reserves.

TEST YOUR KNOWLEDGE: ANSWERS

12 SSAP 22 treats goodwill arising on consolidation in the same way as any other purchased goodwill. The normal accounting treatment is to eliminate goodwill immediately against reserves. Alternatively, purchased goodwill may be carried as an asset in the balance sheet; in this case, the balance must be amortised over the useful life of the goodwill.

13 SSAP 1 defines an associated company as one over which the investing company can exercise significant influence (for example by board representation or by holding equity shares in the associate. A holding of 20% or more of the ordinary shares will give rise to a presumption of associated company status). This definition is in line with the Companies Act 1985 definition of an associated undertaking which is included in its new regulations on consolidated accounts.

14 The additional depreciation adjustment is the difference between:

   (a) depreciation based on the historical cost of a fixed asset; and
   (b) depreciation based on the current cost of the asset.

15 (a) Debtors' collection period = $\dfrac{\text{Average debtors}}{\text{Annual sales}} \times 365$ days

   (b) Finished goods turnover period = $\dfrac{\text{Average finished goods stock}}{\text{Cost of goods sold in year}} \times 365$ days

16 Breakeven sales volume = $\dfrac{\text{Total fixed costs}}{\text{Unit contribution}}$

17 (a) As a deduction, under 'adjustments for items not involving the movement of funds'.
    (b) As a source of funds.
    (c) Nowhere, but the tax actually *paid* during the year would appear as an application of funds.

18 The order is:

   (a) secured creditors with a fixed charge;
   (b) liquidation expenses;
   (c) preferential creditors;
   (d) secured creditors with a floating charge.

19 Value of the company = £100,000 × 5
                         = £500,000

    ∴ Value of each share = $\dfrac{£500,000}{500,000}$
                          = £1

20 The return on investment (or accounting rate of return) method; the payback method; discounted cash flow.

Answers to multiple choice questions

21 D; B affects working capital and A and C are accounting adjustments only.

22 C; see SSAP 12.

TEST YOUR KNOWLEDGE: ANSWERS

23 B; all the others are synonyms for each other.

24 D; 80% × 60% = 48%, ∴ minority interest is 52% (40% direct + (20% × 60%)).

25 C; A has no 'significant influence' over B but although it owns less than 20% of C's equity it *does* have 'significant influence' over C's activities (see SSAP 1).

26 A; distribution costs cannot be included in stock valuations under SSAP 9 but attributable production overheads can.

27 B; dividends payable are declared and recorded net of ACT but dividends receivable are grossed up for disclosure purposes.

28 B; the bad debt write-off has no effect on the trading account but the stock writedown increases cost of sales. Gross profit is therefore £350,000, 35% of sales.

29 B; P/E ratio $= \dfrac{\text{market value per share}}{\text{earnings per share}}$

   Dividend yield $= \dfrac{\text{gross dividend per share}}{\text{market value per share}} \times 100\%$

30 C; the quick ratio excludes stock but the current ratio measures current assets as a proportion of current liabilities.

TABLE OF DISCOUNT FACTORS

TABLE OF DISCOUNT FACTORS FOR THE PRESENT VALUE OF £1

	Year 1	Year 2	Year 3	Year 4	Year 5
7%	0.935	0.873	0.816	0.763	0.713
8%	0.926	0.857	0.794	0.735	0.680
9%	0.917	0.842	0.773	0.709	0.651
10%	0.909	0.826	0.751	0.683	0.620
11%	0.900	0.812	0.731	0.659	0.594
12%	0.893	0.797	0.712	0.636	0.567
13%	0.885	0.783	0.693	0.613	0.543
14%	0.877	0.769	0.675	0.592	0.519
15%	0.870	0.756	0.658	0.572	0.497
16%	0.862	0.743	0.641	0.552	0.476
17%	0.855	0.731	0.624	0.534	0.456
18%	0.847	0.718	0.609	0.516	0.437
19%	0.840	0.706	0.593	0.499	0.419
20%	0.833	0.694	0.579	0.482	0.402
21%	0.826	0.683	0.564	0.467	0.386
22%	0.820	0.671	0.551	0.451	0.370

PRACTICE AND REVISION CHECKLIST

This page is designed to help you chart your progress through this Practice and Revision Kit and thus through the Institute's syllabus. By this stage you should have worked through the Study Text, including the illustrative questions at the back of it. You can now tick off each topic as you revise and try questions on it, either of the practice type or of the full examination type. Insert the question numbers and date you completed them in the relevant boxes. You will thus ensure that you are on track to complete your revision before the exam.

	Revision of Study Text chapter(s) Ch No/Date Comp	*Tutorial questions in Kit* Ques Nos/Date Comp	*Examination style questions* Ques No/Date Comp
The nature and use of accounting statements	1		
The form and content of company accounts	2		
The valuation of assets and liabilities	3		
Group accounts	4		
Limitations of published accounts	5		
Capital reduction, reorganisation and reconstruction	6		
Share and business valuation	7		
Interpretation of accounts: ratio analysis	8		
Interpretation of accounts: funds flow analysis	9		
Business decision making: short run	10		
Business decision making: long run	11		
Forecasts and budgets	12		

Test paper   Date completed

INDEX TO QUESTIONS AND SUGGESTED SOLUTIONS

As far as possible, questions have been listed under the appropriate headings from the syllabus. But some questions span more than one area of the syllabus: where this is the case, a question has been placed under the heading which is most relevant to its content. Questions in italics are *tutorial questions:* see Page 1 for an explanation of the function of such questions.

		Question	Suggested solution
The nature and use of accounting statements			
1	*Tutorial question: Walter Rogers*	37	93
2	*Tutorial question: Separate transactions*	37	93
3	*Tutorial question: Basic*	38	94
4	*Tutorial question: Trend*	39	95
5	*Tutorial question: Laura*	40	97
6	*Tutorial question: Karen Dickson*	41	98
7	*Tutorial question: Trading account*	41	99
The form and content of company accounts			
8	*Tutorial question: Penn*	42	100
9	*Tutorial question: Segmental reporting*	42	101
10	*Tutorial question: Shepparton*	43	102
11	*Tutorial question: Horngren*	44	104
The valuation of company assets and liabilities			
12	*Tutorial question: Barents*	45	107
13	Barber (5/90)	45	108
14	Poynton (10/90)	46	110
15	Harden (5/91)	47	114
16	Rowland (5/91)	49	116
17	Ashmole (10/91)	50	118
18	Attercliffe (5/92)	53	121
Group accounts			
19	*Tutorial question: Hakluyt*	54	123
20	Newman (10/90)	55	124
21	Grimshaw (5/89 and Specimen)	56	125
22	Hagg (5/92)	57	126
Limitations of published accounts			
23	*Tutorial question: Gnomes*	58	128
24	Price (5/91)	58	129

INDEX TO QUESTIONS AND SUGGESTED SOLUTIONS

		Question	Suggested solution
Capital reduction, reorganisation and reconstruction			
25	*Tutorial question: Purchase of own shares*	59	130
26	Harbour (5/89)	59	132
27	Clayton (5/91)	60	133
28	Duke (5/92)	62	135
Share and business valuation			
29	*Tutorial question: Business valuation methods*	62	136
30	Falkus (10/91)	63	138
Interpretation of accounts: ratio analysis			
31	*Tutorial question: Ritt*	64	139
32	Burdon (10/90)	65	141
33	Greenwood (10/90)	65	142
34	Thornville (5/91)	66	144
35	Pinfold (5/91)	68	146
36	Alban and Lamb (10/91)	70	150
Interpretation of accounts: funds flow and cash flow analysis			
37	*Tutorial question: Cash flow statements*	71	154
38	Scapens (5/90)	72	156
39	Notley (5/89)	75	159
40	Whaley (5/92)	76	163
Business decision making: short run			
41	*Tutorial question: George*	78	165
42	Newell (5/90)	78	166
43	Helmore (10/90)	80	168
44	Henley (10/91)	81	170
45	Carburton (5/92)	81	171
46	Fell (5/92)	82	173
Business decision making: long run			
47	Landore (5/90)	83	175
48	Bucknall (10/91)	84	177

INDEX TO QUESTIONS AND SUGGESTED SOLUTIONS

		Question	Suggested solution
Forecasts and budgets			
49	Kaplan (5/90)	85	178
50	Rowan (10/90)	86	181
51	Hobhouse (10/91)	88	183

QUESTIONS

1 TUTORIAL QUESTION: WALTER ROGERS

Walter Rogers is the sole owner of a large wholesalers. He employs a manager to look after the day to day running of the business including the supervision of the other staff.

The following events take place during the year.

(a) Walter issues a cheque from his private bank account to pay a creditor.

(b) Walter pays a cheque representing interest on the business bank deposit account into his own private current account.

(c) Walter takes home some stock for his own use.

(d) Walter receives a rates demand for his house which he settles using a cheque drawn on his private bank account.

(e) Walter wins the football pools and pays the winnings into his own building society account.

(f) Walter decides that since he no longer needs his second car, it might as well be used in the business by his manager.

(g) Walter makes a loan to his brother using some money drawn out of his building society account.

(h) Walter decides that the business should immediately pay all the staff a bonus.

Required

State whether or not each of the above events should appear in the books of the business.

2 TUTORIAL QUESTION: SEPARATE TRANSACTIONS

The following table shows the cumulative effects of a succession of separate transactions on the assets and liabilities of a business.

Transactions		*A*	*B*	*C*	*D*	*E*	*F*	*G*	*H*	*I*	*J*
Assets	£'000	£'000	£'000	£'000	£'000	£'000	£'000	£'000	£'000	£'000	£'000
Buildings	50	50	50	50	50	50	50	50	50	50	50
Equipment	54	60	60	60	60	60	60	60	60	60	60
Stocks	28	28	28	28	28	34	31	31	31	31	31
Trade debtors	34	34	30	30	30	30	35	35	30	20	20
Prepayments	3	3	3	3	3	3	3	3	3	3	3
Bank	14	8	12	12	14	14	14	13	18	27	13
Cash	4	4	4	3	1	1	1	1	1	1	1
	187	187	187	186	186	192	194	193	193	192	178
Liabilities											
Capital	100	100	100	100	100	100	102	101	101	100	102
Loan	60	60	60	60	60	60	60	60	60	60	60
Trade creditors	23	23	23	22	22	28	28	28	28	28	12
Accrued expenses	4	4	4	4	4	4	4	4	4	4	4
	187	187	187	186	186	192	194	193	193	192	178

QUESTIONS

Required

Identify clearly and as fully as you can what transaction has taken place in each case. Do not copy out the table but use the reference letter for each transaction.

3 TUTORIAL QUESTION: BASIC

The following information relates to a business with year end 31 December 19X4.

(a) *Office equipment*

	£
At cost, 1 January 19X4	13,500
Accumulated depreciation 1 January 19X4	4,700
Additions in year at cost	7,200
Disposals in year at cost (NBV £1,700)	2,400

Depreciation policy: 10% per annum on the reducing balance

(b) *Telephone expenses*

	£
Accrued expense at 31 December 19X3	112
Quarterly bills	
1.11.X3 - 31.1.X4 (paid 5.2.X4)	180
1.2.X4 - 30.4.X4 (paid 4.5.X4)	190
1.5.X4 - 31.7.X4 (paid 10.8.X4)	195
1.8.X4 - 31.10.X4 (paid 6.11.X4)	210
1.11.X4 - 31. 1.X5 (paid 5.2.X5)	216

(c) *Rates*

	£
Six months to 31.3.X4 (paid 3.10.X3)	1,200
Six months to 30.9.X4 (paid 4.4.X4)	1,400
Six months to 31.3.X5 (paid 4.10.X4)	1,400

(d) *Debtors*

	£
Provision for doubtful debts at 1 January 19X4	380
Cash received during year from debtor previously written off as bad debt	90
Bad debts written off during year	130
Debtors' balances at 31 December 19X4	24,800

Of the debtors' balances of £24,800 outstanding at 31 December 19X4 £300 is regarded as doubtful. A provision of 2% is required at 31 December 19X4 in respect of balances not specifically provided for.

(e) *Rental income*

The business owns a property which it rents to a local trader. Rent is payable quarterly in advance on 28 February, 31 May, 31 August and 30 November. The following sums were received in 19X4.

			£
2 Jan	Quarter to 28 February		240
26 Feb	Quarter to 31 May		240
31 May	Quarter to 31 August		270
30 Aug	Quarter to 30 November		270

A payment of £270 in respect of the quarter to 28 February 19X5 was not received until January 19X5.

You are required to compute the amounts which would appear in the 19X4 profit and loss account for:

(a) depreciation of office equipment;
(b) telephone expenses;
(c) rates;
(d) bad and doubtful debts;
(e) rental income.

4 TUTORIAL QUESTION: TREND

Trend Limited began trading on 1 April 19X0. The following figures are available for cost and depreciation of plant in the three years to 31 March 19X3.

Year ended 31 March	19X1	19X2	19X3
	£	£	£
(A) Plant at cost	80,000	80,000	90,000
(B) Accumulated depreciation	(16,000)	(28,800)	(36,720)
(C) Net (written down value)	64,000	51,200	53,280

The only other information available is that disposals have taken place at the beginning of the financial years concerned.

	Date of Disposal 12 months ended 31 March	Original acquisition 12 months ended 31 March	Original cost £	Sale proceeds £
First disposal	19X3	19X0	15,000	8,000
Second disposal	19X4	19X0	30,000	21,000

Plant sold was replaced on the same day by new plant. The cost of the plant which replaced the first disposal is not known but the replacement for the second disposal is known to have cost £50,000.

Required

(a) Identify the method of providing for depreciation on plant employed by Trend Ltd, stating how you have arrived at your conclusion.

(b) Reconstruct a working schedule to support the figures shown at line (B) for each of the years ended 31 March 19X1, 19X2 and 19X3. Extend your workings to cover year ended 31 March 19X4.

QUESTIONS

(c) Calculate the figures for cost, accumulated depreciation and net book value for the year ended 31 March 19X4.

(d) Calculate the profit or loss arising on each of the two disposals.

5   **TUTORIAL QUESTION: LAURA**

Laura carries on a business as a clothing manufacturer. The trial balance of the business as on 31 December 19X0 was as follows.

	£	£
Capital account: Laura		30,000
Freehold factory at cost (including land £4,000)	20,000	
Factory plant and machinery at cost	4,800	
Travellers' cars	2,600	
Provision for depreciation 1 January 19X0		
Freehold factory		1,920
Factory plant and machinery		1,600
Travellers' cars		1,200
Stocks 1 January 19X0	8,900	
Trade debtors and creditors	3,600	4,200
Provision for doubtful debts		280
Purchases	36,600	
Wages and salaries	19,800	
Rates and insurance	1,510	
Sundry expenses	1,500	
Motor expenses	400	
Sales		72,000
Balance at bank	11,490	
	111,200	111,200

You are given the following further information.

(a) Stocks on hand as on 31 December 19X0 were £10,800.

(b) Wages and salaries include the following.

| Drawings | £2,400 |
| Motor expenses | £600 |

(c) Provision is to be made for depreciation on the freehold factory buildings, plant and machinery, and travellers' cars at 2%, 10% and 25% respectively, calculated on cost.

(d) On 31 December 19X0, £120 was owing for sundry expenses, and rates paid in advance amounted to £260.

(e) Of the trade debtors, £60 for which provision had previously been made is to be written off. It is thought that the remaining provision will be adequate.

Required

Effect the necessary adjustments at 31 December 19X0 and prepare the balance sheet and profit and loss account at that date.

6 TUTORIAL QUESTION: KAREN DICKSON

Karen Dickson is interested in knowing what effect the following transactions would have on her balance sheet. Since liquidity and profitability are particularly important to her, she wants to know whether each individual item would alter current assets, current liabilities and profit, and if so by how much.

(a) Purchased £2,000 of stock for cash.
(b) Bought £15,000 of machinery by loan repayable over 8 years.
(c) Bought new car for £6,250 by cash.
(d) Karen withdrew £2,750 of cash from the business for private use.
(e) Paid rates demand for £1,400 in cash.
(f) Borrowed £1,000 cash from the bank by way of loan repayable over 5 years.
(g) Depreciated the machinery by £500.
(h) Sold an old car with a book value of £650 for £775 cash.
(i) Bought £8,000 of stock on credit.
(j) Sold stock which had cost £4,000 for £5,000 in cash.
(k) Paid for repairs to the premises costing £820 in cash.

Required

Produce a table, as shown below, giving the effect of each individual transaction by stating whether the current assets, current liabilities and profit would increase or decrease (together with the relevant amount) or stay the same.

Transaction	*Current assets*	*Current liabilities*	*Profit*
(a)	Increase £2,000 Decrease £2,000	Stay the same	Stay the same

7 TUTORIAL QUESTION: TRADING ACCOUNT

On 1 April 19X7 Dorian Ltd had trade debtors of £55,680 and owed its suppliers £41,560. Receipts from credit customers during the year ended 31 March 19X8 were £403,270 and payments to suppliers were £301,770. There were also cash sales totalling £249,830.

Dorian Ltd returned goods costing £7,820 to suppliers and made allowances of £3,510 to customers in respect of goods returned by them.

Bad debts of £4,500 were written off during the year. Discounts received from suppliers were £2,540 and discounts allowed to customers were £5,560.

At 31 March 19X8 there were unpaid invoices from suppliers totalling £42,090 while customers owed Dorian Ltd a total of £56,810.

Stocks of unsold goods at the beginning and end of the year were valued at £30,400 and £31,850 respectively.

QUESTIONS

Required

(a) Calculate Dorian Ltd's total sales for the year ended 31 March 19X8.
(b) Calculate Dorian Ltd's total purchases for the year ended 31 March 19X8.
(c) Prepare Dorian Ltd's trading account for the year ended 31 March 19X8.

8 TUTORIAL QUESTION: PENN

In preparing the annual accounts of Penn plc for the year to 30 June 19X4 you come across a number of problems which you think may require special treatment in the published accounts of the company. A brief summary of each problem is listed below.

(a) A major and fundamental error is discovered which will require an adjustment to last year's profit, that is, that of the year to 30 June 19X3.

(b) There has been a substantial increase in the amount of expenditure incurred on applied research.

(c) The financial director has suggested that an additional amount should be transferred to the deferred taxation account to cover for new originating timing differences arising in the year.

(d) The directors' aggregate emoluments have increased from £55,000 in the previous year to £85,000 in the current year.

(e) The company paid £250 to a major political party.

(f) During the year the company closed one of its largest factories in France.

(g) As from 1 July 19X3 the company's method of pricing the issue of goods to production was changed from a LIFO (last in first out basis) to a FIFO (first in first out) basis.

(h) An interim dividend was paid on 10 January 19X4 on which ACT was paid on 14 April 19X4.

(i) It is now believed that considerable expenditure incurred on developing an existing product during the year is likely to prove highly beneficial to the company.

(j) You have estimated that 30% of the current year's gross profit has been earned as a result of a special and quite unique order.

Required

State how and where you would treat each of the above problems in the published accounts of Penn plc, being careful to explain clearly the reasons for your decision.

9 TUTORIAL QUESTION: SEGMENTAL REPORTING

(a) What do you understand by the term 'segmental reporting' and to what extent do you consider that financial reporting by companies would be improved by further disclosure of segmental information?

(b) What objections and problems arise in the implementation of segmental reporting?

10 TUTORIAL QUESTION: SHEPPARTON

Shepparton Ltd was incorporated on 1 October 19X7. The books were balanced as at 30 September 19X8 and a trial balance was extracted. A profit and loss account was then prepared and the remaining balances, together with the balance from the profit and loss account, are listed below.

	£
Share capital	280,000
Freehold property at cost	305,000
Retained profit at 30 September 19X8	26,500
Plant and machinery at cost	100,000
Bank loan	80,000
Shares in Megon Ltd	6,200
Accumulated depreciation	
Freehold property	10,100
Plant and machinery	20,000
Balance at bank	1,300
Stocks	153,400
Debtors	78,500
Trade creditors	32,100
12% debentures	150,000
Interest payable accrued due	21,300
National Insurance payments outstanding	4,800
Corporation tax due 30 June 19X9	7,700
Prepaid expenses	3,100
Proposed dividend	15,000

The following additional information is provided.

(a) The balance of share capital consists of the proceeds arising from the issue of 200,000 ordinary £1 shares on 1 October 19X7.

(b) The bank loan was raised on 31 December 19X7 and is repayable in four equal annual instalments commencing 31 December 19X8.

(c) The shares in Megon Ltd were acquired as a temporary investment on 5 September 19X8, using cash surplus to immediate operating requirements.

(d) Advance corporation tax may be taken 25/75 as for the purpose of your calculations.

Required

(a) Prepare the balance sheet of Shepparton Ltd at 30 September 19X8 together with relevant notes complying with the requirements of the Companies Act 1985 so far as the information permits.

(b) Discuss the limitations of published accounts from the viewpoint of 'external' users of accounting information.

QUESTIONS

11 TUTORIAL QUESTION: HORNGREN

The following balances have been extracted from the trial balance of Horngren Ltd as at 31 December 19X8.

	£'000
Turnover	10,620
Cost of sales	6,290
Administrative expenses	3,100
Distribution costs	638
Reorganisation costs	396
Revaluation surplus	1,500
Tax on profit on ordinary activities	150
Retained profit on 1 January 19X8	936

Notes

(a) The cost of sales includes development expenditure of £85,000, of which £72,000 was incurred in previous years. The company's policy was, in the past, to capitalise development expenditure which it expected to recover from future revenue. The directors now believe that a policy of writing off such expenditure immediately it is incurred is better designed to give a true and fair view of the company's financial affairs. The company's auditors have agreed to the need for this change.

(b) Administrative expenses and distribution costs include: fees paid to four non-executive directors of £2,000 each; the chairman's salary, £11,000; and salaries paid to the managing director and sales director of £25,000 and £18,000 respectively.

(c) The reorganisation costs comprise £260,000, incurred as the result of closure of one of the company's five operating divisions, and redundancy costs of £136,000 paid to factory workers in order to enable one of the other divisions to become more capital intensive.

(d) The revaluation surplus arose as the result of restating freehold properties at their current value on 1 January 19X9. Administrative expenses include a depreciation charge of £25,000 compared with the £11,000 which would have been charged if the property had remained in the books at historical cost.

Additional information

(a) It was discovered, on 31 January 19X9, that Lumby Ltd, in which Horngren held 50,000 shares as a trade investment, had gone into liquidation on 1 December 19X8. The shares, which had cost 80p each, are now considered valueless.

(b) Horngren Ltd raised a loan of £80,000 at 15% interest on 1 January 19X9.

(c) The directors propose to recommend to the 19X9 Annual General Meeting a dividend of 12p per share on the company's ordinary share capital. The share capital comprise 1,000,000 ordinary shares of 50p each.

Required

(a) Define and distinguish between exceptional items and extraordinary items in company accounts, and state how each should be treated.

(b) Define and distinguish between adjusting and non-adjusting post balance sheets events in company accounts, and state how each should be treated.

(c) Prepare the profit and loss account and statement of retained earnings for Horngren Ltd in respect of 19X8, together with appropriate notes, complying with the Companies Act 1985 and relevant statements of standard accounting practice so far as the information permits.

(d) Compute the profits legally available for distribution by Horngren at 31 December 19X8.

Note. Ignore the tax implications, if any, of notes (a) to (d) and the additional information (a) to (c).

12 TUTORIAL QUESTION: BARENTS

Barents Ltd began trading on 1 January 19X0. It acquired stock-in-trade costing £100,000 in 19X0, £105,000 in 19X1 and £135,000 in 19X2. Balance sheet figures for stock at 31 December, under different valuation methods, are given below.

Stock valuation for balance sheet under various cost flow assumptions

31 December	LIFO	FIFO	*Lower of FIFO cost and net realisable value*
19X0	£40,200	£40,000	£37,000
19X1	£36,400	£36,000	£34,000
19X2	£41,800	£44,000	£44,000

Required

Answer the following questions, clearly indicating how each answer is deduced.

(a) Assuming that in any one year, prices moved only up or down, but not both, in the same year:

    (i) did prices go up or down in 19X0?
    (ii) did prices go up or down in 19X2?

(b) Which inventory method, LIFO or FIFO, would show the highest profit for 19X0?

(c) Which would show the highest profit for 19X2?

(d) Which would show the lowest profit for all three years combined?

(e) For 19X2 how much higher or lower would profit be on the FIFO basis than it would be on the lower of FIFO cost or net realisable value basis?

13 BARBER (20 marks)   5/90

Barber Ltd undertakes long term contract work and makes up its accounts to 31 December each year. The following information is provided relating to a contract to build a sports centre for a local authority.

(a) Contract price, £6,000,000.

(b) Date contract commenced: 1 November 19X7.

QUESTIONS

(c) Financial details at 31 December

	19X7 £'000	19X8 £'000
Total costs to date	350	4,100
Estimated costs to completion	5,000	1,240
Progress payments received	-	3,800
Invoiced sales valued of work completed during the year	-	4,000
Cost of work completed during the year	-	3,600

(d) The contract was completed on 30 May 19X9, by which time total contract costs amounted to £5,400,000. The contract price was received in full by 31 December 19X9.

The company complies with the requirements of SSAP 9 *Stocks and long-term contracts* when preparing its accounts.

Required

(a) Calculate the amount of contract profit, if any, recognised in the accounts for each of the years to 31 December 19X7, 19X8 and 19X9. (5 marks)

(b) Prepare the balance sheet entries in respect of the above contract at 31 December 19X7 and 19X8. (5 marks)

(c) Compare the standard accounting procedures used to recognise profit on the sale of stocks with those used for recognising profit on long term contracts. Explain why the treatment is different. (10 marks)

14 POYNTON (30 marks) 10/90

Poynton Ltd was incorporated some years ago. The trial balance as at 30 June 19X8 contained the following information.

TRIAL BALANCE AS AT 30 JUNE 19X8

	£'000	£'000
Turnover		7,230
Opening stock: first in first out (FIFO) basis	350	
Manufacturing costs	5,000	
Goodwill at cost	120	
Development expenditure	60	
Distribution and administrative costs	1,380	
Plant and machinery at cost less depreciation	2,050	
Net monetary assets	295	
Share capital		1,400
Retained profit at 1 July 19X7		625
	9,255	9,255

The following additional information is made available.

(a) The goodwill arose on the acquisition of the business assets of Hammond & Co on 1 July 19X7. The goodwill is estimated to have a useful economic life of three years from the date of acquisition.

(b) The following information is provided relating to Poynton's stock.

	Value at 1 July 19X7 £'000	30 June 19X8 £'000
FIFO basis	350	400
Average cost basis	302	336

(c) The development expenditure, incurred during the period April-June 19X8, relates to the refinement of one of the company's established products. This change is expected to improve materially the product's marketability and contribution to the overall profitability of Poynton. The improved product was first sold on 1 July 19X8.

Required

(a) Produce summarised profit and loss accounts and appropriation accounts for Poynton Ltd for the year ended 30 June 19X8 and balance sheets at that date, using accounting policies that comply with standard accounting practice and show:

(i) the *highest* reported profit for the year; (9 marks)
(ii) the *lowest* reported profit for the year. (11 marks)

Notes

1 Presentation of the financial statements prepared under (a) should comply with relevant statements of standard accounting practice but need not be in the detailed format necessary for publication purposes.

2 Net monetary assets comprise debtors, cash and creditors.

3 Ignore taxation.

(b) Identify *three* other areas in financial reports (in addition to those considered under (a)) where alternative methods of asset valuation and profit measurement are permissible. To what extent do these alternative methods of asset valuation affect the interpretation of financial statements by banks and other users? (10 marks)

15 HARDEN (30 marks) 5/91

Jim Harden commenced business as a builder and decorator on 1 May 19X0, trading under the name Harden & Co. He has recently approached your bank for an increase in his firm's overdraft facility to help finance its expanding activities. At the time of his visit, he handed in the following financial statement which, he believes, sets out his position at the end of the first year's business.

QUESTIONS

FINANCIAL POSITION OF HARDEN & CO AT 30 APRIL 19X1

Assets

£

Lock-up garage. The freehold cost £5,000 in May 19X0. In addition there was a solicitor's bill, for work undertaken in connection with the purchase, of £600. A friend of mine has just sold his lock-up garage for £6,350. My property is in better condition and worth at least £7,000.   7,000

Motor vehicle. I bought a secondhand van for £3,000 on 1 May 19X0. It should last me for four years but will then probably be worn out. I have looked after it well this year and it is still as good as when I bought it.   3,000

Equipment. I bought my cement mixer and other equipment, which will probably last for five years, from Harwood Ltd when it closed down in May 19X0. I got it for £1,500 but would have had to pay anyone else £2,100.   2,100

Stock. My stock of materials was purchased for £1,200 less trade discounts of £150. It is worth considerably more. I don't think I could buy the materials today for less than £1,400. My friend says that stocks are sometimes shown at what he calls 'net realisable value' in the accounts. I think this is the same as selling price, which would be about £1,750.   1,750

Contract. I am working on an extension, for a customer, and have so far spent £1,700. I have invoiced the customer £2,000 for completed to 30 April at a cost of £1,400. The customer has promised to pay me next month. I expect to incur a further £1,000 in completing the contract, so the profit is £4,000 (the total contract) less costs £2,700.   1,300

Debtors. I am owed £1,350 for decorating work. This includes £250 for a job finished last November. The customer says he is not happy with the work, but I think it is perfectly satisfactory and hope to get the money from him eventually.   1,350

Goodwill. Things have been going well, with sales increasing all the time. My suppliers know I pay on time and my workers are all reliable. Goodwill must be equal to at least a month's sales, which is approximately £8,000.   8,000
        24,500

Liabilities

£

Bank overdraft. This never exceeds £1,000 and stood at just £850 at the end of April. My June bank statement included charges and interest of £60 for the quarter to 31 May. It seems a bit high but I expect I will have to pay it.   850

Loan. I borrowed £5,000 from my brother on 1 November 19X0. I have agreed to pay him back interest at 10% once a year, which is cheaper than I could get money from the bank.   5,000

Trade creditors   250
        6,400

My capital investment at the year end is therefore   18,400

I put £3,000 in the business at the beginning of the year and so I seem to have made a profit of £15,400, which is not bad considering the fact that I take out £200 a week to live on.

Required

Prepare the balance sheet of Harden & Co at 30 April 19X1. The balance sheet should comply with established accounting conventions regarding the valuation of assets and liabilities, and should show movements on the capital account during the year, commencing with the opening balance of £3,000. You should explain the treatment of each of the assets and liabilities included in the balance sheet you prepare.

16 ROWLAND (20 marks) 5/91

The directors of Rowland Ltd are considering the company's estimated financial position at the end of July 19X1. The following information has been prepared.

FORECAST PROFIT AND LOSS ACCOUNT FOR THE YEAR ENDING 31 JULY 19X1

	£'000	£'000
Sales		6,000
Purchases	3,600	
Increase in stock	(100)	
Cost of goods sold		3,500
Gross profit		2,500
Depreciation of plant	300	
Other overhead expenses	2,000	
		2,300
Operating profit		200

FORECAST BALANCE SHEET AS AT 31 JULY 19X1

	£'000	£'000
Fixed assets		
Goodwill		400
Freehold property		1,000
Plant and machinery at cost less depreciation		600
		2,000
Current Assets		
Stock	500	
Trade debtors	750	
Cash	50	
	1,300	
Current liabilities		
Trade creditors	300	
Net current assets		1,000
Total assets less current liabilities		3,000
Debenture repayable 19X9		500
		2,500
Financed by		
Share capital (50p shares)		1,000
Retained profit		1,500
		2,500

QUESTIONS

It is to be assumed that a year consists of twelve months, each of 30 days, and that transactions take place at an even rate throughout the year.

The directors require finance for a planned expansion of activities and have heard that, when deciding to make an advance, it is normal practice for a potential lender to examine certain key financial measurements and performance indicators. The directors are therefore interested in the financial effects of the following possible changes to the estimates.

(a) Making a bonus (capitalisation) issue of three ordinary shares for every one share held at present. The issue is to be made on 1 June 19X1.

(b) Reducing the depreciation charge for the year to £200,000.

(c) Showing the freehold property in the accounts at its recent professional valuation of £3,500,000.

(d) Writing the balance of goodwill off against retained profit.

(e) Offering customers a cash discount of 8% for payment within 30 days. This offer is to take effect for sales made on or after 1 June 19X1. All the company's customers are expected to take advantage of the offer with the volume of sales remaining unaffected.

(f) Extending the period of credit taken from suppliers to two months for purchases made on or after 1 June 19X1.

Required

Taking each of these six courses of action *separately*, set out a statement showing the following.

Course of Action	Operating profit 19X0/X1	Bank balance 31 July 19X1	Working capital 31 July 19X1	Debt:equity ratio 31 July 19X1
(a)				
(b)				
(c)				
(d)				
(e)				
(f)				

For any items unaffected by a course of action, show the original figures derived from the accounts.

17 ASHMOLE (30 marks) 10/91

The final accounts of Ashmole plc for the year ended 30 September 19X1 are in the course of preparation. The company's accountant has produced the following *draft* financial statements.

PROFIT AND LOSS ACCOUNT FOR THE YEAR ENDED 30 SEPTEMBER 19X1

	£'000
Turnover (note (a))	5,168
Cost of sales	3,000
Gross profit	2,168
Distribution costs	317
Administrative expenses (note (b))	1,220
Operating profit	631
Interest payable	80
Profit on ordinary activities before tax	551
Taxation on profits	190
Profit on ordinary activities after tax	361
Ordinary interim dividend paid	80
Retained profit for the year	281

MOVEMENT ON RESERVES FOR THE YEAR ENDED 30 SEPTEMBER 19X1

	Debenture redemption reserve £'000	Retained profits £'000	Profits £'000
At 1 October 19X0	150	714	864
Retained earnings for year to 30 September 19X1	-	281	281
	150	995	1,145

BALANCE SHEET AS AT 30 SEPTEMBER 19X1

	£'000	£'000
Fixed assets		
Intangible asset: goodwill		100
Tangible assets: land and buildings		270
plant and machinery		1,406
		1,776
Current assets		
Stocks	740	
Debtors	290	
	1,030	
Creditors: amounts falling due within one year		
Bank overdraft	16	
Trade creditors	161	
Corporation tax (note (c))	203	
	380	
Net current assets		650
Total assets less current liabilities		2,426
15% debenture loan repayable 1998	500	
Suspense account	(159)	
		341
		2,085
Capital and reserves		
Called up share capital		
Ordinary shares (£1 shares)		800
Preference shares (£1 shares)		140
Reserves		1,145
Total equity		2,085

QUESTIONS

Notes

(a) The figure for turnover includes a profit of £80,000 from the sale of trade investments purchased 31 years ago. The related tax due, £20,000, is included in the corporation tax charge of £190,000.

(b) The administrative expenses include salaries and wages of £102,000 relating to the previous year, which were overlooked as the result of a 'fundamental error' made when preparing the accounts.

(c) The balance sheet figure for corporation tax includes an overprovision, of £13,000, for tax on the profits of the previous year.

The following *additional information* is provided.

(a) The goodwill of £100,000 arose on the purchase of a local business on 1 October 19X0 and is estimated to have a useful economic life of four years.

(b) The land and buildings were revalued at £800,000 on 30 September 19X1. It is now decided to use this figure for the purpose of the accounts.

(c) The balance on the suspense account represents the amount paid on 1 October 19X0 to redeem the preference shares still shown in the balance sheet at £140,000.

(d) The directors propose to make a further transfer of £50,000 to the debenture redemption reserve.

Required

(a) Prepare the final accounts of Ashmole plc in the format given above (including a 'movement on reserves' statement) revised to take account of notes (a) to (c) and additional information (a) to (d). The accounts should be presented in good form and comply with the provisions of relevant SSAPs. The accounts should show clearly the balances on reserve accounts. (20 marks)

(b) There is a disagreement among the board members about whether a final dividend of 20p per share should be declared in addition to the interim dividend already paid. The managing director is of the view that the shareholders are expecting a final dividend, and that anyway 'there is plenty of money in reserves'.

You are required:

(i) to explain whether or not the directors are legally entitled to distribute the balances appearing on each of the reserve accounts shown in your answer to (a);

(ii) to calculate the precise amount legally available for distribution; and

(iii) to comment on the desirability of making the proposed distribution. (10 marks)

Note. Ignore the tax implications, if any, of note (b) and additional information (a) to (d).

QUESTIONS

18 ATTERCLIFFE (30 marks) 5/92

Attercliffe Ltd is a trading company which was incorporated on 1 May 19X1 with an ordinary share capital of £500,000 divided into ordinary shares of £1 each. The published accounts for the year to 30 April 19X2 are in the course of preparation and the directors are keen to report the highest possible profit figure in order to impress investors and potential lenders. The company's recently appointed accountant requests your advice on the appropriate accounting treatment of certain items and provides you with the following information.

(a) Finished stock consists of three main product lines.

Product line	Purchase price, first in first out £	Purchase price, weighted average cost £	Net realisable value £
X	126,500	124,000	175,000
Y	63,000	62,000	71,000
Z	97,100	96,000	90,000

Total purchases for the year amounted to £1,200,000.

(b) Research and development expenditure incurred to date is as follows.

	£
Research expenditure	10,500
Development expenditure	12,000

The expenditure has been incurred in respect of packaging design for a new product which will be launched onto the market in the autumn of 19X2. There is general agreement that the new product will be a financial success.

(c) The company acquired the assets, including goodwill, of a sole trader at the date of incorporation. The goodwill was valued at £40,000 and is expected to have a useful economic life of eight years.

(d) 20,000 ordinary shares in Clipstone Ltd were purchased on 1 November 19X1 at a cost of £37,100 and, since that date, Attercliffe has had a strong representation on Clipstone's board of directors. The share capital of Clipstone Ltd amounts to 60,000 ordinary shares of £1 each. Clipstone Ltd also makes up its accounts to 30 April, and its reported profit for the year ended 30 April 19X2 was £36,000. Clipstone's profit accrued at an even rate during the year and no dividends have been paid or proposed.

(e) The draft calculation of Attercliffe's reported profit for the year to 30 April 19X2 is £180,000, while taxable profit has been estimated at £120,000. The discrepancy between the two figures arises because of 'originating' timing differences: capital allowances claimed exceed the depreciation charge by £60,000 for the year to 30 April 19X2. These timing differences will reverse in future years when the depreciation charged in the accounts will exceed the capital allowances by an equivalent amount.

(f) The directors propose to pay a final dividend of 12p per share.

Required

For each of items (a) to (f) calculate the following amounts.

(a) The amount to be charged against revenue, indicating whether the deduction would appear:

QUESTIONS

      (i)   above the line (in the trading account or profit and loss account); or
      (ii)   below the line (in the appropriation account); or
      (iii) as a deduction from reserves.

(b) The balance, if any, to be carried forward in the balance sheet, indicating whether it would appear as an asset or a liability.

The calculations should be made in accordance with recognised accounting practice and relevant SSAP's.

Present the results of your numerical calculations in tabular format. You should explain the treatments you have used and, where more than one accounting treatment is permissible, you should show the alternatives and identify the one which results in the *higher* reported profit for the year to 30 April 19X2.

Notes

1   The rate of corporation tax is 25% and advance corporation tax 25/75.

2   Ignore any adjustments to profit which might be needed when considering the accounting significance of the information provided under (e) above.

19   TUTORIAL QUESTION: HAKLUYT

Hakluyt plc, a carpet manufacturer and wholesaler, purchased 300,000 of the 400,000 issued ordinary shares of a much smaller company Cook Ltd on 1 January 19X1 when the retained earnings account of Cook Ltd had a credit balance of £36,000.

The latest accounts of the two companies are as follows.

SUMMARY PROFIT AND LOSS ACCOUNTS FOR THE YEAR ENDED
30 SEPTEMBER 19X2

	Hakluyt plc £'000	Cook Ltd £'000
Credit sales	7,220	880
Cost of sales and production services	2,380	420
Gross profit	4,840	460
Expenses, taxation and dividends	4,744	320
Profit retained	96	140
Brought forward from last year	800	96
Carried forward to next year	896	236

SUMMARISED BALANCE SHEETS AS AT 30 SEPTEMBER 19X2

	Hakluyt plc £'000	Cook Ltd £'000
Fixed assets at cost less depreciation	2,833	364
Investment in Cook Ltd	350	–
Current account with Hakluyt plc	–	50
Stock	396	103
Debtors	1,500	185
Bank	60	12
	5,139	714

	£'000	£'000
Share capital	4,000	400
Retained earnings	896	236
Current account with Cook Ltd	45	-
Creditors for goods and services	198	78
	5,139	714

On 28 September 19X2 Hakluyt plc sent a cheque for £5,000 to Cook Ltd. This was not received until 2 October 19X2.

Required

Prepare the consolidated balance sheet of Hakluyt plc and its subsidiary Cook Ltd at 30 September 19X2.

20 NEWMAN (20 marks) 10/90

The summarised balance sheets of Newman Ltd and Gilbert Ltd as at 30 September 19X8 are as follows.

	Newman Limited £'000	*Gilbert Limited* £'000
Freehold properties	-	210
Other fixed assets	3,650	420
Net current assets	1,160	51
	4,810	681
Ordinary share capital (£1 shares)	2,000	300
Reserves at 1 October 19X7	2,600	221
Net profit reported for 19X7/X8	210	160
	4,810	681

Newman Ltd acquired the entire share capital of Gilbert Ltd on 30 September 19X8 for £900,000. The consideration took the form of five newly issued ordinary shares in Newman Ltd for every three shares currently held in Gilbert Ltd. This transaction has not yet been recorded in the books of Newman.

Gilbert Ltd's freehold properties possessed a fair value of £325,000 on 30 September 19X8. There were no significant differences between the book value and fair value of Gilbert's remaining assets at that time.

Required

(a) Prepare the consolidated balance sheet of Newman Ltd and its subsidiary Gilbert Ltd at 30 September 19X8 prepared in accordance with the acquisition method of accounting specified in SSAP 14. (11 marks)

(b) Prepare the consolidated balance sheet of Newman Ltd and its subsidiary Gilbert Ltd at 30 September 19X8 prepared in accordance with the merger method of accounting specified in SSAP 23. (9 marks)

QUESTIONS

Notes

1 Show all workings.

2 Ignore taxation.

3 The balance sheet should be framed, as far as possible, in the format given in the question, so as to show the group net profit reported for 19X7/X8.

21 GRIMSHAW (20 marks) *5/89 and Specimen*

The summarised balance sheets of Dingle Ltd, Eagle Ltd and Fender Ltd are as follows.

BALANCE SHEETS AS AT 31 DECEMBER 19X8

	Dingle £'000	Eagle £'000	Fender £'000
Fixed assets	100	260	720
Current assets	85	170	555
	185	430	1,275
Ordinary share capital (£1 shares)	80	200	500
Retained profit 1 Jan 19X8	70	100	360
Profit for 19X8	20	80	200
Proposed dividend	-	(60)	(150)
	170	320	910
Trade creditors	15	50	215
Proposed dividend	-	60	150
	185	430	1,275

Grimshaw Ltd made the following investments on 1 January 19X8.

Company	Shares acquired	Price paid
Dingle	64,000	£178,000
Eagle	80,000	£151,000
Fender	50,000	£116,000

Required

Calculate separately for each company the amounts (if any) to be included in the group accounts of Grimshaw Ltd in respect of each of the following items:

(a) share of profit reported for 19X8;
(b) goodwill/premium paid on acquisition;
(c) minority interest at 31 December 19X8.

You should explain, briefly, the principles followed when making your calculations. The result of your calculations under (a) to (c) should be presented in the following format.

	Dingle £'000	Eagle £'000	Fender £'000
Share of profit			
Goodwill/premium on acquisition			
Minority interest			

Note. There were no significant differences, on 1 January 19X8, between the book values and market values of the assets of any of the companies.

22 HAGG (20 marks)   5/92

The summarised balance sheets of Hagg Ltd, Oaken Ltd and Greave Ltd at 31 March 19X2 contained the following information.

BALANCE SHEETS AS AT 31 MARCH 19X2

	Hagg Ltd £'000	Oaken Ltd £'000	Greave Ltd £'000
Fixed assets at book value	2,600	2,100	1,300
Investments in subsidiaries	1,300	-	-
Net current assets	1,680	930	1,370
Total assets less current liabilities	5,580	3,030	2,670
16% debenture stock	500	2,000	1,500
	5,080	1,030	1,170
Capital and reserves			
Ordinary share capital (£1 shares)	3,300	500	1,000
Retained profit at 31 March 1991	1,360	320	140
Profit for year to 31 March 1992	420	210	30
	5,080	1,030	1,170

The three companies trade in complementary products and their directors arranged a merger of their activities on 31 March 19X1. The terms of the merger were as follows.

(a) Hagg Ltd issued 500,000 £1 ordinary shares in exchange for the entire share capital of Oaken Ltd.

(b) Hagg Ltd issued 800,000 £1 ordinary shares in exchange for the entire share capital of Greave Ltd.

Required

(a) Prepare the consolidated balance sheet of Hagg Ltd and its subsidiaries as at 31 March 19X2. Use the merger method of consolidation as prescribed in SSAP 23. (8 marks)

(b) Compare the financial position shown in the above balance sheet of Hagg Ltd with that appearing in the consolidated balance sheet prepared under (a). Your comparison should include calculations of the debt equity ratio and calculations of the interest cover.
(8 marks)

(c) Indicate TWO ways in which the financial position disclosed in the consolidated balance sheet might be affected by the use, instead, of the acquisition method of consolidation as prescribed in SSAP 14. (4 marks)

QUESTIONS

23 TUTORIAL QUESTION: GNOMES

Your client Eric runs a gnomes' hospital to which damaged garden gnomes can be brought for repair. He is concerned about the effect of the rising cost of miniature fishing rods on his business and has asked you if he should record his purchases and value his stocks at current or replacement costs so that his accounts reflect inflation.

Required

Write a brief memorandum to Eric explaining the implications of valuing stock at current cost. Give your advice on his proposal.

24 PRICE (20 marks) 5/91

Price Ltd was incorporated on 1 January 19X0 and took over the following business assets of Peter Price.

	£'000
Fixed assets valued at	2,000
Stock valued at	480

Price Ltd started business immediately and its summarised balance sheet, prepared on the historical cost basis at 31 December 19X0, contained the following information.

BALANCE SHEET AS AT 31 DECEMBER 19X0

	£'000
Fixed assets at cost	2,000
Depreciation charge for 19X0	400
	1,600
Stock	600
Net liquid assets	200
	2,400
Financed by	
Share capital	2,000
Net profit for 19X0	400
	2,400

The fixed assets are estimated to have a useful life of five years and a zero residual value at the end of that period. They are depreciated on the straight line basis. Their current replacement cost (as new) at 31 December 19X0 is estimated to be £2,500,000.

The company's accountant has estimated that the current cost of goods sold during 19X0 was £51,000 higher than the historical cost: that is, the COSA (cost of sales adjustment) = £51,000. The replacement cost of stock held at the balance sheet date is £611,000.

Required

(a) Calculate the current cost profit of Price Ltd for 19X0. (4 marks)

(b) Prepare the summarised current cost balance sheet of Price Ltd as at 31 December 19X0, so far as the information permits. (8 marks)

(c) Give separate calculations of the rate of return on net assets at the end of the year, based on the information contained in (i) the historical cost balance sheet shown above and (ii) the current cost balance sheet prepared under (b). (2 marks)

(d) Comment on the difference between the ratios calculated under (c). Explain which ratio you consider the more relevant for the purpose of assessing management's performance.

(6 marks)

25 TUTORIAL QUESTION: PURCHASE OF OWN SHARES

Set out below are the summarised balance sheets of A plc and B Ltd at 30 June 19X5.

	A £'000	B £'000
Capital and reserves		
Called up share capital £1 ordinary shares	300	300
Share premium account	60	60
Profit and loss account	160	20
	520	380
Net assets	520	380

On 1 July 19X5 A plc and B Ltd each purchased 50,000 of their own ordinary shares. A plc purchased its own shares at 150p each. The shares were originally issued at par. The redemption was partly financed by the issue at par of 5,000 10% redeemable preference shares of £1 each. B Ltd purchased its own shares out of capital at a price of 80p each.

Required

Prepare the summarised balance sheets of A plc and B Ltd at 1 July 19X5 immediately after the above transactions have been effected.

26 HARBOUR (20 marks) 5/89

Harbour Ltd is a private company whose shares are owned by the directors and their families. The company's draft balance sheet is as follows.

BALANCE SHEET AS AT 31 MARCH 19X9

	£	£
Fixed assets		
Development expenditure		15,000
Goodwill		12,000
Land and buildings		100,000
Plant and machinery		362,000
		489,000
Current assets		
Stocks	235,000	
Debtors	93,000	
	328,000	
Creditors falling due within one year		
Bank overdraft (secured on fixed assets)	247,000	
Trade creditors	184,000	
	431,000	
Net current liabilities		(103,000)
Total assets less current liabilities		386,000
12% debenture		80,000
		306,000

	£
Capital and reserves	
Ordinary share capital (£1 shares)	400,000
Profit and loss account	(94,000)
	306,000

The company's activities have been rationalised and the loss-making departments closed. The following scheme for financial reorganisation has been drawn up.

(a) Intangible fixed assets to be written off and the remaining assets to be re-stated at the following realistic values.

	£
Land and buildings	161,000
Plant and machinery	200,000
Stocks	162,000
Debtors	88,000

(b) The ordinary share capital to be reduced, as necessary, to enable assets and liabilities to be restated at realistic figures and to clear past losses.

(c) The debenture holders to accept, in full satisfaction of the amount due, 80,000 ordinary shares of £1 each at par.

(d) The directors to subscribe for a further 200,000 ordinary shares of £1 each at par to provide the cash needed to complete the reorganisation.

(e) The bank to convert £200,000 of the overdraft into a loan carrying interest at 14% per annum, repayable in four equal annual instalments commencing 31 December 19X9.

Required

(a) Calculate the amount to be written off the existing share capital. (7 marks)

(b) Prepare revised balance sheet of Harbour Ltd as at 1 April 19X9 giving effect to the proposed scheme for reorganisation. (7 marks)

(c) Assess the proposals from the viewpoint of Harbour's bank. (6 marks)

Note. Assume you are making the calculations and writing the report on 1 April 19X9 and that no other changes occur. Make any assumptions you consider appropriate.

27 CLAYTON (20 marks)   5/91

Clayton Ltd is a supplier of soft furnishing to the retail trade in its immediate locality. The company has suffered over the last two years from a reduction of consumer expenditure. A balance sheet, recently prepared, sets out the following financial position.

QUESTIONS

CLAYTON LIMITED
BALANCE SHEET AS AT 20 APRIL 19X1

	£	£
Fixed assets		
Goodwill		300,000
Leasehold buildings at cost less depreciation		500,000
		800,000
Current assets		
Stock at cost	550,000	
Debtors	380,000	
	930,000	
Current liabilities		
Sundry creditors	590,000	
Bank overdraft secured on leasehold property	650,000	
	1,240,000	
Net current liabilities		(310,000)
		490,000
Financed by		
Share capital		400,000
Reserves		80,000
Retained profit		10,000
		490,000

The company has exceeded its overdraft facility and is known to be suffering severe pressure from creditors, some of whom are threatening to petition for compulsory winding up. The directors advise the bank that there are only two possible options for the company's future. These are:

Scheme 1. A firm offer of £400,000 has been received for the company's leasehold property. The production manager says that the stocks, although worth much more, would only realise approximately £395,000 in a closing down sale. £310,000 of the total amount due from debtors is estimated as recoverable. Liquidation expenses are estimated at £20,000 and sundry creditors include preferential creditors of £220,000.

Scheme 2. The directors, having taken advice, propose to implement a rescue operation which includes a loan of £400,000, already provisionally arranged, from the Wilsden Finance Company Ltd. The bank would be repaid £250,000 immediately and the remainder of the loan would be used to satisfy pressing creditors. The bank has been asked to accept a 20% debenture in exchange for the balance remaining due. The debenture would be repayable in four annual instalments of £100,000, commencing 20 April 19X2, with interest due for the preceding year paid on the same date.

Assume that:
(a) the current rate of interest on all borrowing is 14%;
(b) the calculations are being made on 20 April 19X1 and either scheme could be put into effect immediately.

Required
(a) Prepare a numerical analysis of the two schemes from the viewpoint of the company's bank.
(14 marks)

(b) Discuss briefly the advantages/disadvantages of the two schemes from the bank's point of view.
(6 marks)

A table of discount factors can be found on Page 29.

QUESTIONS

28   DUKE   (20 marks)   5/92

The forecast balance sheet of Duke Ltd as at 31 May 19X2 is as follows.

FORECAST BALANCE SHEET AS AT 31 MAY 1992

	£
Fixed assets and net current assets	1,023,000
Capital and reserves	
Ordinary shares of £1 each	500,000
Share premium account	36,000
Revaluation reserve	175,000
Retained profit (all distributable)	312,000
	1,023,000

The company plans to redeem 100,000 ordinary shares (£1 nominal value) at £1.20 per share on 1 June 19X2. These shares were initially issued at par.

Required

(a) State the value of Duke's 'permanent' capital at 31 May 19X2 (the amount of its capital and undistibutable profits).   (3 marks)

(b) Starting from the forecast balance sheet above, prepare TWO revised balance sheets, at 1 June 19X2, taking account of the planned redemption on the separate assumptions that:

  (i) no further share issue is planned;
  (ii) an issue of 50,000 ordinary shares is made on 1 June 19X2 at £1.70 each.
  (11 marks)

(c) Explain the nature and purpose of the accounting adjustments made to the balance sheets you have prepared under (b).   (6 marks)

Note. Assume that the share issue and the redemption occur on 1 June 19X2 and that no other transactions take place.

29   TUTORIAL QUESTION: BUSINESS VALUATION METHODS

(a) Name seven methods of valuing a business.

(b) State the circumstances (if any) in which each method is most useful.

(c) A company has annual earnings of £200,000 and a price/earnings ratio of 8. Comparable companies have a dividend yield of 10% and an earnings yield of 20%. Its payout ratio is 50%. Its net assets have a book value of £950,000 and a replacement cost of £1,250,000. On liquidation its net assets would probably fetch £750,000. Its cost of capital is 16%. If you were thinking of buying 10% of this company's shares how much would you be willing to pay?

30 FALKUS (20 marks) 10/91

Falkus plc plans to diversify its activities and has under consideration the possible acquisition of a number of different private companies. One such company is Fanshawe Ltd, in respect of which the following information has been obtained.

(a) PROFIT AND LOSS APPROPRIATION ACCOUNT FOR 19X0

	£
Net profit	72,000
Less dividends	18,000
Retained profit	54,000

BALANCE SHEET AS AT 31 DECEMBER 19X0

	£
Freehold property at cost less depreciation	29,000
Machinery at cost less depreciation	125,000
Stocks	63,000
Net monetary assets	17,000
	234,000
Financed by	
Share capital (£1 ordinary shares)	100,000
Reserves	134,000
	234,000

(b) The freehold property is estimated to be currently worth £150,000. The machinery and stocks might be expected to sell for £50,000 and £52,000, respectively, in a forced sale. The cost of replacing each of these assets is put at: machinery £180,000; stocks £75,000.

(c) Shares in quoted companies operating in the same line of business as Fanshawe have an average price/earnings ratio of 10 and a dividend yield of 6%.

Required

(a) Calculate the value to be placed on one £1 ordinary share in Fanshawe Ltd based on the information provided above. You should summarise the results of your calculations in the following manner.

Valuation of one £1 ordinary share

   (i)   Break-up basis
   (ii) Replacement cost basis
   (iii) Dividend yield basis
   (iv) Price/earnings basis   (10 marks)

(b) Discuss the meaning and significance of each of the four valuations and comment on their relevance in the light of the proposed takeover by Falkus plc. (10 marks)

Note. Ignore taxation.

QUESTIONS

31 TUTORIAL QUESTION: RITT

The summarised balance sheets of Ritt Ltd at the end of two consecutive financial years were as shown below.

SUMMARISED BALANCE SHEETS AS AT 31 MARCH

	19X6 £'000	19X6 £'000	19X7 £'000	19X7 £'000
Fixed assets (at written down values)				
Premises	50		48	
Plant and equipment	115		196	
Vehicles	42		81	
		207		325
Current assets				
Stock	86		177	
Debtors and prepayments	49		62	
Bank and cash	53		30	
	188		269	
Current liabilities				
Creditors and accruals	72		132	
Proposed dividends	20		30	
	92		162	
Working capital		96		107
Net assets employed		303		432
Financed by				
Ordinary share capital	250		250	
Reserves	53		82	
Shareholders' funds		303		332
Loan capital: 7% debentures		–		100
		303		432

Turnover was £541,000 and £675,000 for the years ended 31 March 19X6 and 19X7 respectively. Corresponding figures for cost of sales were £369,000 and £481,000 respectively.

At 31 March 19X5, reserves had totalled £21,000. Ordinary share capital was the same at the end of 19X5 as at the end of 19X6.

Required

(a) Calculate, for each of the two years, the ratios listed below.

　　Gross profit/turnover percentage
　　Net profit/turnover percentage
　　Turnover/net assets employed
　　Net profit/net assets employed percentage
　　Current assets/current liabilities
　　Quick assets/current liabilities

　　Note. Calculations should be correct to one decimal place.

(b) Comment on each of the figures you have calculated in (a) above, giving probable reasons for the differences between the two years.

32 BURDON (20 marks)   10/90

Burdon Ltd and Jennings Ltd are two separate companies engaged in similar lines of business carried on in different geographical areas of the UK. Each company banks with Newbank plc. Their business activities are cyclical and the level of operating profit before interest charges might, in any single year, be expected to vary upwards or downwards by up to 50% compared with the results achieved in 19X1.

Figures for 19X1 are as follows.

	Burdon Ltd £'000	Jennings Ltd £'000
Operating profit before interest charges	800	750
Shareholders' equity	3,500	1,500
16% secured loans from Newbank plc, repayable 19X6	500	2,500

Required

(a) Calculate the rate of return on shareholders' equity and the debt: equity ratio, for each company for 19X1. (6 marks)

(b) Calculate the possible variations in the rate of return on shareholders' equity, so far as the information permits. (6 marks)

(c) Give a critical assessment of the financial structure of each company from the viewpoint of (i) the shareholders and (ii) the bank, based on the information provided and the calculations made under (a) and (b). (8 marks)

Note. Ignore taxation.

33 GREENWOOD (20 marks)   10/90

Your bank has been approached separately by two companies, Greenwood Ltd and Westport Ltd, to provide finance for the purchase of shares owned by one of their directors who wishes to retire. This course of action is permissible under the Companies Act 1985. Each company requires £300,000 to finance the share acquisition. The summarised accounts of the companies for the year ended 30 September 19X1 are as follows.

SUMMARISED PROFIT AND LOSS ACCOUNTS
FOR THE YEAR ENDED 30 SEPTEMBER 19X1

	Greenwood £'000	Greenwood £'000	Westport £'000	Westport £'000
Turnover		4,820		5,200
Less cost of sales		2,800		3,000
Gross profit		2,020		2,200
Depreciation	250		100	
Other overheads (including interest)	1,250		1,480	
		1,500		1,580
Net profit		520		620

QUESTIONS

BALANCE SHEETS AS AT 30 SEPTEMBER 19X1

	Greenwood £'000	Westport £'000
Freehold properties	1,000	100
Other fixed assets	1,200	1,000
Net current assets	900	1,100
	3,100	2,200
Debentures repayable 19X9	500	800
	2,600	1,400
Financed by		
Share capital (ordinary shares)	2,000	500
Reserves	600	900
	2,600	1,400

The level of trading activity is steady and each company expects profits for each of the next few years to be roughly in line with those achieved in the year to 30 September 19X1. The directors of each company plan to pay out the entire profits in the form of dividends.

Required

(a) Set out the following calculations, for each company, expressed in tabular format.

	Greenwood	Westport
Net profit percentage	....	....
Gross profit margin	....	....
Debt: equity ratio	....	....
Total funds generated from operations	....	....

(8 marks)

(b) State which calculations under (a), if any, favour Greenwood and which calculations, if any, favour Westport. (4 marks)

(c) Based on the results of your findings under (a) and (b), together with any other calculations you consider appropriate, explain to which company you would be more willing to grant loan facilities. (8 marks)

34 THORNVILLE (30 marks) 5/91

Thornville Ltd is a company, formed ten years ago, which supplies computer software to businesses located in the west of England and south Wales. The company is run by Peter and John Sutton who, together with members of their family, have owned the entire share capital, which amounts to £50,000 (100,000 shares with a nominal value of 50p each), since incorporation.

Peter and John visited your bank yesterday to request an increase in the overdraft facility, which currently stands at £90,000. They point to the substantial annual increase in both turnover and profit, in most years, as evidence of the continuing viability of their company. The following information is taken from the management accounts for the last five years.

QUESTIONS

(a) PROFIT AND LOSS ACCOUNT
FOR THE YEAR TO 31 MARCH

	19X1 £'000	19X2 £'000	19X3 £'000	19X4 £'000	19X5 £'000
Turnover	2,460	2,706	2,977	3,274	3,601
Gross profit	775	852	893	949	1,008
Trading overheads					
Directors' remuneration	100	100	86	86	86
Wages and salaries	368	412	421	461	470
Depreciation	75	70	65	40	35
Interest charges	12	12	12	16	21
Other overheads	180	204	237	286	299
Operating profit	40	54	72	60	97
Corporation tax	10	13	18	20	29
Profit after tax	30	41	54	40	68

(b) Figures for shareholders' equity, long-term liabilities (a 12% debenture repayable 19X8), the bank balance (overdraft) and a price index constructed internally to measure the *average* price of goods *sold* are as follows.

31 March	Shareholders' equity £'000	12% Debenture £'000	Bank balance/ (overdraft) £'000	Price index for goods sold sold
19X0	150	100	42	100
19X1	180	100	45	104
19X2	221	100	37	108
19X3	275	100	44	115
19X4	255	100	(30)	128
19X5	323	100	(60)	144

(c) The following additional information, relating to the figures stated in the above accounts, came to light during discussions with Peter and John Sutton.

(i) The directors explain that apparent performance suffered during 19X3/X4 due to the omission from stock at 31 March 19X4 of certain items, worth £21,000, located in the loading bay.

(ii) The depreciation charge includes £20,000 in respect of goodwill amortised for each of the years to 31 March 19X3. In 19X3/X4 the company changed its accounting policy and instead wrote off the remaining balance of £60,000 against reserves.

Required

Prepare a full appraisal of the financial information provided by the directors of Thornville Ltd. The following items should be included in your appraisal.

(a) A clear indication of any adjustments necessary to enable valid comparisons to be made, year by year, between the figures for gross profit, net profit and shareholders' equity.

(b) The following accounting ratios based on the figures you have revised under (a) above:

QUESTIONS

   (i)   gross profit percentage
   (ii) net profit percentage (pre-tax)
   (iii) return on year end equity (pre-tax)
   (iv) interest cover
   (v)   total debt: equity ratio.

(c) Any other calculations you consider appropriate.

Notes

1 Ignore Advance Corporation Tax.
2 Assume none of the adjustments affects the corporation tax charge for the year.

35   PINFOLD   (30 marks)   5/91

The forecast accounts of Pinfold Ltd for the year to 30 June 19X1 show the following financial results which the directors are confident will be achieved.

PROFIT AND LOSS ACCOUNT
FOR THE YEAR ENDED 30 JUNE 19X9

	£'000
Turnover	4,800
Direct materials	1,800
Direct labour and variable overheads	1,500
Contribution	1,500
Fixed overheads	1,200
Net profit	300

BALANCE SHEET AS AT 30 JUNE 19X1

	£'000	£'000
Fixed assets (at cost less depreciation)		1,000
Current assets		
Stocks		
Raw materials	150	
Work in progress	425	
Finished goods	275	
Cash	50	
	900	
Current liabilities		
Trade creditors	225	
Working capital		675
Total assets less current liabilities		1,675
Financed by		
Shareholders equity		1,675

The company's accountants are preparing the budget for the year to 30 June 19X2. There is a strong demand for the company's products, and it is estimated that an increase of up to 25% in the *volume* of sales can be achieved, which would have consequential implications for the selling price and operating costs. The following information is provided.

QUESTIONS

(a) The selling price can be increased by 11% with effect from 1 July, assuming the existing level of activity, or 2.5% if the directors decide to aim for a 25% increase in the volume of activity. All sales are made for cash.

(b) Direct material costs per unit are expected to increase by 6%, due to rising prices, with effect from 1 July 19X1. However, a 25% increase in the level of activity would enable the directors to negotiate a 4% trade discount on all purchases. Materials are held in stock for one month before being transferred to production. Suppliers allow 45 days credit.

(c) Direct labour and variable overheads per unit are expected to increase by 8%, with effect from 1 July 19X1, following the completion of wage negotiations presently in progress. Payments for labour and variable overheads are made on the last day of each month.

(d) Fixed overheads are expected to rise by 10% for the 12 months commencing 1 July 19X1.

(e) Factory processing takes two months. Production is carried out at a steady rate throughout the year. Materials are introduced at the start of processing; labour and overheads are then incurred at an even rate during the processing period.

(f) Finished goods are held in stock for one month awaiting sale.

(g) Stocks are matched with sales on the first in first out (FIFO) basis. Work in progress and finished goods are valued on the variable (marginal) cost basis for the purpose of the management accounts.

(h) Operating cash requirements will increase from £50,000 to £52,000 if activity remains at existing levels, but will rise to £65,000 if activity rises by 25%.

Required

(a) Prepare budgeted profit and loss accounts for the year to 30 June 19X2 in the format given in the question, on the alternative assumptions that:

   (i) the volume of sales will remain unchanged;
   (ii) the volume of sales will increase by 25%.

Ignore changes in the value of opening and closing stocks for the purpose of the above calculations. (8 marks)

(b) Calculate the expected additional investment in working capital, compared with the forecast position at 30 June 19X1, as the result of implementing each of the two plans examined under (a). (10 marks)

(c) Compare the two plans, indicating the advantages/disadvantages to the company and paying particular attention to their relative profitability and the possible ways of financing the additional working capital requirements. (12 marks)

Notes

1. Make all calculations to the nearest £'000.
2. Assume that a year consists of twelve months of 30 days each.
3. Present your answers to (a) and (b) in columnar format.
4. Ignore taxation.

QUESTIONS

36 ALBAN AND LAMB (30 marks)   10/91

Alban and Lamb are partners in a firm called Alban Lamb & Co which acts as agents for the sale of commercial premises and domestic dwellings and also manages properties on behalf of clients. Alban deals entirely with the sale of commercial and domestic dwellings and spends time equally on these two activities, while Lamb, who works part time, is client property manager. The partners share profits equally after allowing for salaries which appear in the revenue account below.

The following information is provided for the year to 30 June 19X1 together with some comparative figures for the previous financial year.

REVENUE ACCOUNT FOR THE YEAR ENDED 30 JUNE

	19X1 £	19X0 £
Revenue		
Commissions received: commercial properties	36,000	
domestic properties	63,000	
managed properties	29,500	
	128,500	123,000
Expenditure		
Advertising: commercial properties	14,200	
domestic properties	15,500	
Rent collection costs	4,100	
Cleaning managed properties	3,700	
Salary of: Alban	24,000	
Lamb	10,800	
Other salaries	22,500	
Finance charges (19X0: £2,500)	3,200	
General administration costs	33,000	
	131,000	102,400
Surplus/(deficit)	(2,500)	20,600

BALANCE SHEET AS AT 30 JUNE

	19X1 £	19X0 £
Assets		
Freehold premises	85,000	20,000
Furniture and equipment	9,400	5,100
Debtors	11,100	6,000
Bank balance		4,200
	105,500	35,300

	£	£
Financed by		
Capital: Alban	36,450	5,200
Lamb	34,250	3,000
Trade creditors	9,300	5,900
Value added tax (VAT) outstanding	3,400	1,200
Bank overdraft	2,100	-
Loan from financial institution	20,000	20,000
	105,500	35,300

It is discovered that the freehold premises, previously stated at cost, were revalued during the year to 30 June 19X1 and that the figure for trade creditors, at 30 June 19X1, includes £2,500 in respect of a recently acquired photocopier. It is estimated that staff, other than Alban and Lamb, spend an equal amount of time on each of the three areas of activity.

Alban and Lamb have approached your bank and requested an increase in the firm's overdraft limit from £7,500 to £15,000 for a six month period. They point out that the overdraft shown in the balance sheet is very modest when compared with total balance sheet assets of £105,000 including a freehold property valued at £85,000.

Required

(a) Prepare a report for the bank on the financial progress and position of the firm in the light of the request for an increased overdraft facility. The report should be based on the accounting ratios listed below, an analysed revenue account showing the results of each activity, and any other calculations you consider relevant.

Accounting ratios

(i) Net profit percentage (margin).
(ii) Interest cover.
(iii) Rate of return on partners' capital investment.
(iv) Liquidity (quick) ratio.
(v) Gearing ratio. (25 marks)

(b) Identify five limitations of ratio analysis. You should illustrate the limitations, where possible, by reference to the information you have given in answer to (a) above.
(5 marks)

Note. A recommendation on whether to grant the overdraft is not required.

37 TUTORIAL QUESTION: CASH FLOW STATEMENTS

The directors of Arc Ltd have decided to implement the terms of FRS 1 *Cash flow statements* in the accounts at the earliest opportunity. The following information is available.

PROFIT AND LOSS ACCOUNT FOR THE YEAR ENDED 31 DECEMBER

	19X0 £'000	19X1 £'000
Operating profit	9,400	20,640
Interest paid	–	(280)
Interest received	100	40
Profit before taxation	9,500	20,400
Taxation	3,200	5,200
Profit after taxation	6,300	15,200
Dividends		
Preference (paid)	100	100
Ordinary: interim (paid)	1,000	2,000
final (proposed)	3,000	6,000
Retained profit for the year	2,200	7,100

QUESTIONS

BALANCE SHEET AS AT 31 DECEMBER

	19X0 £'000	19X1 £'000
Fixed assets		
Plant, machinery and equipment, at cost	17,600	23,900
Less accumulated depreciation	9,500	10,750
	8,100	13,150
Current assets		
Stocks	5,000	15,000
Trade debtors	8,600	26,700
Prepayments	300	400
Cash at bank and in hand	600	-
	14,500	42,100
Current liabilities		
Bank overdraft	-	16,200
Trade creditors	6,000	10,000
Accruals	800	1,000
Taxation	3,200	5,200
Dividends	3,200	6,000
	13,000	38,400
Net assets	9,600	16,850
Share capital		
Ordinary shares of £1 each	5,000	5,000
10% preference shares of £1 each	1,000	1,000
Profit and loss account	3,000	10,100
	9,000	16,100
Loans		
15% debenture stock	600	750
	9,600	16,850

Additional information

(a) The directors are extremely concerned about the large bank overdraft as at 31 December 19X1, and they attribute this mainly to the increase in trade debtors as a result of alleged poor credit control.

(b) During the year to 31 December 19X1, fixed assets originally costing £5,500,000 were sold for £1,000,000. The accumulated depreciation on these assets as at 31 December 19X0 was £3,800,000.

Required

(a) Prepare a cash flow statement for the year to 31 December 19X1 using the format laid out in FRS 1.

(b) Compare FRS 1 with SSAP 10 and state whether you feel the use of cash flow statements will improve the standard of financial reporting, with reference to your answer in (a).

38 SCAPENS (30 marks) 5/90

The following accounting information is provided for Scapens which trades in electrical goods.

PROFIT AND LOSS ACCOUNT FOR THE YEAR ENDED 31 MARCH

	19X2 £'000	19X1 £'000
Turnover	6,375	5,920
Cost of sales	4,311	4,070
Gross profit	2,064	1,850
Administrative expenses	1,174	995
Distribution costs	640	627
Trading profit before interest	250	228
Interest payable	65	18
Profit on ordinary activities before tax	185	210
Tax on profit on ordinary activities	55	60
	130	150
Extraordinary item	70	-
	200	150
Dividends	150	120
Retained profit for the year	50	30

BALANCE SHEET AS AT 31 MARCH

	19X2 £'000	19X2 £'000	19X1 £'000	19X1 £'000
Fixed assets				
Tangible assets (note 1)		2,532		2,450
Current assets				
Stocks	989		700	
Debtors	64		60	
Cash at bank and in hand	98		12	
	1,151		772	
Creditors: amounts falling due within one year				
Bank overdraft	-		75	
Trade creditors	140		185	
Proposed dividends	150		120	
Other creditors (including taxation)	76		77	
	366		457	
Net current assets		785		315
Total assets less current liabilities		3,317		2,765
Debentures and loans	600		100	
Provisions for liabilities and charges (note 2)	652		150	
		52		50
Net assets		2,665		2,615
Capital and reserves				
Called up share capital		2,000		2,000
Share premium account		200		200
Profit and loss account		465		415
		2,665		2,615

QUESTIONS

Notes

1 *Tangible fixed assets*

	Properties Leasehold £'000	Properties Freehold £'000	Vehicles etc £'000	Total £'000
Net book value at 31 March 19X1	30	2,200	220	2,450
Additions	-	100	120	220
Sales at book value	-	-	(20)	(20)
Depreciation charged	(18)	(40)	(60)	(118)
Net book value at 31 March 19X2	12	2,260	260	2,532

Vehicles sold during the year raised £9,000. The directors' report states that the company's properties have a current market value of £4m.

2 These provisions are for estimated future warranty costs.

The following financial information, in respect of the year to 31 March 19X2, is provided by the Trade Association to which Scapens belongs.

	Upper quartile*	Median quartile*	Lower quartile*
Working capital (current) ratio	2.9:1	2.5:1	2.0:1
Ratio of long term debt to equity	2%	5%	10%
Rate of stock turnover	45 days	50 days	60 days
Total asset turnover	2.3:1	2.0:1	1.9:1
Rate of return on shareholders' equity	12%	8%	6%

* The meaning of these terms is as follows.

Upper quartile
The average of the best 25% of ratios achieved by members of the Trade Association.

Median quartile
The average of the middle 25% of ratios achieved by members of the Trade Association.

Lower quartile
The average of the worst 25% of ratios achieved by members of the Trade Association.

Future warranty costs
The directors are of the opinion that the company is making good progress, and point to the increase in trading profit to £250,000 and the fact that there has also been an improvement in the cash position. The directors have approached the bank for finance to help purchase the freehold of one of the company's leasehold properties, whose lease runs out on 30 September 19X2. The asking price for the property is £200,000.

Required

Prepare a report for the bank on the financial progress and position of Scapens plc. Your report should include a statement of funds for the year ended 31 March 19X2, and also a comparison of the information obtained from the Trade Association with corresponding ratios computed for Scapens plc.

Note. Ignore advance corporation tax.

39 NOTLEY (30 marks) 5/89

Notley Ltd was incorporated in May 19X7 to purchase and sell a single product, and it plans to commence business operations on 1 July 19X7. The business is to be managed by two directors who, in June 19X7, will together subscribe equally for the entire issued share capital consisting of 60,000 ordinary shares of £1 each, at par. Fixed assets costing £54,000 and stocks costing £30,000 will be acquired in June 19X7 and paid for in July.

The directors have made arrangements for venture capital to be provided, if required, in the form of a five-year loan carrying interest at 12% per annum. The amount of the loan will be equal to the estimated cash deficiency, if any, at 30 September 19X7, and will be advanced on 1 October 19X7. The bank has agreed to provide overdraft facilities to meet any cash deficiencies not covered by this arrangement. Interest on venture capital will be payable, annually, on 30 September. Ignore interest on any bank overdraft.

The estimated revenue account for the year to 30 June 19X8 (which does not take account of interest on venture loan capital) is as follows.

ESTIMATED REVENUE ACCOUNT

	£'000	£'000	Comment
Sales		500	Credit period: 1½ months
Cost of stock sold	300		Credit period on purchases: one month
Direct labour costs (variable with turnover)	50		Payable on the last day of each week
Variable expenses	60		Payable one month after the date incurred
Fixed expenses	24		Payable quarterly in advance: first payment 1 July 19X7
Directors' remuneration	48		£2,000 (each) payable on last day of each month
Depreciation	9		Fixed assets' estimated life: six years
		491	
Net profit		9	

The following additional information is provided.

(a) Sales will accrue at an even rate during the six months to 31 December 19X7 and are estimated at £200,000. Thereafter, and for the foreseeable future, sales are estimated at £50,000 per month.

(b) Purchases each month will be sufficient to replace items sold.

(c) The market rate for the services provided by each of the two directors is estimated at £1,600 per person per month.

(d) The entire profit is to be distributed as dividends.

Required

(a) Prepare a cash forecast for each of the four quarters to 30 June 19X8 showing the estimated accumulated cash surplus or deficit at the end of each quarter. (8 marks)

QUESTIONS

(b) Explain the difference between the forecast trading profit for the year to 30 June 19X8 and the expected change in the cash balance over the same twelve-month period. You should support your explanation with an appropriate numerical calculation. (10 marks)

(c) Assess the prospects of Notley Ltd from the viewpoint of the two directors. You should include in your assessment an estimate of profit for the year to 30 June 19X9.
(12 marks)

Notes

1. Assume that a year consists of 48 weeks, a quarter of 12 weeks and a month of 4 weeks.
2. Ignore taxation.

40 WHALEY (30 marks) 5/92

Whaley plc is a retail organisation with outlets in a number of large towns and cities in the Midlands. The company requires finance for prospective acquisitions and has approached your bank for medium-term finance, comprising a four-year secured loan of £5 million. The following information is extracted from the published accounts for the year to 31 March 19X2.

BALANCE SHEET AS AT 31 MARCH

	19X2 £'000	19X1 £'000
Fixed assets		
Tangible assets	35,760	20,400
Investments at cost	700	1,500
	36,460	21,900
Current assets	6,700	6,280
Creditors: amounts falling due within one year		
Current corporation tax	1,423	1,200
Proposed dividends	500	500
Other payments due	2,800	1,910
Net current assets	1,977	2,670
Total assets less current liabilities	38,437	24,570
Creditors falling due after one year	10,000	10,000
	28,437	14,570
Capital and reserves		
Called up share capital (£1 ordinary shares)	20,000	10,000
Reserves	8,437	4,570
	28,437	14,570

PROFIT AND LOSS ACCOUNT FOR THE YEAR ENDED 31 MARCH

	19X2 £'000	19X1 £'000
Turnover	46,150	44,090
Cost of goods sold	37,310	36,210
Gross profit	8,840	7,880
Administrative expenses	3,220	2,611
Distribution costs	520	509
Operating profit	5,100	4,760
Finance charges	1,480	1,610
Profit on ordinary activities before tax	3,620	3,150
Taxation	1,243	1,200
Profit on ordinary activities after tax	2,377	1,950
Extraordinary profit	420	-
Profit after tax	2,797	1,950
Dividends paid	800	800
Dividends proposed	500	500
Retained profit for the year	1,497	650

TANGIBLE FIXED ASSETS

	Freehold land and buildings £'000	Machinery vehicles, etc £'000	Total £'000
Cost or valuation			
At 1 April 19X1	25,440	4,900	30,340
Additions	3,600	710	4,310
Surplus on revaluation	4,170	-	4,170
At 31 March 19X2	33,210	5,610	38,820
Depreciation			
At 1 April 19X1	8,200	1,740	9,940
Provided during year	800	520	1,320
Surplus on revaluation	(8,200)	-	(8,200)
At 31 March 19X2	800	2,260	3,060
Net book amounts			
At 1 April 19X1	17,240	3,160	20,400
At 31 March 19X2	32,410	3,350	35,760

Notes

1 *Revaluation method*
   The freehold land and buildings were professionally revalued on 2 April 19X1. The depreciation charged prior to revaluation was found to be unnecessary and has been written back to reserves.

2 *Extraordinary profit*
   The company sold investments with a book value of £800,000 for £1,400,000. The corporation tax charge due in respect of this capital gain is estimated at £180,000.

3 *Bonus issue*
   The directors made a bonus issue, on 1 January 19X2, of one new ordinary share, fully paid, for every share held at 31 December 19X1.

QUESTIONS

Required

(a) Reconcile the balance on reserves at 31 March 19X1 with the balance a year later.
(6 marks)

(b) Prepare a statement of source and application of funds for the year ended 31 March 19X2, so far as the information permits.
(6 marks)

(c) Calculate of the following ratios in respect of the year ended 31 March 19X2, together with corresponding calculations for the previous year.

   (i) Gearing ratio (calculated as creditors due after one year: equity).
   (ii) Net profit percentage.
   (iii) Gross profit margin.
   (iv) Total asset turnover.
   (v) Return (pre-tax) on shareholders' equity.
   (vi) Working capital (current) ratio.
(6 marks)

(d) A discussion of the financial progress and position of Whaley plc, from the bank's point of view, based on your calculations made in answer to requirements (a) to (c). State whether you consider that the bank should provide the finance requested. (12 marks)

Note. Ignore advance corporation tax.

41 TUTORIAL QUESTION: GEORGE

George manufactures commemorative medals. The following data relates to 19X0.

	£
Selling price	50
Variable production cost	30
Variable selling cost	5
	15
Fixed production cost, based on annual sales of 20,000 medals	5
Fixed selling costs based on annual sales of 20,000 medals	1
	9

Required

(a) Calculate the level of production needed for George to break even.

(b) George is thinking of doubling his production. To do so, he will have to occupy additional premises at a cost of £210,000. What will be the breakeven point?

42 NEWELL (20 marks) 5/90

Newell Ltd manufactures widgets for sale in the UK market at £50 each. The head office is located in Wokingham, whilst factory buildings are rented in Wokingham, Oxford and Glasgow to manufacture this product. The following estimates have been prepared for the year to 30 June 19X1.

FORECAST OUTPUT: YEAR ENDED 30 JUNE 19X1

	Units
Wokingham	48,000
Oxford	32,000
Glasgow	60,000
	140,000

FORECAST OPERATING STATEMENT: YEAR ENDED 30 JUNE 19X1

	Head office £'000	Woking-ham £'000	Oxford £'000	Glasgow £'000	Total £'000
Sales		2,400	1,600	3,000	7,000
Variable costs		1,440	1,040	1,800	4,280
Fixed costs					
Factory		600	500	700	1,800
Administration	140	20	15	25	200
Re-allocated costs	(140)	48	32	60	-
	-	2,108	1,587	2,585	6,280
	-	292	13	415	720

The managing director is very disappointed with the forecast results for the Oxford factory and asks the financial controller to explore possible alternatives. The following points arise.

(a) There is no spare capacity at the Glasgow factory, but capacity available at Wokingham is sufficient to enable the production of 60,000 widgets in total. Additional costs of £5 per unit would be incurred to transport the widgets to customers of the Oxford factory. The fixed factory costs of Wokingham would increase to £700,000 and the administration costs to £25,000.

(b) An overseas company, Leyton SA, is keen to market its own widgets in the UK. It would be possible for Newell to enter into a contract for Leyton to supply some of Newell's existing customers. Leyton would pay a commission of £3 per unit to Newell.

Required

(a) Prepare a report containing calculations which indicate the financial effects of the policy options open to the management of Newell listed below. Each of the policy options should be considered separately.

   (i)   Close the Oxford factory.

   (ii) Implement option (i) and *also* expand output at Wokingham.

   (iii) Implement option (i) and *also* contract with Leyton to supply former customers of the Oxford factory.

   (iv) Implement option (ii) and *also* contract with Leyton to supply former customers of the Oxford factory. (16 marks)

(b) Which one of the options in (a) would you recommend management to follow, assuming the principal criterion is profit maximisation? Explain your choice. (4 marks)

QUESTIONS

Note. You may assume that, if production is discontinued at Oxford, steps can be taken to eliminate fixed costs incurred locally, and that the disposal value of equipment will be just sufficient to cover any costs associated with closure.

43 HELMORE (30 marks)   10/90

Helmore Ltd has traded for some years, confining its activities to the south west of England. The planning department has prepared the following budgeted information for the calendar year 19X1.

(a) *Revenue and expenditure*

	£
Selling price per unit	20
Variable cost per unit	12
Fixed costs per annum	300,000

(b) Both production and sales are expected to amount to 50,000 units, and this means that the company should be able to operate at full productive capacity throughout the year.

The planning department has also discovered that there exists a strong demand for the company's product in the north of England provided the selling price in that region does not exceed £18 per unit. Helmore Ltd is able to arrange additional facilities which will increase total capacity to 80,000 units per annum, but this will produce an annual increase in fixed costs of £150,000 per annum. Additional packaging costs, designed to distinguish the product sold in the north of England from that marketed in the south west, will cause variable costs per unit for those goods sold in the north to rise to £13. The planning department estimates that demand in the north of England will be at least 5,000 units per annum and may be as much as 40,000 units per annum.

Required

(a) Assuming the company continues to trade only in the south west of England, prepare calculations for 19X1 of:

  (i) budgeted profit;
  (ii) the break-even point, in units;
  (iii) the margin of safety, expressed as a percentage.   (10 marks)

(b) Assuming the company wishes to examine the possible extension of its activities to the north of England, prepare a table showing the expected results for 19X1, at output intervals of 10,000 units, over the range of activity zero to 80,000 units. Indicate on the table the point, or points, at which the company breaks even.

For the purpose of preparing the table, you should assume that the first 50,000 units of production are sold in the south west and that all extra production will be used to supply the north of England.   (8 marks)

(c) Assess the results obtained under (a) and (b), and include your advice to the management of Helmore Ltd concerning whether it should sell its product in the north of England.
                                                                              (12 marks)

QUESTIONS

44 HENLEY (20 marks) 10/91

The management of Henley Ltd intends to expand its scale of operations and the planning department has produced the following estimates for two new products for 19X2, each of which uses the same grade of skilled labour.

	Product A	Product B
Sales volume per annum	12,000	10,000
	£	£
Sales price per unit	45	40
Costs per unit: direct materials	11	14
direct labour, £5 per hour	15	10
variable overheads	4	3
Fixed costs per annum	80,000	70,000

In addition, you discover that:

(a) salesmen are entitled to a commission of 5% on each item sold;

(b) the fixed costs represent an allocation of business overheads which Henley will incur whether or not it decides to proceed with either or both of the above products.

Required

(a) Prepare an operating statement showing, for each product line, the forecast contribution per unit and forecast total contribution and net profit, assuming the estimated sales volume per annum is achieved. (8 marks)

(b) Explain what you understand by the term 'limiting factor'. (4 marks)

(c) Assuming that the company is able to engage sufficient skilled labour to work no more than 26,000 hours during 19X2, use limiting factor analysis to help plan production for the year. (8 marks)

45 CARBURTON (30 marks) 5/92

Carburton Ltd manufactures a standard product, designated XL, which sells for £70 per unit. The company normally produces and sells 16,000 units per annum, representing 80% of total available capacity. The cost forecasts for the twelve months commencing 1 June 19X2, set out below, have been prepared on the assumption that the company operates at its normal level of activity throughout that period. The estimated costs at full capacity are provided for the purpose of comparison.

Level of activity	80%	100%
Costs	£	£
Direct materials	480,000	600,000
Direct labour	80,000	100,000
Production overhead	260,000	300,000
Administration costs	220,000	220,000

The production overheads contain both fixed and variable costs.

QUESTIONS

The demand for XL has recently weakened, and the sales manager is doubtful whether it will be possible to operate at much more than 60% of full capacity during the forthcoming year.

From time to time Carburton Ltd also manufactures specialist machinery, SM, for which it holds a registered patent. The SM machine is constructed by workers, specifically engaged for that purpose, in a part of the factory which otherwise remains vacant. An SM machine has been completed for a customer, for an agreed price of £50,000, at a cost of £42,000. The customer has since gone into liquidation and is unable to proceed with the planned acquisition. The sales manager has produced three possible schemes for the disposal of the SM machine. These schemes have the following financial implications.

Scheme 1 Sell the SM machine, as it stands, to Roche Ltd at a 20% discount on the price of £50,000.

Scheme 2 An offer of £56,000 has been received from Renishaw Ltd for the SM machine, provided it is re-designed to meet Renishaw's specifications. It is estimated that the following additional costs will be incurred during the conversion process; direct materials, £7,000; direct labour, £4,000.

Scheme 3 Convert the SM machine to a general purpose model which the sales manager is confident can be sold for £54,000. The conversion costs in this case are: direct materials, £6,000; direct labour, £1,500. Under this option, advertising costs will be incurred amounting to £1,000.

Required

(a) (i) Calculate the contribution arising from the sale of each unit of XL. (6 marks)

    (ii) Prepare an operating statement which sets out the expected revenues, costs, contribution and profit at:

        (1) 60% of total capacity - the sales manager's estimate;
        (2) 80% of total capacity - the normal level of output. (5 marks)

    (iii) Calculate the break-even point, in units, for the sale of product XL. (4 marks)

    (iv) Calculate the relevant (marginal) costs and revenues for each of the three possible schemes for dealing with the SM machine. (5 marks)

(b) Advise Carburton's management on the financial implications of your calculations under (a) above. (10 marks)

Note. There are no stocks of XL at either the beginning or the end of the year.

46 FELL (20 marks)   5/92

J Fell is the owner of a firm which supplies and assembles garden sheds. Fell urgently needs to replace his office computing system and plans to make the acquisition on 1 July 19X2. The cost of the new system is £30,000. Fell is in the process of selling some land surplus to business requirements for £40,000, and he estimates that this transaction will be completed at around the end of the current calendar year. The firm's overdraft, on which interest is charged at 1.5% per month, is close to the limit of £20,000 and is normally fully utilised.

The following schemes are under consideration as a means of financing the required computing facility between 1 July 19X2 and 31 December 19X2.

Scheme 1 Hire a comparable computing system for £800 per month, payable on the first day of each month July to December.

Scheme 2 Purchase the system, on 1 July, and finance it by raising a short-term loan of £30,000. This scheme would involve an initial arrangement fee of £1,000 and an interest charge of 20% per annum, charged on a six-monthly basis.

Scheme 3 Offer customers a 2.5% cash discount for immediate payment. The company currently collects its debts, on average, one month after the date of sale. It is estimated that 25% of all customers would choose to take the discount offer. The offer would apply to all sales made from 1 July 19X2, which are estimated to amount to £160,000 per month.

Required

(a) Calculate the financial implications of each of the three schemes. (12 marks)

(b) Evaluate each of the three schemes, drawing attention to any matter which Fell should consider before reaching a decision. (8 marks)

Note. Ignore taxation and compound interest.

47 LANDORE (20 marks) 5/90

Landore Ltd has two investment projects under consideration, each involving an initial outlay on plant (which will last for five years) of £240,000 and on working capital of £10,000. The company is able to arrange finance for one, but not both, of these projects.

The estimated net cash inflows for the two projects are as follows.

Year	Project 1 £'000	Project 2 £'000
1	80	60
2	80	200
3	90	90
4	100	10
5	50	15

Required

(a) Prepare a numerical analysis of each of the two projects using the following methods of capital project appraisal:

 (i) accounting rate of return;
 (ii) net present value (the appropriate discount rate is 15%). (10 marks)

(b) Discuss the relative merits of the two methods of capital project appraisal used above. Advise the management of Landore Ltd which project should be chosen. (10 marks)

QUESTIONS

Notes

1   Assume that the initial investment will be made at the beginning of year one, and that annual net cash inflows arise at the year end.

2   Make your calculations to the nearest £'000.

3   Ignore taxation.

A table of discount factors will be found on Page 29.

48 BUCKNALL   (20 marks)   10/91

The directors of Bucknall Ltd have decided to undertake a programme of expansion. They have under consideration two mutually exclusive three year projects, and intend to invest in the project which offers the greater financial gain. The initial capital investment, and the annual cash flows which are expected to arise from each project, are as follows.

	Project Y £	Project Z £
Capital investment	10,000	16,000
Annual cash flows Year		
1	4,897	7,596
2	4,897	7,596
3	4,897	7,596

The cost of capital is 15%.

Required

(a) Calculate the net present value (NPV) of each project.   (8 marks)

(b) Calculate the discounted cash flow (DCF) yield or internal rate of return (IRR) of each project.   (6 marks)

(c) Compare and comment on the results of your calculations under (a) and (b). Identify which project should be preferred by management.   (6 marks)

Note. The capital investment will be undertaken immediately and the annual cash flows may be assumed to arise at the year end. Ignore taxation.

TABLES OF FACTORS

Present value of £1

Years	15%	16%	17%	18%	19%	20%	21%	22%	23%	24%
1	0.870	0.862	0.855	0.847	0.840	0.833	0.826	0.820	0.813	0.806
2	0.756	0.743	0.731	0.718	0.706	0.694	0.683	0.671	0.661	0.650
3	0.658	0.641	0.624	0.609	0.593	0.579	0.564	0.551	0.537	0.525

Present value of £1 received per year for three years

15%	16%	17%	18%	19%	20%	21%	22%	23%	24%
2.284	2.246	2.210	2.174	2.139	2.106	2.073	2.042	2.011	1.981

49 KAPLAN (30 marks) 5/90

Kaplan Ltd is a well established private company whose balance sheet at 31 December 19X8, was as follows.

	19X8 £'000	19X8 £'000	19X7 £'000	19X7 £'000
Fixed assets at cost		1,370		1,250
Accumulated depreciation		500		450
		870		800
Current Assets				
Stock	285		280	
Debtors	296		302	
Cash at bank	56		12	
	637		594	
Current liabilities				
Creditors	131		128	
Corporation tax due 30 September	35		30	
	166		158	
Net current assets		471		436
		1,341		1,236
Financed by				
Share capital		1,000		1,000
Plant replacement reserve		200		150
Retained profit		141		86
		1,341		1,236

The profits derived from existing activities during 19X8 are expected to be repeated during the current financial year and next year.

In addition, the directors plan to expand the company's range of business operations by selling glass conservatories imported from abroad. The following estimates have been prepared for this plan.

(a) Advertising costs will amount to £10,000 in June 19X9 and £1,000 in each month that follows. The advertising agency is expected to allow one month's credit.

(b) Sales of conservatories are estimated at £30,000 per month during the months of July-September 19X9, inclusive, and £45,000 per month thereafter.

(c) An initial stock of conservatories costing £60,000 will be purchased and paid for in June 19X9. Commencing July 19X9, sufficient conservatories will be purchased and paid for each month to replace items sold.

(d) The sales price of conservatories is to be fixed at 50% above purchase price.

(e) Customers will be required to pay 80% of the sales price on installation and 20% one month later.

(f) Installation costs are expected to be £2,000 per month during the months of July-September, inclusive, and £3,000 per month thereafter. These costs are to be paid immediately they are incurred.

(g) General administration expenses, also paid immediately they are incurred, will amount to £6,000 per month commencing July.

(h) Provision is to be made for corporation tax at the rate of 25% on forecast profit before tax.

Required

(a) Reconstruct the profit and loss appropriation account of Kaplan Ltd for 19X8. (5 marks)

(b) Prepare a monthly cash flow forecast for the new project for each of the six months from 1 July to 31 December 19X9. (8 marks)

(c) Calculate the estimated bank balance, or overdraft, of the company at 31 December 19X9. (4 marks)

(d) Provide a profit forecast for the new project for the six month period to 31 December 19X9 (monthly figures are not required). (5 marks)

(e) Write a brief report, for the company's bank, on the profitability and financial implications of the new project. (8 marks)

Notes

1 The bank has agreed to provide overdraft facilities if required.

2 Ignore advance corporation tax and bank interest payable if any.

50 ROWAN   (30 marks)   10/90

The directors of Rowan Ltd arrive at your bank on 15 October 19X8 to inform you of a dispute about wages to be paid to production workers for the year commencing 1 April 19X9. These employees have decided to go on strike commencing 1 November 19X8, and the directors estimate that the strike will last one month, during which time the strikers will not be paid. It is expected that production and sales for November will be totally lost (no goods will be produced and no deliveries will be made during that month) and it will not be possible to increase production and sales in future months to make up the shortfall. Activity for December onwards is expected to be in line with the original forecast. The directors suspect that the company will require overdraft facilities as a result of the industrial action, and seek your advice.

The following plans, calculations and estimates were prepared in September 19X8 before the industrial dispute arose.

(a) MONTHLY CASH FORECAST FOR THE EIGHT
MONTHS COMMENCING 1 OCTOBER 19X8

	Oct £'000	Nov £'000	Dec £'000	Jan £'000	Feb £'000	Mar £'000	April £'000	May £'000
Receipts								
Sales of stock	30	50	52	60	60	52	55	48
Plant sold	-	10	-	-	-	-	-	-
	30	60	52	60	60	52	55	48
Payments								
Materials	12	20	21	24	24	21	22	19
Direct factory wages	11	12	12	10	11	10	12	11
Other factory expenses								
Fixed	1	1	1	1	1	1	1	1
Variable	4	4	4	3	4	3	4	4
General expenses	4	4	5	4	5	5	5	5
Salesmen's salaries	5	5	5	5	5	5	5	5
Salesmen's commission	3	3	3	3	3	3	2	2
	40	49	51	50	53	48	51	47
Monthly surplus/(deficit)	(10)	11	1	10	7	4	4	1
Brought forward	12	2	13	14	24	31	35	39
Carried forward	2	13	14	24	31	35	39	40

(b) Customers receive, and suppliers allow, two months' credit.

(c) The plant to be sold has a book value of £12,000.

(d) Direct factory wages, other variable factory expenses and salesmen's salaries are paid during the month they are incurred. Salesmen's salaries will continue to be paid during November 19X8.

(e) Fixed factory expenses and general expenses are paid after a time lag of one month.

(f) Salesmen's commission is paid on the basis of deliveries made during the previous month.

(g) The depreciation charge for the six months to 31 March 19X9 is £12,000.

(h) The company's stock is maintained at a steady level of £30,000.

Required

(a) Calculate the forecast profit for the six month period to 31 March 19X9, assuming the strike had not occurred. A monthly cash forecast is not required. (8 marks)

(b) Prepare a revised monthly cash forecast for each of the four months commencing 1 November 19X8, assuming the strike lasts for one month. (7 marks)

(c) Calculate the effect of the strike on forecast profit for the six month period to 31 March 19X9. (5 marks)

(d) Write a short report for the management of Rowan Ltd on the financial implications of the strike. The report should be based on your calculations under (a), (b) and (c) and any other information you consider relevant. (10 marks)

QUESTIONS

51 HOBHOUSE (30 marks)   10/91

Hobhouse Ltd is a private company which installs double glazing in domestic and commercial premises. Reginald Jones is its managing director and he and his wife own all the shares. The recession produced a downturn in demand, and cash flow problems resulted in the company approaching the bank for funds at the beginning of 19X0. The bank granted overdraft facilities with an initial limit of £5,000 that has since been increased to £10,000.

The summarised balance sheet as at 30 September 19X1 contained the following information.

BALANCE SHEET AS AT 30 SEPTEMBER 19X1

	£	£
Offices and equipment at cost less depreciation		14,500
Current assets		
Stock of double glazing units	8,000	
Work in progress (note 1)	10,000	
	18,000	
Current liabilities		
Deposits from customers (note 2)	3,600	
Trade creditors	8,000	
Bank overdraft	7,500	
	19,100	
Net current liabilities		(1,100)
		13,400
Financed by		
Share capital		2,000
Retained profit		11,400
		13,400

Notes

1. £8,000 materials + £2,000 labour
2. Jobs commenced in September (£18,000 × 20%)

In order to consider the company's requirements for the forthcoming year, the bank has requested the provision of:

(i) a monthly cash flow forecast for the twelve month period commencing 1 October 19X1;

(ii) a profit forecast showing the expected total profit for the twelve month period ending 30 September 19X2 (monthly figures are not required);

(iii) calculations of the expected ratio of current assets to current liabilities at the end of each of the four quarters, commencing 31 December 19X1. *Note.* It is a condition of the overdraft that this ratio should not fall below 0.8:1.

The following forecasts and further information are provided in respect of the year to 30 September 19X2.

(a)

		Value of jobs commenced	Purchases of double-glazing units	Wages paid re jobs commenced this month	last month
		£	£	£	£
19X1	October	22,500	10,000	2,500	2,000
	November	22,500	10,000	2,500	2,500
	December	22,500	10,000	2,500	2,500
19X2	January	18,000	8,000	2,000	2,500
	February	18,000	8,000	2,000	2,000
	March	27,000	12,000	3,000	2,000
	April	45,000	20,000	5,000	3,000
	May	45,000	20,000	5,000	5,000
	June	45,000	20,000	5,000	5,000
	July	27,000	12,000	3,000	5,000
	August	27,000	12,000	3,000	3,000
	September	27,000	12,000	3,000	3,000

(b) Customers pay a deposit of 20% of the job at the outset and the balance on completion. Jobs take one month to complete and, on average, work commenced in any month is 50% complete at the end of the month. Work in progress is valued at materials and labour cost.

(c) Salesmen receive a commission of 12% on the value of jobs commenced during any month and are paid at the end of the month.

(d) All materials are transferred to jobs immediately they are commenced. Purchases of units are sufficient to replace items transferred to jobs commenced during the month. Suppliers allow one month's credit.

(e) Wages paid each month comprise 50% of the wages cost of jobs commenced the previous month and 50% of the wages cost of jobs commenced the current month. Total wages cost always amounts to one half of materials cost.

(f) General expenses, paid in cash, amount to £5,500 each month, including an allowance for interest and directors' remuneration.

(g) The annual depreciation charge is £3,000.

Required

(a) Prepare the financial statements and calculations required by the bank to appraise expected financial developments over the twelve months ending 30 September 19X0 (see (i), (ii) and (iii) above). (26 marks)

(b) Comment on the forecast ratios you have calculated under (a), in terms of the condition relating to the ratio laid down by the bank. (4 marks)

SUGGESTED SOLUTIONS

SUGGESTED SOLUTIONS

1 TUTORIAL QUESTION: WALTER ROGERS

(a) Would appear (assuming 'a creditor' is a business creditor).
(b) Would appear.
(c) Would appear.
(d) Would not appear.
(e) Would not appear.
(f) Would appear.
(g) Would not appear.
(h) Would appear.

2 TUTORIAL QUESTION: SEPARATE TRANSACTIONS

The transactions are identified and described as follows.

Transaction A
Equipment has been purchased at a cost of £6,000 and has been paid for immediately by cheque from the bank account.

Transaction B
Trade debtors of the business have paid £4,000 and this has been banked. The effect has been to reduce one asset, trade debtors, and to increase another asset, bank account.

Transaction C
Cash of £1,000 has been sent to trade creditors to pay off £1,000 of debts owing. The asset of cash has been reduced, and the liability of the trade creditors is also reduced.

Transaction D
Cash in hand of £2,000 has been paid in to the bank account. This keeps the cash secure and makes it available for the paying out of cheques.

Transaction E
Stocks amounting to £6,000 have been purchased from trade creditors (suppliers) on credit and will be paid for later following the trade creditors usual terms of trade.

Transaction F
Stocks have been reduced by £3,000 whilst trade debtors have been increased by £5,000, the balancing credit being an increase of £2,000 in the capital account. This means that stock originally costing £3,000 has been sold at a profit of £2,000 to trade debtors (customers) who have not yet paid for them.

Transaction G
£1,000 has been paid out of the bank account on some item of expense (unidentified) which has had the effect of reducing the owners' capital by £1,000.

Transaction H
Trade debtors have paid in to the business £5,000 of the total amount they owe, and the business has paid the money into the bank account.

SUGGESTED SOLUTIONS

Transaction I

The business has received £9,000 (increase in bank account) and accepted the money as settlement of trade debtors of £10,000 (reduction in trade debtors accounts). The difference of £1,000 Dr has reduced the owners' capital. The loss of £1,000 may have been a bad debt or a discount allowed.

Transaction J

The business has paid the trade creditors £14,000 in settlement of £16,000 of outstanding accounts. The balance of £2,000 is a discount received and this has increased the owners' capital.

3 TUTORIAL QUESTION: BASIC

> *Tutorial note.* This question is designed to revise your knowledge of (a) depreciation and (b) the accruals concept. Remember that the accruals concept states that the profit and loss account for a year should include all expenses relating to that year, whenever paid. Note how in (b), (c) and (e) each payment is analysed between amounts relating to 19X4 and amounts relating to 19X3 or 19X5. Only the former amounts are charged to profit and loss account in 19X4.

(a) *Depreciation of office equipment*

	£
At 1 January 19X4	
Cost	13,500
Less accumulated depreciation	4,700
Net book value	8,800
Less net book value of disposals in year	1,700
	7,100
Add cost of additions in year	7,200
NBV of assets in use at 31 December 19X4	14,300

∴ Depreciation charge = 10% × £14,300
 = £1,430

(b) *Telephone expenses*

	£	£
Quarter to 31 January 19X4	180	
Less relating to year ended 31 December 19X3	112	
		68
Quarter to 30 April 19X4		190
Quarter to 31 July 19X4		195
Quarter to 31 October 19X4		210
Quarter to 31 January 19X5	216	
Less relating to year ended 31 December 19X5*	72	
		144
Amount charged to 19X4 P & L account		807

* This is an estimated figure. Of the three months to 31 January 19X5 only two fall in 19X4. One third of the quarter's bill is therefore allocated to 19X5.

SUGGESTED SOLUTIONS

(c) *Rates*

	£	£
Six months to 31 March 19X4	1,200	
Less three months to 31 December 19X3	600	
Balance - three months to 31 March 19X4		600
Six months to 30 September 19X4		1,400
Six months to 31 March 19X5	1,400	
Less three months 1.1.X5 - 31.3.X5	700	
Balance: three months 1.10.X4 - 31.12.X4		700
Amount charged to 19X4 P & L account		2,700

(d) *Bad and doubtful debts*

	£	£
Bad debts written off during year		130
Less recovery of debt previously written off		90
Profit and loss charge for bad debts		40
Provision for doubtful debts at 31 December 19X4		
Balances specifically provided for	300	
General provision for remainder of		
balances (2% × (£24,800 - £300))	490	
	790	
Less already provided at 1 January 19X4	380	
Profit and loss charge for doubtful debts		410
Total charge to 19X4 P & L account		450

(e) *Rental income*

	£	£
Quarter to 28 February 19X4	240	
Less amount relating to December 19X3		
(one third)	80	
Balance (1.1.X4 - 28.2.X4)		160
Quarter to 31 May 19X4		240
Quarter to 31 August 19X4		270
Quarter to 30 November 19X4		270
Quarter to 28 February 19X5	270	
Less amount relating to January, Febryart 19X5		
(two thirds)	180	
Balance (1.12.X4 - 31.12.X4)*		90
Amount charged to 19X4 P & L account		1,030

* It does not matter that this amount was not received until 19X5. The £90 would be included as a debtor in the balance sheet at 31 December 19X4 (or, more properly, the balance sheet would show a debtor of £270 (amount receivable from tenant) and a creditor of £180 (19X5 income received in advance)).

4 TUTORIAL QUESTION: TREND

> *Tutorial note*. This question tests your understanding of depreciation by asking you in effect to work backwards: given the amounts of depreciation charged, to calculate the method being used. The most common method (straight line) is ruled out, because accumulated depreciation does not increase evenly over years 1 and 2.

SUGGESTED SOLUTIONS

(a) *Depreciation method*

19X1 depreciation charge is £16,000, 20% of £80,000.

19X2 depreciation balance is £28,800. No new assets have been purchased so:

	£
Original cost of assets	80,000
19X1 depreciation	(16,000)
	64,000
19X2 depreciation (28,800-16,000)	(12,800)
	51,200

$\frac{12,800}{64,000}$ = 20%. Therefore method is 20% reducing balance.

(b) *Depreciation schedule*

19X1	Charge to 31 March 19X1	16,000
	Balance at 31 March 19X1	16,000
19X2	Charge to 31 March 19X2	12,800
	Balance at 31 March 19X2	28,800
	Disposal during year to March 19X3 (W1)	(5,400)
	Depreciation charge	13,320
19X3	Balance per question	36,720
	Disposal (W2)	(14,640)
	Depreciation charge (W3)	17,584
	Closing balance 31 March 19X4	39,664

(c) *Year ended 31 March 19X4*

			£
A	Plant at cost (90 - 30 + 50)		110,000
B	Depreciation accumulated (part b)		(39,664)
C	Net written down value		70,336

(d) *Profit on disposal*

	First disposal £	Second disposal £
Cash received	8,000	21,000
WDV (W1, W2)	9,600	15,360
Profit/(loss)	(1,600)	5,640

Workings

1 *First disposal*

	£
Original purchases year to 19X1	15,000
Depreciation	(3,000)
	12,000
Depreciation to March 19X2	(2,400)
Written down value	9,600

Therefore loss on disposal £(8,000 - 9,600) = £1,600 (see below).

2 Second disposal

	£
Purchase year to 19X1	30,000
Depreciation 19X1	(6,000)
	24,000
Depreciation 19X2	4,800
	19,200
Depreciation 19X3	(3,840)
Written down value	15,360

Therefore profit on disposal £(21,000 - 15,360) = £5,640 (see below).

3 Depreciation charge 19X4

	£
Written down value 19X3	53,280
Disposal at WDV (W2)	(15,360)
Purchase	50,000
	87,920
20% reducing balance	£17,584

5 TUTORIAL QUESTION: LAURA

TRADING AND PROFIT AND LOSS ACCOUNT FOR THE YEAR ENDED 31 DECEMBER 19X0

	£	£
Sales		72,000
Cost of sales		
Opening stock	8,900	
Purchases	36,600	
	45,500	
Less closing stock	10,800	
		34,700
Gross profit		37,300
Expenses		
Wages and salaries £(19,800 - 2,400 - 600)	16,800	
Rates and insurance £(1,510 - 260)	1,250	
Motor expenses £(400 + 600)	1,000	
Sundry expenses £(1,500 + 120)	1,620	
Depreciation: factory 2% × (£20,000 - £4,000)	320	
plant	480	
cars	650	
		22,120
Net profit		15,180

SUGGESTED SOLUTIONS

BALANCE SHEET AS AT 31 DECEMBER 19X0

	Cost £	Dep'n £	NBV £
Fixed assets			
Factory	20,000	2,240	17,760
Plant	4,800	2,080	2,720
Cars	2,600	1,850	750
	27,400	6,170	21,230
Current assets			
Stocks		10,800	
Debtors £(3,600-60)	3,540		
Less provision £(280-60)	220		
		3,320	
Prepayment (rates)		260	
Cash at bank		11,490	
		25,870	
Current liabilities			
Trade creditors	4,200		
Accruals (sundry expenses)	120		
		4,320	
Net current assets			21,550
			42,780
Capital			
Opening balance			30,000
Add: net profit for year		15,180	
less drawings		2,400	
retained profit for year			12,780
Closing balance			42,780

6 TUTORIAL QUESTION: KAREN DICKSON

Transaction	Current assets	Current liabilities	Profit
(a)	Increase £2,000 Decrease £2,000	Stay the same	Stay the same
(b)	Stay the same	Stay the same	Stay the same
(c)	Decrease £6,250	Stay the same	Stay the same
(d)	Decrease £2,750	Stay the same	Stay the same
(e)	Decrease £1,400	Stay the same	Decrease £1,400
(f)	Increase £10,000	Stay the same	Stay the same
(g)	Stay the same	Stay the same	Decrease £500
(h)	Increase £775	Stay the same	Increase £125
(i)	Increase £8,000	Increase £8,000	Stay the same
(j)	Decrease £4,000 Increase £5,000	Stay the same	Increase £1,000
(k)	Decrease £820	Stay the same	Decrease £820

SUGGESTED SOLUTIONS

7 TUTORIAL QUESTION: TRADING ACCOUNT

> *Tutorial note.* Part (a) of the question requires total sales to be calculated. This should be done by first posting all the figures regarding sales and debtors to a debtors control account. After all the figures have been entered, including the opening and closing balance, the total sales figure will be the amount needed to balance the debtors control account. Don't be put off by the ledger accounts below. You could reach the same result arithmetically.
>
> Part (b) of the question requires total purchases to be calculated. This should be done by posting all the figures regarding purchases and creditors to a creditors control account. The total purchases figure will be the amount needed to balance the account.

(a) **DEBTORS CONTROL ACCOUNT**

		£			£
1.4.X7	Balance b/d	55,680	1.4.X7	Bank	403,270
1.4.X7 to 31.3.X8	Total sales (by deduction)	417,970	to	Returns inwards	3,510
			31.3.X8	Bad debts	4,500
				Discounts allowed	5,560
			31.3.X8	Balance c/d	56,810
		473,650			473,650

Total sales figure is as follows.

	£
Credit sales (as above)	417,970
Cash sales given in the question	249,830
	667,800

(b) **CREDITORS CONTROL ACCOUNT**

		£			£
1.4.X7	Bank	301,770	1.4.X7	Balance b/d	41,560
to	Returns outwards	7,820	1.4.X7	Total purchases	
31.3.X8	Discounts received	2,540	to 31.3.X8	(by deduction)	312,660
31.3.X8	Balance c/d	42,090			
		354,220			354,220

(c) **DORIAN LTD TRADING ACCOUNT**
FOR THE YEAR ENDED 31 MARCH 19X8

	£	£
Sales		667,800
Less returns		3,510
		664,290
Opening stock	30,400	
Purchases	312,660	
Less returns	7,820	
	335,240	
Less closing stock	31,850	
Cost of goods sold		303,390
Gross profit		360,900

SUGGESTED SOLUTIONS

8 TUTORIAL QUESTION: PENN

(a) A major and fundamental error in the previous year's accounts requires a prior year adjustment under the rules of SSAP 6. Such items should be disclosed as a movement on reserves in the statement of retained profits. The balance of reserves brought forward would be adjusted; the error would not affect the reported profit for the current year. *Note.* FRS 3 would also require a prior year adjustment.

(b) SSAP 13 and the Companies Act 1985 forbid the treatment of research expenditure as an asset. All such expenditure should be written off as incurred. Disclosure should be made as an exceptional item if material.

(c) Transfers to deferred taxation should be disclosed as part of the taxation charge in the profit and loss account, usually by way of note. The balance on the deferred taxation account should be disclosed in the balance sheet under the heading 'Provisions for liabilities and charges'.

(d) When directors' emoluments exceed £60,000 additional disclosure is required, and is usually presented as a note to the profit and loss account. The following details are necessary:

   (i) the number of directors whose emoluments fall within separate bands of £5,000;
   (ii) the emoluments of the chairman;
   (iii) the emoluments of the highest-paid director, if the highest-paid director is not also the chairman;
   (iv) the number of directors who waived emoluments and the aggregate amount waived.

(e) Political contributions in excess of £200 must be disclosed in the directors' report together with the name of the political party concerned.

(f) The closure of a large factory is likely to be a material and non-recurring event and until recently would have fallen within the definition of an *extraordinary* item in SSAP 6. Under FRS 3, however, such items should normally be treated as *exceptional* items. Exceptional items are disclosed by way of note to the profit and loss account (see Study Notes).

(g) This is a change of accounting policy which, if its effects are material, would fall within the definition of a prior year adjustment in SSAP 6. The disclosure of prior year adjustments has been described in (a) above; in this case the comparative figures would require similar adjustment. In addition SSAP 2 requires that the reasons for changing the accounting policy should be disclosed. *Note.* The FRS 3 definition of prior year adjustments would require the same treatment.

(h) The net dividend paid during the year would be shown as part of the total dividends disclosed in the profit and loss appropriation account. Any ACT paid during the year would be offset against the eventual liability, if any, for corporation tax on the year's profits.

(i) Unlike research expenditure (see (b) above) development expenditure need not always be written off as incurred. In circumstances defined by SSAP 13 such expenditure may be carried forward as an intangible fixed asset in the balance sheet. The key circumstances in which such carry forward is permissible are when the project has been assessed as technically and commercially feasible and the related costs are separately identifiable.

(j) This appears to be an exceptional item, since although it is material and non-recurring it falls within the normal activities of the company. It should be included in the profit on ordinary activities before taxation and its nature and amount described in a note. *Note.* FRS 3 would require this treatment.

SUGGESTED SOLUTIONS

9 TUTORIAL QUESTION: SEGMENTAL REPORTING

(a) Segmental reporting can be defined as 'the analysis of general corporate information between separate divisions or classes of business which are individually of economic significance'.

Companies legislation has now made limited progress towards these aims: the Companies Act 1985 requires companies to disclose for each 'class of business' (undefined) the amount of turnover and pre-tax profit or loss, and for each geographical market the amount of turnover.

SSAP 25 extends the Companies Act requirements on analysis of turnover and profits as follows:

(i) the result as well as turnover must be disclosed for *all* segments;

(ii) 'result' for these purposes is profit or loss before tax, minority interests and extraordinary items;

(iii) each segment's net assets should be disclosed (so that return on capital employed can be calculated);

(iv) segmental turnover must be analysed between sales to customers outside the group and inter-segment sales/transfers (where material).

Like the CA 1985, SSAP 25 requires analysis by two types of segment, class of business and geographical market.

Identifying segments could be difficult and the SSAP gives as a rule of thumb the dictum that a segment should normally be regarded as material if its third party turnover is ≥ 10% of the entity's total third party turnover or its profit is ≥ 10% of the combined results of all segments in profit (or its loss is ≥ 10% of the combined results of all loss making segments) or its net assets are ≥ 10% of total net assets of the entity.

The trend towards increased segmental reporting reflects growing awareness among users of accounts that information about the company as a whole may be inadequate for their needs. Rates of profitability, opportunities for growth, future prospects and risks to investments may vary greatly among industry and geographical segments. Information by segment is likely to assist shareholders and potential investors in assessing future profitability. Employees and trade unions may find such information useful in wage negotiations and in assessing future employment prospects.

(b) Segmental reporting has been criticised on a number of grounds.

(i) It is difficult and to some extent arbitrary to identify the segments on which reporting would be based. This difficulty was recognised in *The corporate report* which suggested various possible criteria (see (a) above).

(ii) Problems arise in allocating common income and costs among the different segments. The difficulties are made worse when there is a significant amount of inter-segment activity and care would be needed in establishing a system of transfer pricing between segments. Equally it would be necessary to provide reconciliations between the sum of the information on individual segments and the aggregated information in the financial statements.

SUGGESTED SOLUTIONS

(iii) Concern is sometimes expressed that disclosing information about segments may weaken an enterprise's competitive position because more detailed information is made available to competitors, customers, suppliers and others. The Companies Act 1985 and SSAP 25 include an exemption from the already very limited disclosure prescribed in cases, where, in the opinion of the directors, such disclosure 'would be seriously prejudicial to the interests of the company'.

10 TUTORIAL QUESTION: SHEPPARTON

> *Tutorial note.* Although you are no longer required to produce the Companies Act formats in the examination, such questions provide valuable experience in producing accounts in the 'good form' the examiner requires.

(a) BALANCE SHEET AS AT 30 SEPTEMBER 19X8

	Notes	Cost £	Dep'n £	Net £
Fixed assets				
Freehold property		305,000	10,100	294,900
Plant and machinery		100,000	20,000	80,000
		405,000	30,100	374,900
Current assets				
Stocks			153,400	
Debtors	1		86,600	
Investments	2		6,200	
Cash at bank			1,300	
			247,500	
Creditors: amounts falling due within one year				
Bank loan			20,000	
Trade creditors			32,100	
Other creditors including taxation and social security	3		53,800	
			105,900	
Net current assets				141,600
Total assets less current liabilities				516,500
Creditors: amounts falling due after more than one year				
Debenture loan	4		150,000	
Bank loan	5		60,000	
				210,000
				306,500
Capital and reserves				
Called up share capital				
200,000 ordinary shares of £1 each				200,000
Reserves				
Share premium account			80,000	
Profit and loss account			26,500	
				106,500
				306,500

NOTES TO THE BALANCE SHEET

1 *Debtors*

	£
Trade creditors	78,500
Prepaid expenses	3,100
ACT recoverable (£15,000 × 25/75)	5,000
	86,600

The £5,000 ACT will be recoverable after a period of more than twelve months.

2 *Investments*

This comprises an investment in the shares of an unlisted company.

3 *Other creditors including taxation and social security*

	£
Corporation tax	7,700
National Insurance	4,800
Proposed dividend	15,000
ACT on proposed dividend	5,000
Interest payable	21,300
	53,800

4 *Debenture loan*

This is a 12% debenture repayble in ... [date not given in question].

5 *Bank loan*

This is repayable by instalments, all of which fall due in less than five years.

(b) *The principal limitations of published accounts*

(i) Published accounts are almost always, since the withdrawal of SSAP 16, based on historical costs. The values of assets are not current and the balance sheet therefore does not provide a realistic valuation of the company. Depreciation charges do not represent the true value of the asset used. Holding gains are included in profit. The effect of inflation on capital maintenance is not shown. Comparisons over time are unrealistic. Many of these difficulties were reduced by the system of current cost accounting advocated by SSAP 16, but the system as a whole was eventually discarded as unsatisfactory.

(ii) Many external users of accounts (such as creditors or potential investors) are less interested in the historical picture provided by accounts than in the company's future prospects. Historical results are often an inadequate basis for estimating future profitability, and as yet there is no requirement for companies to publish forecast financial information.

(iii) The variety of possible accounting treatments makes it difficult to compare companies with different accounting policies. Accounting standards are meant to limit the areas of difference, but in practice they are often fairly permissive documents. For example, SSAP 22 allows companies to write off purchased goodwill immediately or to amortise it gradually over an undefined period. Companies with several 'blocks' of purchased goodwill may even adopt different policies in respect of each block.

SUGGESTED SOLUTIONS

(iv) Various forms of off balance sheet finance (factoring debts, discounting bills receivable, leasing and more elaborate schemes) enable companies to disguise the true extent of their liabilities while remaining within the law.

11 TUTORIAL QUESTION: HORNGREN

> *Tutorial note.* This question was set in a format which will not recur under the new syllabus as you are not now required to prepare published accounts in Companies Act 1985 format. However, you are required to know how to calculate items for inclusion in published accounts and to present your answers in 'good form'. This is still, therefore, a useful test.
>
> It is important in tackling this question to be able to recognise the difference between:
>
> (a) exceptional and extraordinary items;
> (b) adjusting and non-adjusting post balance sheet events; and
> (c) current and prior year charges/credits arising from a change in accounting policy.
>
> Although in practice many companies have to date treated redundancy costs in a *continuing* business segment as an *extraordinary* item, strictly speaking this is an *exceptional* item. SSAP 6 classified the costs of *closing down* a business segment as extraordinary. However, FRS 3, which supersedes SSAP 6, states that *all* such costs should normally be treated as exceptional not extraordinary (see Study Notes).

(a) Extraordinary items were defined by SSAP 6 as 'material items which derive from events or transactions that fall outside the ordinary activities of the company and which are therefore expected not to recur frequently or regularly'. Exceptional items are items which are also material and infrequent but they derive from the ordinary activities of the business. The Companies Act 1985 refers to transactions that are 'exceptional by virtue of size or incidence though they fall within the ordinary activities of the company'.

The difference between extraordinary and exceptional items is therefore whether or not the transaction is outside or within the ordinary activities of the business. Inevitably, there will be a problem of different interpretations. Examples such as making a special provision for pensions, expenses of reorganisation, deficits on the revaluation of fixed assets and profits or losses on the sale of fixed assets or investments have been treated as both exceptional and extraordinary, depending on the outlook of the companies concerned.

The Companies Act 1985 requires companies to show extraordinary income, extraordinary charges and extraordinary profit or loss in the profit and loss account or in notes to the account. The Act also requires that particulars of any extraordinary income or charges in the year should be given. These particulars will presumably be a short narrative description. SSAP 6 merely requires that the profit and loss account should show profit before extraordinary items, extraordinary items less attributable taxation, and profit after extraordinary items, and that the nature as well as the size of the items should be disclosed.

SSAP 6 requires that the nature and size of exceptional items should also be disclosed but does not specify any particular format for this disclosure. The Companies Act 1985 repeats the SSAP 6 requirement, and is also not specific. The Act requires that 'the effect shall be stated' of any exceptional items.

Note. FRS 3 has now changed the definition of extraordinary items, making them much rarer. Extraordinary items are now defined as 'material items possessing a high degree of abnormality which arise from events or transactions that fall outside the ordinary activities of the reporting entity and which are not expected to recur.' See Study Notes for further details.

(b) SSAP 17 defines adjusting events and non-adjusting events as follows.

Adjusting events are post balance sheet events which provide additional evidence of conditions existing at the balance sheet date. They include events which because of statutory or conventional requirements are reflected in financial statements. (In this context, post balance sheet events are themselves defined by SSAP 17 as 'those events, both favourable and unfavourable, which occur between the balance sheet date and the date on which the financial statements are approved by the board of directors'.)

Non-adjusting events are post balance sheet events which concern conditions which did not exist at the balance sheet date.

The accounting treatment of material post balance sheet events prescribed by SSAP 17 is as follows.

(i) Adjusting events should be accrued for in the financial statements by altering the relevant accounts figures. The accounts should also be altered if a post balance sheet event indicates that application of the going concern principle in preparing the accounts is not appropriate.

(ii) Non-adjusting events should not lead to alteration of the accounts figures, but such events should be disclosed if non-disclosure would affect the ability of the users of financial statements to reach a proper understanding of the financial position or if they represent the reversal or maturity after the year end of a transaction entered into before the year end, the substance of which was primarily to alter the appearance of the company's balance sheet. In such cases disclosure should be made of:

(1) the nature of the event; and

(2) an estimate of the financial effect, or a statement that it is not practicable to make such an estimate.

The estimate of the financial effect should be disclosed before taking account of taxation, and the taxation implications should be explained where necessary for a proper understanding of the financial position.

SUGGESTED SOLUTIONS

(c) HORNGREN LIMITED
PROFIT AND LOSS ACCOUNT FOR THE YEAR ENDED 31 DECEMBER 19X8

	Notes	£'000	£'000
Turnover			10,620
Cost of sales (6,290-72+136 + 260)			6,614
Gross profit			4,006
Administrative expenses			3,100
Distribution costs			638
Profit on ordinary activities before activities	1		268
Tax on profit on ordinary activities			150
Profit on ordinary activities after taxation			118
Extraordinary losses	3		40
Profit for the financial year			78
Dividend proposal	4		120
Retained loss for the year			(42)
Retained profit brought forward			
As previously stated		936	
Prior year adjustment	5	(72)	
			864
Retained profit carried forward			822

HORNGREN LIMITED
NOTES TO THE FINANCIAL STATEMENTS FOR THE YEAR
ENDED 31 DECEMBER 19X8 (EXTRACTS)

1 Profit is stated after charging or crediting   £'000
   the following items.

Exceptional items	
Redundancy costs	136
Closure of operating division	260
Directors' emoluments (see below)	62
Depreciation	x + 25

2 *Directors' emoluments*   £'000

Fees	8
Other emoluments	54
	62

Chairman	11
Highest paid director	25

The emoluments of the other directors fell within the following ranges.

	Number
£Nil - £5,000	4
£15,001 - £20,000	1

3 *Extraordinary losses*   £'000

Cost of trade investment written off   40
  (50,000 × 80p)

	4	*Dividend proposed*	£'000
		Final ordinary dividend proposed of 12p per share	<u>120</u>

5 *Prior year adjustment*

The company's accounting policy for development expenditure has been changed in the year. Previously development expenditure was capitalised and amortised over the expected life of the project to which it related. The directors now feel that a policy of writing off such expenditure as it is incurred will give a truer and fairer view and this policy has been adopted. £72,000 of expenditure incurred in prior years has been written off against reserves brought forward and an extra charge of £13,000 has been made against profit for the financial year.

6 *Fixed assets (extract)*

The freehold properties were revalued to current market value on 1 January 19X8 by £x. Depreciation of freehold property for the year would have been £11,000 based on historical cost.

7 *Revaluation reserve* £'000

At 31 December 19X7 —
Surplus on revaluation as at
1 January 19X8 <u>1,500</u>
At 31 December 19X8 <u>1,500</u>

8 *Post balance sheet events*

The company received a loan of £80,000 at an annual rate of interest of 15% on 1 January 19X9.

(d)
	£'000
Retained profit at 31 December 19X8	822
Add excess of depreciation on revalued assets over depreciation on historical cost (25-11)	14
Add proposed dividend (not yet approved by the shareholders in general meeting)	<u>120</u>
	<u>956</u>

12 TUTORIAL QUESTION: BARENTS

(a) In times of rising prices the year end stock valuation is higher under FIFO than it is under LIFO. This is because under FIFO the stock valuation is based on the assumption that the stock remaining on hand at the year end is the most recently purchased. Under LIFO, the stock on hand is valued at prices prevailing perhaps months previously, leading to a lower valuation when prices are rising. The converse is true when prices are falling.

SUGGESTED SOLUTIONS

(i) In 19X0, year end stock has a higher value under LIFO. Prices must have fallen during the year.

(ii) In 19X2, year end stock has a higher value under FIFO. Prices must have risen during the year.

(b) 19X0 was the first year of trading and opening stock therefore does not affect the calculation. The highest profit figure will come from the method which gives the highest valuation for closing stock, namely LIFO.

(c) We know that cost of sales = opening stock + purchases - closing stock. Since the purchases figure is the same under both methods, the lowest cost of sales (and therefore the highest profit) comes from the method which gives the lowest value for opening stock less closing stock.

	LIFO £	FIFO £
Opening stock	36,400	36,000
Less closing stock	(41,800)	(44,000)
	(5,400)	(8,000)

The figure for FIFO is lower (minus £8,000 compared with minus £5,400) and therefore the profit under FIFO is higher.

(d) Stock movements for 19X0 and 19X1 do not affect the problem. Only the stock at the end of the three year period is relevant. Since the LIFO valuation at 31 December 19X2 is lower, the LIFO profit for the period will be lower.

(e) As in part (c) the answer to this question depends on the movement in stock over the year.

	FIFO cost £	Lower of FIFO cost and NRV £
Opening stock	36,000	34,000
Less closing stock	(44,000)	(44,000)
	(8,000)	(10,000)

The cost of sales is £2,000 higher on the basis of FIFO cost and therefore profit would be £2,000 lower on that basis.

13 BARBER

> *Tutorial note.* The examiner commented that answers to this question illustrated candidates' tendency not to read the question carefully. 'Many candidates seemed to feel obliged, for no obvious reason, to preface their remarks by a long discussion on the reason for revising SSAP 9. The information provided was interesting but of absolutely no relevance to this question, earned zero marks, and reduced the amount of time available for answering the matters which should have been discussed.' You will find it helpful to read the Chief Examiner's *Signpost* article on this subject in February 1989's *Banking World*.

SUGGESTED SOLUTIONS

(a) As at 31 December 19X7, the contract has been under way for two months and no invoices have been submitted or progress payments received. The contract still has 17 months to run. It would therefore be imprudent to take any profit in the 19X7 accounts.

As at 31 December 19X8, however, the contract is close enough to completion to warrant recognition of profit.

Expected profit on contract	£'000
Contractual price	6,000
Costs to date	4,100
Estimated costs to completion	1,240
Expected profit	660

No loss is foreseen at 31 December 19X8. Attributable profit is calculated as the difference between attributable turnover and the cost of earning that turnover.

		£'000
Turnover	(= invoiced sales value of work completed)	4,000
Cost of sales	(= cost of work completed)	3,600
Attributable profit		400

By 31 December 19X9 the contract is complete and so the full profit can be recognised in the accounts. The entries in the 19X9 profit and loss account will be as follows.

	£'000
Turnover (= contract price less turnover already recognised): (6,000 - 4,000)	2,000
Cost of sales (= total contract costs less cost of sales already charged): (5,400 - 3,600)	1,800
Attributable profit: (total contract profit (6,000 - 5,400) less amount recognised earlier (400))	200

(b)

	19X7 £'000	*19X8* £'000
Balance of costs on contract account	350	4,100
Transfer to cost of sales (cumulative)	-	3,600
Long-term contract work in progress	350	500
Turnover (cumulative)	-	4,000
Progress payments	-	3,800
Amounts recoverable on long-term contracts	-	200

Included, therefore, within 'Stocks' and 'Debtors' in the balance sheet will be the following amounts to be aggregated with other long-term contract related items which will then require separate disclosure.

	19X7 £'000	*19X8* £'000
Stocks	350	500
Debtors	-	200

(c) It would be inappropriate to value stock and work in progress at above cost as this would mean recognising profit before it has been earned (that is, on sale). Stock is therefore valued for inclusion in the balance sheet at the lower of cost and net realisable value.

SUGGESTED SOLUTIONS

Net realisable value is sales price less the costs incurred in making a sale. This is an appropriate valuation when a stock item cannot be sold for as much as it cost, as to value such items at cost would not ensure that the fall in their value is charged against profit.

This valuation policy has the advantage of *prudence* and *objectivity*. There are clear criteria for determining when profit should be recognised and when stock should be written down, thus removing the risk that stock will be valued inconsistently.

However, if a long-term contract is valued at cost, the profit on that contract is only recognised when the contract is completed whereas that profit has been earned over the whole period of the contract. Thus, the accruals concept is not applied. SSAP 9 therefore permits the recognition of profit earned to date on long-term contracts as they proceed as soon as the outcome of the contract can be assessed with reasonable certainty. This proviso ensures that profit is not recognised until it is prudent to do so. Again on grounds of prudence, a foreseeable loss must be charged against profit as soon as it is foreseen and in full.

To avoid conflict with the Companies Act 1985 valuation rules, the contract balances themselves are no longer valued inclusive of profit. Instead, the proportion of the contract value earned in the period is recorded as turnover and the costs incurred in earning that turnover are included in the cost of sales. The cumulative proportion of the contract value earned to date is set against the progress payments received and any excess is treated as a debtor. Excess progress payments are deducted from the balance of costs incurred on the contract not yet transferred to cost of sales; if these are insufficient excess payments are recorded as part of creditors. Foreseeable losses are also deducted from contract work in progress and any excess is shown as a provision.

This rather convoluted treatment reflects the difference between the relatively simple operation of buying and selling stocks (or selling them after transformation into finished goods) and the complex operation of undertaking a long-term contract. In the latter case there is a contractual liability to recompense the company for work done, quite a different situation from that of holding stocks which customers have indicated that they *may* buy. In addition, only to record profit on completion could mean that the profit and loss accounts for two periods when activity levels were the same would not be comparable if in one period no contracts were completed and in the other many were.

14 POYNTON

> *Tutorial note.* This is not a difficult question if you know the requirements of the relevant SSAPs. However, the examiner commented that answers were generally poor, not just because of difficulties with the specific adjustments required but because of difficulty with preparing balance sheets. Your basic accounting technique *must* be sound if you are to cope successfully with this paper. The trickiest point in part (a) is recognising that, while a *combination* of the FIFO and average cost bases of valuing stock will produce the highest and lowest profits possible arithmetically, it is not possible to mix them in practice. Additionally, a change from FIFO to average cost valuation for opening stock necessitates a prior year adjustment (see note 4).
>
> We have incorporated detailed notes in our solution explaining the difference between the accounting treatments adopted. This is *not* a requirement of the question and you should not therefore have commented on your answer - if you did, you wasted time and effort for which no marks would have been awarded in the exam!

SUGGESTED SOLUTIONS

(a) POYNTON LIMITED
SUMMARISED PROFIT AND LOSS ACCOUNTS
FOR THE YEAR ENDED 30 JUNE 19X8

	Highest £'000	*Lowest* £'000
Turnover	7,230	7,230
Cost of sales (note 1)	4,950	4,966
Gross profit	2,280	2,264
Distribution costs and administrative expenses	1,380	1,380
Amortisation of goodwill (120 ÷ 3) (note 2)	-	40
Development expenditure written off (note 3)	-	60
	1,380	1,480
Retained profit for the year	900	784
Retained profit brought forward (note 4)	625	577
Goodwill written off against reserves (note 2)	(120)	-
	1,405	1,361

SUMMARISED BALANCE SHEET AS AT 30 JUNE 19X8

	Highest £'000	£'000	*Lowest* £'000	£'000
Fixed assets				
Intangible assets				
Development costs		60		-
Goodwill		-		80
Tangible assets		2,050		2,050
		2,110		2,130
Net current assets				
Stocks	400		336	
Net monetary assets	295		295	
		695		631
Total assets less current liabilities		2,805		2,761
Capital and reserves				
Share capital		1,400		1,400
Profit and loss account		1,405		1,361
		2,805		2,761

Notes

1 *Cost of sales*

Cost of sales is charged with (increased by) a decrease in stock over the period and credited with (reduced by) an increase. Profit will therefore be highest if that valuation method is chosen which produces the smallest decrease or highest increase. It is not permissable under the Companies Act 1985 or SSAP 2 to use one method of valuation for opening stock and another for closing stock.

	FIFO £'000	*Average cost* £'000
Opening stock	350	302
Closing stock	400	336
Increase	50	34

SUGGESTED SOLUTIONS

Here, the FIFO valuation reduces cost of sales by more than the average cost valuation.

Cost of sales is therefore as follows.

	Highest £'000	Lowest £'000
Manufacturing costs	5,000	5,000
Less increase in stocks	50	34
	4,950	4,966

2 *Goodwill*

SSAP 22 allows purchased goodwill to be treated in either of two ways. It can be amortised over its estimated economic life which reduces profit for the year in the same way as depreciation. Alternatively, it can be deducted from reserves. This does not affect profit for the year at all and thus this treatment results in higher reported profit.

3 *Development expenditure*

Under SSAP 13 development expenditure may either be written off as incurred or (if it meets the criteria laid down in the SSAP) it may be treated as a fixed asset and amortised over the life of the product it relates to. Amortisation would begin here in July 19X8 and so none need be charged in 19X7/X8.

4 *Reserves brought forward*

Since last year's accounts showed closing stock at FIFO valuation, this year's should, if average cost valuation is adopted, incorporate a prior year adjustment as required by SSAP 6 because of the change in accounting policy.

	£'000
Profit and loss account as at 1 July 19X7 as previously stated	625
Decrease in profit in respect of closing stock (valued lower on average cost basis): 350 - 302	48
Profit and loss account as at 1 July 19X7 restated	577

(b) *Tutorial note.* Obviously, many different asset valuation methods could have been chosen. In our answer we have discussed the revaluation of fixed assets, the choice of consolidation method in preparing group accounts and brand accounting. The examiner commented that answers to this part of the question were poor, because students failed to answer the question asked and merely discussed the different methods used under requirement (a).

Revaluation of fixed assets

Company law permits but does not require the inclusion in the balance sheet of certain fixed and current assets at valuation. Usually only fixed assets are revalued, most commonly because land and buildings have increased in value. There is no requirement in any current SSAP or in law to revalue all assets or to keep valuations up to date. SSAP 12 does, however, require that depreciation on revalued assets should be calculated on the basis of the revalued amount and not on cost.

Thus, a balance sheet figure for fixed assets may represent a hotch potch of unexpired costs and part-depreciated revaluations, possibly long out of date. Many commentators argue that such figures do not help the reader to understand the state of a company's affairs. Although the financial statements must include details of revaluations and material differences between market and book value of assets, the balance sheet itself often gives no clue either to the historical costs incurred by the company or to the current value of assets. This means that users who wish to assess the company's true worth, gearing and financial security must amass current value information for themselves if they have sufficient information or influence on the company so to do. This is time consuming and expensive and does not give the assurance of objectivity that *audited* current valuations would give.

Additionally, because depreciation may be based on historical costs or out of date valuations, profit is not reduced by the true cost of assets consumed in the period. Profit could be overstated as a consequence and distributions (that is, dividend payments) could erode the company's operating capability by reducing its capital in real terms.

Consolidation methods

Another area where choice is currently permitted is in consolidation of a business which its parent company has merged with rather than acquired. In such a case, SSAP 23 and the Companies Act permit either the acquisition or the merger method to be applied. This can make a considerable difference to the group accounts.

The acquisition method requires that an acquired company's assets and liabilities should be stated at fair value as at acquisition and that the difference between these fair values and the fair value of consideration should be treated as goodwill, which must either be amortised or written off against reserves. All pre-acquisition profits and other reserves are eliminated from the consolidated accounts.

The merger method requires that the merged companies simply add together their assets, liabilities and reserves at book value and adjust consolidated reserves to eliminate or add the difference between the parent company's investment and the subsidiary's share capital. No pre- and post-acquisition distinction arises and so the combined business's profit and loss account shows combined current and prior year results even if the combination took place part of the way through the year.

Thus, the user of consolidated accounts must refer extensively to the notes to find out:

(i) which method has been used for which combinations;
(ii) what fair value adjustments have been made (acquisitions method);
(iii) what the analysis of profit was between businesses in the year of combination (merger method).

Within the same set of accounts, some combinations may have been accounted for by the merger method and some by the acquisition method, in which case a further distinction arises between those in which goodwill is to be amortised and those in which it is eliminated against reserves. This makes it difficult to attach any value to the consolidated accounts.

Brand accounting

Finally, brand accounting is a recent phenomenon whereby companies with valuable portfolios of branded products (such as Hovis bread or Paxo stuffing) have begun to attribute a value to these brands and to treat them as intangible assets in the balance sheet. There are currently no Companies Act provisions on this practice nor is there an accounting standard in issue on the topic. Companies can therefore adopt any valuation method they please and many have chosen not to amortise brands. Most controversially, some have chosen to capitalise brands which have been developed internally and not acquired (which, by

SUGGESTED SOLUTIONS

implication, have been given an objective valuation on the basis of which a purchase price was fixed). Many valuations are on the basis of estimated future earnings rather than separately identifiable costs incurred in developing brands.

The result is that shareholders' funds are greatly increased and the balance sheet looks stronger. Additionally, goodwill calculated on acquisitions of companies with large brand portfolios becomes much less significant because brands are treated as part of the separable net assets of such companies rather than as part of the goodwill.

The problem for users of accounts is therefore that there is no consistency in this area and, many would argue, insufficient prudence. While some consider that capitalisation of brands results in a more meaningful balance sheet, others feel that brands are *too* intangible and too subject to the whims of fickle consumers to be treated as fixed assets.

15 HARDEN

> *Tutorial note*. This is not a difficult question as long as you make sure that your notes do not simply show where you got the figures for your balance sheet but also explain *why* each is the most appropriate figure.
>
> The examiner said that the main errors made by candidates were:
>
> (a) capitalising goodwill;
> (b) giving the cost of equipment as £2,100, not £1,500;
> (c) not deducting trade discount from the cost of materials;
> (d) 'the inclusion of the contract at either cost or total selling price or at one of a number of other unidentifiable figures';
> (e) failure to accrue bank interest and charges, or accruing £60, not ($\frac{3}{4}$ × £60);
> (f) accruing a full year's interest, not six months;
> (g) failure to realise that profit can be calculated as a balancing figure.

HARDEN & CO
BALANCE SHEET AS AT 30 APRIL 19X1

	Notes	£	£
Fixed assets			
Lock-up garage	1		5,600
Motor vehicle	2		2,250
Equipment	3		1,200
			9,050
Current assets			
Stocks			
Materials	4	1,050	
Work in progress	5	300	
Debtors			
Amounts recoverable on contracts	5	2,000	
Trade debtors	6	1,100	
		4,450	
Current liabilities			
Bank overdraft	7	850	
Trade creditors		250	
Accruals	7,8	290	
		1,390	

SUGGESTED SOLUTIONS

	Notes	£	£
Net current assets			3,060
Total assets less current liabilities			12,110
Long-term loan	8		5,000
			7,110
Proprietor's capital			
Introduced as at 1 May 19X0			3,000
Profit for the year (balancing figure)		14,510	
Drawings (£200 × 52)		10,400	
			4,110
As at 30 April 19X1			7,110

Notes

1. **Lock-up garage**

   This is shown at cost. It is permissible to show fixed assets at valuation, adding the surplus to proprietor's capital (or charging a deficit against profit) but cost has been used here on grounds of prudence. No depreciation has been charged because no information has been given to make this possible. If the garage is held on a lease, the cost should be amortised over the lease term; if freehold, the cost should be depreciated over the estimated useful life of the garage. The solicitors' fees can be capitalised as they are not for routine work but to enable the firm to purchase the garage.

2. **Motor vehicle**

   This is shown at net book value (¾ × £3,000), representing cost less one full year's depreciation charge. It is assumed that there will be no residual value at the end of its four year useful life and that a straight line charge is appropriate. The vehicle's good condition is irrelevant except inasmuch as this indicates that the depreciation charge need not be increased. Again, it is assumed that a straight line charge is appropriate and that a revaluation would be imprudent.

3. **Equipment**

   Equipment is stated at net book value (4/5 × £1,500). A straight line depreciation charge has been made, assuming no residual value. The only relevant cost is the *actual* cost. The higher cost quoted is not said to be the current value of the equipment, so would still be irrelevant even if a revaluation was mooted.

4. **Stocks of materials**

   Stocks are valued under SSAP 9 at the lower of cost and net realisable value. Harden & Co's accounts need not comply with recognised accounting standards by law or professional requirements, but these must be regarded as indicating best practice for all accounting purposes. Accordingly, raw materials are valued at cost less trade discount. Only if the net realisable value (selling price less cost of putting goods into a saleable condition) had been less than cost would that have been the more prudent valuation. Replacement cost is an alternative basis of valuation used in current cost accounts but historical cost is more usual.

5. **Contract**

   This has again been valued in accordance with SSAP 9. The contract is treated as long-term because its duration spans two accounting periods. Credit for profit earned to date is taken by treating the invoiced amount as a debtor balance. The uninvoiced portion is valued at cost.

SUGGESTED SOLUTIONS

6 Trade debtors

The disputed invoice should, for prudence, be provided against and therefore not shown as an asset. Accordingly, only certainly recoverable debts are shown as assets here.

7 Bank overdraft

Two thirds approximately of the interest and charges for the quarter to 31 May was incurred in the accounting period to 30 April, and so should be charged against profit for that period. £40 ($\frac{2}{3}$ × £60) is therefore accrued as a liability as at 30 April.

8 Long-term loan

No mention of repayment terms is made and so it is assumed that this is a long-term loan. Half the interest payable in November 19X1 was incurred in the six months to 30 April 19X1 and so £250 ($\frac{6}{12}$ × 10% × £5,000) must be accrued as at 30 April.

9 Goodwill

Mr Herman has not purchased goodwill and so best accounting practice (as indicated by SSAP 22 and the Companies Act 1985) requires that he should not capitalise his estimate of the value of the goodwill in his business. Any such estimate must be subjective in the absence of an arm's length transaction putting a value on goodwill.

16 ROWLAND

> *Tutorial note.* We give detailed explanation of our figures to help you, but you were not required by the question to explain your figures at all. It is always sensible to show workings so that you get credit for a correct method even if your arithmetic lets you down but you shouldn't have wasted time explaining your workings. On the whole this question was well answered by candidates in the examination.

Course of action	Operating profit 19X0/X1 £'000	Bank balance 31 July 19X1 £'000	Working capital 31 July 19X1 £'000	Debt: equity ratio 31 July 19X1 (note 3)
(a)	200	50	1,000	1 : 5.0
(b)	300	50	1,000	1 : 5.2
(c)	200 *	50	1,000	1 : 10.0
(d)	200	50	1,000	1 : 4.2
(e)	120 (note 1)	260 (note 1)	920 (note 1)	1 : 4.8
(f)	200	350 (note 2)	1,000 (note 2)	1 : 5.0

SUGGESTED SOLUTIONS

* It is to be expected that the buildings element (not the land) in the freehold property would be depreciated and so an increase in the depreciation charge ought to be made on revaluation. However, no information is given to enable this to be done.

Notes

1   *Sales/debtors: scheme (e)*

   Monthly sales are to be assumed as $\frac{1}{12}$ of £6m = £500,000. The settlement discount to be deducted from 19X0/X1 profit would ∴ be 2 × 8% × £500,000 = £80,000, reducing operating profit to £120,000.

   The new policy can be expected to reduce debtors turnover to one month as all customers are expected to settle within 30 days. Provision must be made for the settlement discount and so the debtors balance will be £500,000 × 92% = £460,000. This is £290,000 less than the current estimate, reducing working capital.

   More cash will be collected in June and July than would currently be expected. £750,000 represents 1½ months sales and so it would seem that currently debtors take 1½ months credit. If it is assumed that all June sales will be paid by the end of July under the new policy, then £250,000 of late June sales which would previously have been outstanding at the end of July can now be expected to be paid for in July. However, all June sales will be paid for net of discount (£500,000 × 8% = £40,000). So the net cash inflow will be £250,000 - £40,000 = £210,000. The bank balance will therefore be £260,000.

   To summarise, working capital will decrease by £290,000 - £210,000 (£80,000), in other words by the discount claimed (or to be claimed) in both months.

2   *Purchases/creditors: scheme (f)*

   There is no effect on profit, simply on cash flow. One month's purchases cost £300,000 (£3.6m ÷ 12) and so year end creditors will now be £600,000 (June and July). The bank balance will increase by £300,000 (which would have been paid in July under the old credit terms) to £350,000. Working capital will therefore be £1m - £300,000 + £300,000 = £1m.

3   *Debt: equity ratio*

Course of action	(a) £'000	(b) £'000	(c) £'000	(d) £'000	(e) £'000	(f) £'000
Original forecast	2,500	2,500	2,500	2,500	2,500	2,500
Add reduction in depreciation		100				
Add revaluation reserve (3,500 - 1,000)			2,500			
Deduct goodwill				(400)		
Deduct settlement discount					(80)	
Revised equity	2,500	2,600	5,000	2,100	2,420	2,500
Debt	500	500	500	500	500	500
Debt: equity ratio	1:5.0	1:5.2	1:10.0	1:4.2	1:4.8	1:5.0

SUGGESTED SOLUTIONS

17 ASHMOLE

> *Tutorial notes*
>
> (a) There is a case for treating the gain on sale of investments as an extraordinary item but in our opinion it is not a sufficiently material item and so it is here netted off against administrative expenses. It would probably be disclosed in the notes as an exceptional item. FRS 3 would not allow treatment as an extraordinary item.
>
> (b) The tax charge is overstated and must be reduced by the amount of the 19X0 overprovision.
>
> (c) Goodwill could, under SSAP 22, either be written off against reserves or amortised over its useful life. Since the question hints that the latter is the preferred option, it is the one adopted here.
>
> (d) The preference shares were redeemed at a premium but presumably issued at par (no share premium account). The nominal value of the shares redeemed must be credited to a new capital redemption reserve and the premium must be deducted from retained profits.

(a) ASHMOLE PLC
PROFIT AND LOSS ACCOUNT FOR THE YEAR ENDED 30 SEPTEMBER 19X1

	£'000	£'000
Turnover (5,168 - 80)		5,088
Cost of sales		3,000
Gross profit		2,088
Distribution costs	317	
Administrative expenses (1,220 - 102 - 80 + 25)	1,063	
Operating profit		708
Interest payable		80
Profit on ordinary activities before tax		628
Tax on profit on ordinary activities (190 - 13)		177
Profit on ordinary activities after tax		451
Ordinary interim dividend paid		80
Retained profit for the year		371

Note. The amortisation of goodwill and the profit on the sale of investments have been shown in administrative expenses.

ASHMOLE PLC
MOVEMENTS ON RESERVES FOR THE YEAR ENDED 30 SEPTEMBER 19X1

	Debenture redemption reserve £'000	Retained profits £'000	Capital redemption reserve £'000	Reservation reserve £'000	Total £'000
At 1 October 19X0					
As previously stated	150	714	-	-	864
Prior year adjustment	-	(102)			(102)
As restated	150	612			762
Transfer on redemption of preference shares		(140)	140		-
Premium paid on redemption of preference shares		(19)			(19)
Transfer to debenture redemption reserve	50	(50)			-
Retained earnings for the year		371			371
Revaluation of land and buildings				530	530
At 30 September 19X1	200	774	140	530	1,644

ASHMOLE PLC
BALANCE SHEET AS AT 30 SEPTEMBER 19X1

	£'000	£'000
Fixed assets		
Intangible asset		
Goodwill (100 × ¾)		75
Tangible assets		
Land and buildings		800
Plant and machinery		1,406
		2,281
Current assets		
Stocks	740	
Debtors	290	
	1,030	
Creditors: amounts falling due within one year		
Bank overdraft	16	
Trade creditors	161	
Corporation tax (203 - 13)	190	
	367	
Net current assets		663
Total assets less current liabilities		2,944
Creditors: amounts falling due after more than one year		
15% debenture loans, repayable 19X8		500
		2,444
Capital and reserves		
Called up share capital		
Ordinary £1 shares		800
Reserves		1,644
		2,444

SUGGESTED SOLUTIONS

(b) The directors wish to pay a dividend (make a distribution) of 20p × 800,000 = £160,000. By law this can only be paid from accumulated realised profits less accumulated realised losses. In addition, as a public company Ashmole plc can only make a distribution if its net assets will be not less than its aggregate share capital and undistributable reserves *after* the distribution. The undistributable reserves are the capital redemption reserve and the revaluation reserve. The debenture redemption reserve is maintained voluntarily and is built up from retained profits. (It is assumed that Ashmole plc's memorandum and articles place no restriction on the use of the debenture redemption reserve.) Therefore, Ashmole plc has distributable reserves of £974,000 (aggregate of debenture redemption reserve and retained profits).

	£'000
Net assets before distribution	1,644
Less dividend	160
Net assets after distribution	1,484
Called up share capital	800
Undistributable reserves	
Capital redemption reserve	140
Revaluation reserve	530
	1,470

By a narrow margin, Ashmole plc would be allowed to make the distribution.

Ashmole plc would then have retained profits of £614,000, of which £211,000 was earned in 19X0/X1. There would be no need to raid the debenture redemption reserve, which would be imprudent and short-termist.

However, the dividend would presumably have to be paid from the overdraft. There is no obvious source of cash other than net trading receipts (no investments, for example). The company's current ratio is very satisfactory but the heavy investment in stock means that its short-term liquidity is not so good. Although the corporation tax is not due for another nine months or so, it would be unwise not to set cash aside for it as soon as possible.

The cost of borrowing to pay the dividend must be calculated, looking at how quickly net trading receipts could be expected to reduce the overdraft.

On the other hand, *not* to pay a dividend (especially when a profit has been made) is bound to affect market confidence in the company and this should also be considered. The total dividend for the year does not represent an unduly high payout (53% of profit for the year).

Other considerations are the company's investment plans for the foreseeable future and their expected sources of funding. Currently, even with a £160,000 increase in the overdraft, gearing is low, but any other new borrowing would increase gearing to riskier levels. Any increase in equity funding would result in higher dividend levels in future and the directors would have to consider whether a 30p full year dividend would be a feasible marker for the future, given that markets tend to expect a steady increase in payout over the years.

18 ATTERCLIFFE

> *Tutorial note.* Presentation was a problem in this question. You need to tabulate your answer carefully and neatly. There were many common errors in the examination, showing that candidates were not adequately knowledgeable about the accounting treatment of these items.

AS AT 30 APRIL 19X2

	Profit and loss account £		Balance sheet £
(a) *Above the line (cost of sales)*		*Asset (stocks)*	
(i) FIFO	920,500	(i) FIFO	279,500
(ii) Average cost	924,000	(ii) Average cost	276,000
(b) *Above the line*		*Asset*	
(i) Research and development	22,500	(i)	-
(ii) Research	10,500	(ii) Development	12,000
(c) *Above the line*		*Asset*	
(i) Goodwill	5,000	(i) Goodwill	35,000
Adjustment to reserves			
(ii) Goodwill	40,000	(ii) Goodwill	-
(d) *Above the line*		*Asset*	
Profit of associate (W3)	6,000	Investment at cost	37,100
		Add profit share	6,000
			43,100
(e) *Below the line*		*Liability*	
Tax charge (120,000 × 25%)	30,000	Taxation creditor	30,000
Transfer to deferred tax		Deferred tax account	15,000
(£60,000 × 35%)	15,000		
(f) *Below the line*		*Liabilities*	
Dividend payable		Dividend due	60,000
(£0.12 × 500,000)	60,000	ACT due	20,000
ACT payable (£60,000 × 25/75)	20,000	*Asset*	
		ACT recoverable	20,000

Workings

1 Cost of sales

	FIFO £	Average cost £
Opening stock	-	-
Purchases	1,200,000	1,200,000
Less closing stock (W2)	(279,500)	(276,000)
	920,500	924,000

2 Stock

	FIFO £	Average cost £
X	126,500	124,000
Y	63,000	62,000
Z	90,000	90,000
	279,500	276,000

SUGGESTED SOLUTIONS

3 *Associate company*

Profit: 1 November 19X1 to 30 April 19X2 = £36,000 × $\frac{6}{12}$ = £18,000

Group share = £18,000 × 20,000/60,000 = £6,000.

Reasons for different treatment

(a) Either FIFO or average cost is permitted as a valuation method for stock by SSAP 9 *Stocks and long-term contracts*. However, whichever of these methods is chosen, stock may only be valued at the lower of cost and not realisable value, when calculated on an individual item bases. Hence product line Z will be valued at £90,000 in both circumstances.

(b) The usual treatment of research and development costs is to write them off immediately, according to SSAP 13 *Accounting for research and development*. As an alternative the SSAP does allow development expenditure to be capitalised in the balance sheet thus giving a higher profit than the first methods. It is quite likely that the development costs here would meet the criteria laid down in the standard.

(c) SSAP 22 *Accounting for goodwill* recommends that goodwill on acquisition should be written off to reserves immediately. An alternative treatment is allowed, however, whereby the goodwill can be amortised over its useful life through the profit and loss account. The former method is better for current profits.

(d) SSAP 1 *Accounting for associated companies* requires the equity method to be used when accounting for an associated company. This means that the group share of the associate's profit is shown in the consolidated profit and loss account, while in the balance sheet the value of the investment is shown at cost plus the group share of post acquisition profits.

(e) The tax charge for the year is based on the taxable profits of the business. The deferred tax charge is required by SSAP 15 to reflect the timing difference which has produced a lower taxable profit than the reported profit. The amount of tax transferred to the deferred tax account will eventually become payable.

(f) Companies which pay a dividend are required, under tax law, to pay an advance on their corporation tax bill. The advance corporation tax (ACT) is calculated by multiplying the total dividend payable by a fraction based on the prevailing income tax rate.

The ACT is a liability at the year end, but it is also a deferred asset as it can be recovered by deducting the amount of ACT paid from the corporation tax paid to the revenue for the year ended 30 April 19X3.

SUGGESTED SOLUTIONS

19 PRACTICE QUESTION: HAKLUYT

**CONSOLIDATED BALANCE SHEET
AS AT 30 SEPTEMBER 19X1**

	£'000	£'000
Tangible fixed assets (2,833 + 364)		3,197
Current assets		
Stock (396 + 103)	499	
Debtors (1,500 + 185)	1,685	
Bank (60 + 12 + 5 in transit)	77	
	2,261	
Current liabilities		
Trade creditors (198 + 78)	276	
Net current assets		1,985
Total assets less current liabilities		5,182
Minority interest (W2)		(159)
		5,023
Capital and reserves		
Called up share capital		4,000
Profit and loss account (W3)		1,023
		5,023

Workings

£'000

1 Goodwill arising on consolidation

	£'000
Share capital of Cook Ltd	400
Reserves at date of acquisition	36
Net assets of Cook Ltd at date of acquisition	436
Share of net assets acquired by group (75%)	327
Purchase consideration	350
∴ Goodwill	23

2 Minority interest at 30 September 19X2

	£'000
Share capital of Cook Ltd	400
Reserves at 30 September 19X2	236
	636
Share owned by minority (25%)	159

3 Consolidated profit and loss reserve at 30 September 19X2

	£'000	£'000
Retained earnings of Hakluyt plc		896
Retained earnings of Cook Ltd		
Shown in draft accounts	236	
Less pre-acquisition reserves	36	
Post acquisition reserves	200	
Group share (75%)		150
		1,046
Less goodwill (W1) written off in accordance with SSAP 22		23
		1,023

SUGGESTED SOLUTIONS

20 NEWMAN

> *Tutorial note.* The examiner commented that the main errors were, in part (a), failure to include the revaluation reserve in the goodwill calculation and the treatment of net profit for the year as post-acquisition; in part (b), failure to calculate the merger reserve and use of acquisition method techniques.

NEWMAN LIMITED
CONSOLIDATED BALANCE SHEET AS AT 30 SEPTEMBER 19X8

(a) *Acquisition method*

	£'000	£'000
Freehold properties		325
Other fixed assets (3,650 + 420)		4,070
Net current assets (1,160 + 51)		1,211
		5,606
Capital and reserves		
Ordinary share capital (W1)		2,500
Reserves		
As at 1 October 19X7	2,600	
Share premium on new issue of shares (W1)	400	
Retained profit for the year	210	
Goodwill written off (W2)	(104)	
As at 30 September 19X8		3,106
		5,606

(b) *Merger method*

	£'000	£'000
Freehold properties		210
Other fixed assets		4,070
Net current assets		1,211
		5,491
Capital and reserves		
Ordinary share capital (W1)		2,500
Reserves		
As at 1 October 19X7 (2,600 + 221)	2,821	
Retained profit for the year (210 + 160)	370	
Merger reserve	(200)	
		2,991
		5,491

Workings

1 *Newman Ltd's share capital*

	£'000
Shares in issue before combination	2,000
Issued to shareholders in Gilbert Ltd	
⁵/₃ × 300,000	500
	2,500

Share premium on new issue = £400,000 (£900,000 − £500,000).

2 Goodwill arising on consolidation

	£'000
Consideration given	900
Fair value of Gilbert's assets (325 + 420 + 51)	796
Goodwill arising on consolidation	104

In accordance with SSAP 22's preferred treatment, goodwill has been written off against reserves.

3 Merger adjustment

	£'000
Nominal value of shares issued	500
Nominal value of shares acquired	300
Merger adjustment	200

This adjustment is needed because, under the merger method, the amount at which Newman Ltd records its investment in the shares of Gilbert Ltd is the nominal value of shares issued as consideration (£500,000). No share premium need be recorded because merger relief is available under s 131 CA 1985. The shares acquired, however, against which the investment of £500,000 is to be cancelled, have a nominal value of £300,000. The £200,000 imbalance is simply deducted from reserves to make the balance sheet balance.

21 GRIMSHAW

	Dingle £'000	Eagle £'000	Fender £'000
Share of profit	16	32	15
Goodwill/premium on acquisition	58	31	–
Minority interest	34	–	–

Dingle

Grimshaw has acquired 80% of the capital of Dingle, which must therefore be accounted for as a subsidiary company. In 19X8 Grimshaw will take credit for 80% of Dingle's profit of £20,000, ie £16,000.

Goodwill is calculated as follows.

	£'00
Net assets of Dingle Ltd on acquisition	
Share capital	80
Retained profit at 1 January 19X8	70
	150

Share of net assets acquired by Grimshaw (80%)	120
Price paid	178
Difference = goodwill	58

The minority interest at 31 December 19X8 will be equal to 20% of Dingle's net assets at that date, 20% of £170,000 = £34,000.

SUGGESTED SOLUTIONS

Eagle

The 80,000 shares acquired in Eagle Ltd represent 40% of the company's share capital. Eagle is therefore not a subsidiary company and should be accounted for as an associated company.

In the consolidated profit and loss account for 19X8 Grimshaw will take credit for 40% of Eagle's profit for the year: 40% × £80,000 = £32,000.

Goodwill is calculated in the same way as for Dingle.

	£'000
Net assets of Eagle Ltd on acquisition	
Share capital	200
Retained profit at 1 January 19X8	100
	300
Share of net assets acquired by Grimshaw (40%)	120
Price paid	151
Difference = goodwill	31

Because Eagle is not a subsidiary company, Grimshaw does not consolidate its net assets in the group balance sheet. As a result, no question of minority interest arises.

Fender

The 50,000 shares acquired in Fender Ltd represent only 10% of the company's share capital. Fender therefore does not qualify even as an associated company, much less as a subsidiary; it is merely an investment.

The appropriate accounting treatment is to take credit in the profit and loss account only for dividends received and receivable, which in 19X8 amount to 10% × £150,000 or £15,000.

No goodwill on acquisition and no minority interest should be disclosed.

22   HAGG

> *Tutorial note.* Answers to this question were quite good in the examination, although among frequent errors were the inclusion of the investment in subsidiaries as an asset and summing all the share capitals to give a consolidated total. In other words, candidates failed to cancel intercompany items.

SUGGESTED SOLUTIONS

(a) **HAGG LIMITED**
CONSOLIDATED BALANCE SHEET AS AT 31 MARCH 19X2

	£'000
Fixed assets (2,600 + 2,100 + 1,300)	6,000
Net current assets (1,680 + 930 + 1,370)	3,980
	9,980
16% debenture stock (500 + 2,000 + 1,500)	4,000
	5,980
Capital and reserves	
Ordinary share capital	3,300
Retained profit at 31 March 19X1 (1,360 + 320 + 140)	1,820
Profit for the year to 31 March 19X2 (420 + 210 + 30)	660
Merger reserve (W)	200
	5,980

Working £'000

Nominal value of shares acquired (1,000 + 500)	1,500
Nominal value of shares issued (800 + 500)	1,300
Reserve	200

(b)

	Hagg Limited	
	Single company	*Consolidated*
Debt/equity ratio	$\frac{500}{5,080}$	$\frac{4,000}{5,980}$
	= 0.1:1	= 0.7:1
Interest cover	$\frac{500 \text{ (W1)}}{500 \times 16\%}$	$\frac{1,300 \text{ (W2)}}{4,000 \times 16\%}$
	= 6.25 times	= 2.03 times

Workings

1. Profit before tax = 420 + (16% × 500) = 500
2. Profit before tax = 420 + 210 + 30 + (16% × 4,000) = 1,300

The consolidated balance sheet has a far higher debt/equity ratio than that of the single company, due to the addition of the debentures of Oaken and Greave Ltd. The debentures are not cancelled on consolidation as they are held by external parties. The share capital of the other two companies is cancelled, however, as an intercompany transaction

It is not possible to say whether the figures for debt/equity or interest cover are acceptable unless more is known about the business or industry of the group.

(c) The financial position would be affected in any of the following ways by using the SSAP 14 acquisition method.

   (i) Only post-acquisition profits of Oaken Ltd and Greave Ltd will be shown in the consolidated results.

SUGGESTED SOLUTIONS

(ii) The investment in the subsidiaries would be stated at the fair value of the consideration paid for them under acquisition accounting. In merger accounting the nominal value of the shares issued as consideration was used. In acquisition accounting, the use of fair values means that a share premium account must be created, which does not arise in merger accounting.

(iii) A figure for goodwill will be produced using acquisition accounting which would have to be eliminated from reserves or amortised over its useful life.

(iv) In acquisition accounting, the assets of the acquired company must be restated at fair value. This may increase depreciation charges.

23 TUTORIAL QUESTION: GNOMES

Tutorial note. This suggested solution is purposely long and detailed to give you a chance to revise the problems of accounting for price changes. The important points to mention are:

(a) prudence
(b) profits retention
(c) consistency
(d) *not* an 'inflation' accounting policy
(e) not as straightforward to use in practice.

MEMORANDUM

To: Eric
From: Bank manager

You have asked me to comment on the possibility of recording purchases and valuing stock at current or replacement cost rather than at historical cost (what it costs you to buy them). My comments are as follows.

(a) Your profits would decrease under this valuation basis as the value of cost of sales would increase. This can be considered prudent as it reflects the loss in value of your working capital as a result of price increases in the period.

For example, if during the year you were able to sell 1,000 units purchased for £10,000 less than current prices, you will need that £10,000 now to replace stocks. Under historical cost accounting, however, this loss in 'operating capability' is not recognised.

(b) Such an accounting policy would also result in an increase in the value of stock on the balance sheet. This could be considered imprudent since stock is normally valued at the lower of cost and net realisable value.

(c) Your suggested policy will not be consistent as you will still be recording all other expenses and all revenue at historical amounts. This would not be a problem if these other items were unaffected by price increases, but this is unlikely.

(d) Your suggested policy will not have the result 'that your accounts reflect inflation'. Inflation is a *general* increase in prices giving rise to a fall in the value of money. Using current costs to establish cost of sales but not other items in the accounts does not result in a 'current cost profit'. An alternative system of accounting for changing prices is to try to restate all items in stable monetary units but this is not as useful for you as a manager as a current cost approach.

(e) Finally, on a practical note, your policy would not be acceptable to the Inland Revenue, nor would it be as easy to apply as historical cost accounting.

You might find it most useful to prepare your accounts as normal using historical costs but to keep a memorandum record of the current cost of your stocks so that you can manage your working capital accordingly.

24 PRICE

> *Tutorial note.* Do not be put off by the dreaded words 'current cost'; most of the information needed for parts (a) and (b) is given to you, and on the whole this is a straightforward question.

(a) PRICE LIMITED
CURRENT COST PROFIT FOR THE YEAR ENDED 31 DECEMBER 19X0

	£'000	£'000
Historical cost profit		400
Deduct: cost of sales adjustment	51	
depreciation adjustment (W1)	100	
		151
Current cost profit		249

(b) PRICE LIMITED
CURRENT COST BALANCE SHEET AS AT 31 DECEMBER 19X0

	£'000
Fixed assets	
Replacement cost	2,500
Accumulated depreciation (W1)	500
Net book value	2,000
Stock at replacement cost	611
Net liquid assets	200
	2,811
Capital and reserves	
Share capital	2,000
Current cost reserve (W2)	562
Current cost profit	249
	2,811

SUGGESTED SOLUTIONS

(c) *Return on net assets*

			Historical cost	Current cost
$\dfrac{\text{Profit}}{\text{Long-term capital}}$	$= \dfrac{400}{2,400} \times 100\%$		16.7%	
$\dfrac{\text{Profit}}{\text{Long-term capital}}$	$\dfrac{249}{2,811} \times 100\%$			8.9%

(d) The return on capital earned on a historical cost basis is nearly double the current cost return. This is principally because current cost profit is significantly lower than historical cost profit, because of the increase in the replacement costs of stocks and fixed assets over the year. This is not allowed for in calculating historical cost profit, but current cost profit does allow for the need to maintain operating capability and so will usually report lower profits in times of rising prices.

Additionally, the capital base is usually understated in historical cost accounts, so that a historical cost return will always appear higher than when current costs are used.

The current cost return, if properly understood, is more useful than the historical cost return, precisely because it takes into account *current* costs and values, rather than a random collection of historical costs.

Workings

1 *Depreciation adjustment*

	£'000
Replacement cost of fixed assets	2,500
Current cost depreciation charge (2,500 ÷ 5)	500
Historical cost depreciation charge	400
Depreciation adjustment	100

2 *Current cost reserve*

	£'000
Revaluation of fixed assets	500
Revaluation of closing stock	11
Cost of sales adjustment	51
	562

25 TUTORIAL QUESTION: PURCHASE OF OWN SHARES

Workings for A plc

	£
Cost of redemption (50,000 × £1.50)	75,000
Premium on redemption (50,000 × 50p)	25,000

No premium arises on the new issue

SUGGESTED SOLUTIONS

	£	£
Distributable profits		
Profit and loss account before redemption		160,000
Premium on redemption (must come out of distributable profits, no premium on original issue)		(25,000)
		135,000
Remainder of redemption costs	50,000	
Proceeds of new issue (5,000 × £1)	(5,000)	
Remainder out of distributable profits (= transfer to CRR)		(45,000)
Balance on profit and loss account		90,000

Transfer to capital redemption reserve

	£
Nominal value of shares redeemed	50,000
Proceeds of new issue	(5,000)
Transfer to CRR from profit and loss account	45,000

A PLC
BALANCE SHEET AS AT 1 JULY 19X5

	£'000
Capital and reserves	
Preference shares	5
Ordinary shares	250
Share premium	60
Capital redemption reserve	45
	360
Profit and loss account	90
	450
Net assets (520 − 75 + 5)	450

Workings for B Ltd

	£
Cost of redemption (50,000 × 80p)	40,000
Discount on redemption (50,000 × 20p)	10,000
Cost of redemption	40,000
Distributable profits	(20,000)
Permissible capital payment (PCP)	20,000
Transfer to capital redemption reserve	
Nominal value of shares redeemed	50,000
PCP	20,000
Balance on capital redemption reserve	30,000

B LIMITED
BALANCE SHEET AS AT 1 JULY 19X5

	£'000
Capital and reserves	
Ordinary shares	250
Share premium	60
Capital redemption reserve	30
	340
Net assets (380 − 40)	340

SUGGESTED SOLUTIONS

26 HARBOUR

> *Tutorial note.* There are two fairly straightforward ways of tackling part (a) of the question. The simplest is perhaps to set out a revised balance sheet after the re-organisation (to complete part (b) first). The revised share capital would emerge as a balancing figure and the amount to be written off could easily be calculated. Alternatively, the adjustments to asset values may be listed and totalled; the total downward adjustment will equal the amount to be written off share capital. This is the approach adopted below.

(a) *Adjustments to balance sheet values*

	£'000
Intangible fixed assets (12 + 15)	(27)
Land and buildings	61
Plant and machinery	(162)
Stocks	(73)
Debtors	(5)
Profit and loss account	(94)
Amount to be written off share capital	(300)

(b) **REVISED BALANCE SHEET AS AT 1 APRIL 19X9**

	£'000	£'000
Fixed assets		
Land and buildings		161
Plant and machinery		200
		361
Current assets		
Stocks	162	
Debtors	88	
Cash at bank (W1)	153	
	403	
Creditors: amounts falling due within one year		
Bank loan	50	
Trade creditors	184	
	234	
Net current assets		169
Total assets less current liabilities		530
Creditors: amounts falling due after more than one year		150
		380
Capital and reserves		
Called up share capital (W2)		380

(c) The bank has to consider whether the proposed scheme offers sufficient security for the funds which it has invested. If the conclusion is unfavourable, the bank's alternative is presumably to press for immediate repayment of the £247,000 overdraft; this would inevitably lead to the company's liquidation. In the event of liquidation, the bank would recover the outstanding amount because it is secured on fixed assets of sufficient value.

SUGGESTED SOLUTIONS

Although liquidation is a straightforward way for the bank to recover its money it should clearly be seen as a last resort. The bank's aim should be to keep customers and to help them rather than to force them into extinction.

In fact it is very doubtful whether such a course would be necessary. The proposed re-organisation involves an immediate repayment of £47,000 to the bank, with the balance to be paid off in equal annual instalments over the next four years. Clearly the bank would wish to renew its security, probably by means of a fixed charge on land and buildings and a floating charge over the remaining assets of the company. It would also be important to review the company's financial prospects.

(i) Have adequate forecasts and budgets been prepared? Do the assumptions on which they are based appear reasonable?

(ii) Have *all* loss-making operations been discontinued? Do the financial forecasts include provision for any consequential costs of such closures (for example redundancy payments)?

(iii) Is the cash projected to be available sufficient to meet any new investment in fixed assets and working capital that may be necessary?

(iv) Is management sufficiently skilled to direct operations more profitably than in the past?

Workings

1 *Cash at bank*

	£'000
Bank overdraft per original balance sheet	247
Less amount re-classified as loan	200
	47
Cash introduced by directors	200
Cash at bank per revised balance sheet	153

2 *Called up share capital*

	£'000
Share capital per draft balance sheet	400
Less amounts written off	300
	100
New share capital	
Issued to debenture holders	80
Issued to the directors	200
	380

27 CLAYTON

> *Tutorial note.* Although the overdraft is secured on the leasehold, the offered price is less than the balance sheet value, let alone the full amount of the overdraft. The balance of the overdraft is therefore unsecured as there is apparently no floating charge.
>
> Remember that goodwill is now valueless, as no one has offered anything for it, and that the shareholders are at the bottom of the list for repayment. Their reserves are irrelevant.

SUGGESTED SOLUTIONS

(a) *Scheme 1: liquidation*

	£'000
Bank overdraft	650
Proceeds on disposal of leasehold	400
Balance, unsecured	250
Proceeds on disposal of stock	395
Debtors	310
	705
Liquidation expenses	(20)
Preferential creditors	(220)
Available for unsecured creditors	465
Total unsecured creditors	
Bank	250
Sundry (590 - 220)	370
	620

∴ The bank can expected to receive the following in all.

	£
From sale of security	400,000
Balance = $\frac{465}{620} \times 250$ (75p in the £)	187,500
	587,500

Scheme 2

Since Scheme 1 results in an immediate cash flow, Scheme 2 cash flows must be stated in terms of present values to enable a valid comparison to be made.

Year	Capital £	Interest £	Discount value @ 14% £	Present value £
0	250,000	–	1.000	250,000
1	100,000	80,000	0.877	157,860
2	100,000	60,000	0.769	123,040
3	100,000	40,000	0.675	94,500
4	100,000	20,000	0.592	71,040
				696,440

(b) Scheme 1 results in a lower payout to the bank but has the advantage of increased certainty over the amount to be received and the timing. The valuations of stock and debtors appear to be realistic and a firm offer has been received for the leasehold.

The success of Scheme 2 depends on the current management's ability to keep the business going, which must be in doubt, given the current problems. A high interest burden will put pressure on profits. (The interest rate on the finance company loan is likely to be at least 20%.)

It would be more satisfactory to see an equity injection, given that shareholders' equity (after goodwill is written off) will be less than half of the bank's debenture loan and the finance company loan, resulting in unacceptably high gearing. Cash flow forecasts should be prepared to show where both the £100,000 repayments and the finance company repayments are to come from.

SUGGESTED SOLUTIONS

Finally, the company will have no security to offer the finance company other than a floating charge over debtors and stocks, which the bank will also want to ensure a reasonable margin on its security for its debenture. Perhaps the directors could provide guarantees backed by their personal assets.

Conclusion

Scheme 1 is probably to be preferred, in spite of its apparently lower return, because it is less risky.

28 DUKE

> *Tutorial note.* Although part (a) of this question was well answered in the exam, many candidates failed to make a transfer to the CRR, or transferred the wrong amount, in part (b). Remember, the CRR transfer is made to *preserve* permanent capital.

(a) The amount of 'permanent' capital at 31 May 19X2 is as follows.

	£
Ordinary shares £1 each	500,000
Share premium account	36,000
Revaluation reserve	175,000
	711,000

(b) BALANCE SHEETS AS AT 1 JUNE 19X2

	No further shares £	50,000 share issue £
Fixed assets and net current assets	903,000 (W1)	988,000 (W2)
Capital and reserves		
Ordinary shares of £1 each	400,000	450,000
Share premium account	36,000	71,000 (W3)
Revaluation reserve	175,000	175,000
Capital redemption reserve	100,000 (W4)	15,000
Retained profit	192,000	277,000
	903,000	988,000

Workings

1 *Fixed assets: no further shares*

	£
As at 31 May	1,023,000
Less cash for redemption (100,000 × £1.20)	120,000
	903,000

2 *Fixed assets: share issue*

	£
Assets from (W1) above	903,000
Add proceeds from share issue (£50,000 × £1.70)	85,000
	988,000

135

SUGGESTED SOLUTIONS

3   *Share premium account*

	£
At 31 May	36,000
Premium on issue (70p × 50,000)	35,000
	71,000

4   *Capital redemption and retained profits*

	No new issue £	New issue £
Value of share redeemed	100,000	100,000
Proceeds of new issue	-	85,000
Transfer to capital redemption reserve	100,000	15,000
Share premium	20,000	20,000
	120,000	35,000
Retained profits 31 May	312,000	312,000
Retained profits 1 June	192,000	277,000

(c) The Companies Act 1985 allows a company to redeem ordinary shares (and therefore issue redeemable shares), but under strict rules. The rules are there to maintain the capital base of the company, mainly for the sake of the creditors. To ensure this, redemption of shares is only allowed if the cost is met by the proceeds of a fresh issue, by distributable reserves, or by a combination of the two.

The capital redemption is required to account for the transfer from distributable reserves. In a case where there is no new issue of shares, the transfer to the CRR will be equal to the nominal value of the shares redeemed. Where a new issue of shares takes place to finance the redemption, then the amount transferred will be the difference between the nominal value of the shares redeemed and the proceeds of the new issue.

29   TUTORIAL QUESTION: BUSINESS VALUATION METHODS

(a) (i)   Break-up value basis
    (ii) Book value basis
    (iii) Replacement cost basis
    (iv) Earnings yield basis
    (v)   Price/earnings basis
    (vi) Dividend yield basis
    (vii) Future cash flows basis

(b) (i)   Break-up value is the lowest price which the owners of the business will accept since otherwise they might just as well liquidate the company.

   (ii)   Book value is not a useful measure if based on historical cost accounts except as the lowest approximate value of net assets on a going concern basis. It ignores intangible assets not on the balance sheet and surpluses over historical cost or latest revaluation not yet recorded.

   (iii) Replacement cost values put a valuation in perspective by showing how much it would cost to set up an equivalent business from scratch.

   (iv)   Earnings yield basis valuations are useful in indicating a company's value based on its past or predicted future earnings record rather than the value of its assets. Asset-based valuations must be based on historical accounts and are useful in indicating the security of the investment rather than in giving a realistic view of a shareholder's likely return. A share purchase is essentially a purchase of a future earnings stream as much as an investment for capital growth; and capital growth will be as likely to arise from earnings growth than from increased asset backing.

(v) The price/earnings basis is useful for the same reasons as the earnings yield method but is easier to use as all quoted companies have a P/E ratio in the *Financial Times* whereas earnings yield is not published in the FT. It is therefore simpler to estimate the P/E ratio of an unquoted company than its earnings yield.

(vi) The dividend yield basis of valuation is the first choice for valuing a minority holding as minority shareholders cannot influence distribution policy. Although it is important to look at asset values and earnings to establish dividend cover and asset backing which are of great importance in assessing the risks attached to a share investment, nevertheless the company's past and likely future distribution policy is of most importance.

(vii) Likely future cash flows are an important factor in valuing a business which is to be taken over by another company, as a valuation based on historical profits or even likely future profits under the old management will not be relevant where major changes would be made by the new owner. In this case, the potential acquiror would estimate the initial cash investment in the company (*not* the share purchase but new capital investment) and the expected cash flows over, say, the first five years of ownership. These flows are discounted at the relevant cost of capital and the net present value of all the flows represents the most that is worth paying for the shares. In essence, this is just the same approach as the company would use in deciding whether or not to make any investment.

(c)

	Valuation basis	Formula	Value
(i)	Break-up value	Net assets at break-up value × 10%	£75,000
(ii)	Book value	Net assets at book value × 10%	£95,000
(iii)	Replacement cost	Net assets at replacement cost × 10%	£125,000
(iv)	Earnings yield	$\dfrac{\text{Earnings}}{\text{Earnings yield}} \times 10\%$	£100,000
(v)	Price/earnings	Earnings × P/E × 10%	£80,000
(vi)	Dividend yield	$\dfrac{\text{Dividend}}{\text{Dividend yield}} \times 10\%$	£100,000
(vii)	Future cash flows*	$\dfrac{\text{Earnings}}{\text{Cost of capital}} \times 10\%$	£125,000

* Because expected cash flows are not expected to change in the future, the earnings stream is a *perpetuity*. The value of a perpetuity is determined by dividing annual earnings by the required rate of return. This is obvious if you rearrange the formula because you then see that an investment of £125,000 producing £20,000 per annum has a yield (return) of 16% pa.

The most meaningful valuation here is that produced on the dividend yield basis. 10% is a small holding giving no effective control over a company's policies and so the most relevant factor in fixing the share price is the likely dividend stream. The asset backing for the shares is also of interest as it gives an indication of the risk of the

SUGGESTED SOLUTIONS

investment. A company whose high share price arises from high expectations of profits but has comparatively low net assets relative to its market capitalisation must be a higher risk investment than a company with high net assets, especially in times of recession and high inflation and interest rates.

30 FALKUS

> *Tutorial note.* This is a very straightforward question of its type which should have caused you no problems if you have revised this topic carefully.

(a)

		Valuation of one £1 ordinary share
(i)	Break-even basis	£2.69
(ii)	Replacement cost basis	£4.22
(iii)	Dividend yield basis	£3.00
(iv)	Price/earnings basis	£4.80

Workings

1 *Break-up and replacement cost*

	£	£
Freehold	150,000	150,000
Machinery	50,000	180,000
Stocks	52,000	75,000
Net monetary assets	17,000	17,000
	269,000	422,000
Number of ordinary shares in issue	100,000	100,000
Value per share	£2.69	£4.22

2 *Dividend yield basis*

$$\text{Dividend per share} = \frac{£18,000}{100,000} = 18p$$

$$\text{Dividend yield} = \frac{\text{dividend}}{\text{share price}}$$

$$\therefore \text{Share price} = \frac{\text{dividend}}{\text{dividend yield}} = 18p \div 6\% = £3.00$$

3 *Price/earnings basis*

Fanshawe Ltd is a private company. The P/E ratio applicable to quoted companies in a comparable line of business is too high to apply in valuing Fanshawe's shares. A reduction of at least ⅓ should be made to allow for the reduced marketability of the shares.

SUGGESTED SOLUTIONS

Earnings = net profit = £72,000

EPS (earnings per share) = 72p
Price/earnings ratio = price per share ÷ EPS

∴ Price = EPS × P/E ratio = 72p × 10 × ⅔ = £4.80

(b) A break-up valuation represents the lowest price a seller should accept, as he could otherwise obtain more by winding the company up.

Similarly, a replacement cost valuation represents the highest price a buyer should pay, as he could in theory save money by setting up a similar business from scratch. The valuation here is not altogether realistic as no value is placed on goodwill, which in a continuing business should be a significant asset.

Thus, Falkus should expect to pay at least £2.69 per share but would probably not wish to pay much more than £4.22, depending on the value of goodwill.

The dividend yield basis is probably the most relevant for a minority shareholder as it indicates the value of the income stream which can be expected from the shares and whose size a minority interest could not expect to influence. However, a controlling interest would give the power to set dividend levels, to determine the profit to be retained in the business and to impose management charges etc. The dividend yield value is therefore of less interest, unless Falkus intends to leave Fanshawe much to itself.

The price/earnings basis shows the approximate price which Fanshawe's shares might fetch if it were to go public. This valuation method works on the assumption that the market value of a share represents the number of years' purchase of earnings available for distribution which investors feel confident to make. It is similar to the dividend yield basis but, because it looks at earnings rather than dividends, is more suitable in calculating the value of a controlling interest, since (as stated above) the old management's dividend policy will no longer be relevant.

31 TUTORIAL QUESTION: RITT

(a) (i) *Gross profit percentage*

	19X6 £'000	19X7 £'000	Increase %
Turnover	541	675	24.7
Cost of sales	369	481	30.3
Gross profit	172	194	
Gross profit percentage	$\frac{172}{541} \times 100$ = 31.8%	$\frac{194}{675} \times 100$ = 28.7%	

SUGGESTED SOLUTIONS

(ii) *Net profit percentage*

	19X6 £'000	19X7 £'000
Reserves c/f	53	82
Reserves b/f	(21)	(53)
Dividends proposed	20	30
Net profit	52	59

Net profit percentage

$\frac{52}{541} \times 100 = 9.6\%$ $\frac{59}{675} \times 100 = 8.7\%$

(iii) *Turnover: net assets employed*

$\frac{541}{303} = 1.8$ times $\frac{675}{432} = 1.6$ times

(iv) *Net profit: net assets employed*

$\frac{52}{303} \times 100 = 17.2\%$ $\frac{59}{432} \times 100 = 13.7\%$

(v) *Current assets: current liabilities*

188:92   269:162

∴ Current ratio = 2:1   1.7:1

(vi) *Quick assets: current liabilities*

	£'000	£'000
Current assets	188	269
Less stock	(86)	(177)
	102	92

∴ 'Quick' ratio   102:92   92:162
                 = 1.1:1 = 0.6:1

(b) The reduction in *gross profit/turnover* percentage is due to the fact that cost of sales has risen 30% in 19X7, whilst turnover has only increased 25%. This could be because material and labour costs have risen, or that the sales mix has changed, and there are higher sales of less profitable lines.

The *net profit/turnover* percentages are very much in line with the gross profit percentages discussed above. This indicates that other expenses have been in line with the increase in turnover. More detailed analysis might reveal higher costs in certain areas, compensated by lower ones in others.

Turnover has not increased in line with the increased investment, resulting in a lower *turnover/net assets* ratio. The accounts show an increase in fixed assets of £118,000 in plant and equipment and vehicles which should eventually be reflected in sales. The reasons why this has not occurred need to be further investigated. There has also been an increase of £11,000 in working capital, mainly accounted for by stock. The result of this may be increased sales in the early part of the 19X7/X8 financial year.

The *net profit/net assets* employed percentage is a direct function of the previous two ratios and confirms the fact that increased investment has not improved profitability.

The ratio of current assets to current liabilities has worsened. Creditors have increased by 83%, partly matched by a 106% increase in stock, but other current assets have not maintained this increase; cash deposits have gone down. However, the increase in debtors

The ratio of current assets to current liabilities has worsened. Creditors have increased by 83%, partly matched by a 106% increase in stock, but other current assets have not maintained this increase; cash deposits have gone down. However, the increase in debtors is in line with the increase in turnover (26%) which suggests credit control has been maintained at 19X6 standards, whereas creditors have increased out of all proportion to cost of sales figures. The implication is that the company may have been overtrading, running down its cash levels and leaving longer to pay its creditors, whilst keeping high stock levels and extending credit to customers.

The *quick assets/current liabilities* ratio reveals the full extent of the company's precarious position at 31 March 19X7. Quick assets are only just over 50% of current liabilities. The combination of investment in fixed assets and stock has put a strain on the liquidity of the company.

32 BURDON

> *Tutorial note.* The most common mistakes were failure to deduct interest charges from profits, reversal of the debt:equity ratio and treating the return to debentureholders as variable (not using the same interest figure in (b) as in (a)).

(a) Return on equity (ROE) = $\dfrac{\text{earnings}}{\text{equity}}$

Earnings = profit after tax and interest

	Burdon £'000	Jennings £'000
Interest on loans		
16% × 500	80	
16% × 2,500		400
∴ ROE =	$\dfrac{800-80}{3,500} \times 100$	$\dfrac{750-400}{1,500} \times 100$
=	20.6%	23.3%
Debt: equity ratio =	$\dfrac{500}{3,500} \times 100$	$\dfrac{2,500}{1,500} \times 100$
= $\dfrac{\text{long-term loans}}{\text{equity}}$ =	14.3%	166.7%

(b) Operating profit: 50% increase = 800 × 1.5   750 × 1.5

    = 1,200   1,125

Return on equity = $\dfrac{1,200-80}{3,500+400} \times 100$ $\dfrac{1,125-400}{1,500+375} \times 100$

    = 28.7%   38.7%

Operating profit: 50% decrease = 800 × 0.5   750 × 0.5

    = 400   375

Return on equity = $\dfrac{400-80}{3,500-400} \times 100$ $\dfrac{375-400}{1,500-375} \times 100$

    = 10.3%   -2.2%

SUGGESTED SOLUTIONS

Return on equity may therefore
vary between: 10.3% and 28.7%   -2.2% and 38.7%

(c) *Equity shareholders' viewpoint*

Burdon Ltd has low gearing and is therefore less vulnerable than Jennings Ltd to cyclical downturns in profit. Even if profit halves, its interest cover is still five times (400 ÷ 80). Because it has a high proportion of equity in its long term capital, its equity shareholders do not benefit as much as Jennings Ltd from an increase in profit, in terms of return on equity, because the denominator of the fraction (that is, equity) is higher than in a highly geared company. However, in absolute terms (that is, looking at profit available for distribution) they are always better off than Jennings Ltd's shareholders because interest costs are so much lower. Thus, Burdon Ltd's shareholders have less risk of reduced dividends and earnings than Jennings Ltd's shareholders. Jennings Ltd's shareholders, however, have the chance of a very high return on their stake in the company.

Bank's viewpoint

The bank's concerns are:

(i) interest cover;
(ii) security available for loan.

A highly geared company is a risky customer for a bank because its interest cover is lower and because if profits fall, cash flow will fall, thus reducing the funds available to repay the loan when it falls due without forced asset sales. Assuming that operating profit before interest is equivalent to a net cash inflow, several successive years of low profits would result in an annual cash deficit for Jennings Ltd which would reduce the value of its net assets and prevent it from accumulating a fund of cash and near-cash (or liquid) assets from which to repay its loan. It would also look much less attractive to investors and lenders who could otherwise be asked to advance more equity or debt capital to replace the loan. Thus Jennings Ltd's loan will require careful monitoring to ensure that adequate security is always available to cover the loan and that no breach has occurred of terms in the loan agreement requiring gearing or current ratios to be maintained at or above a stated safe level. Burden Ltd's loan would require less close monitoring as its profits are more than adequate to cover its interest payments and its loan represents a much smaller proportion of its net assets.

33 GREENWOOD

> *Tutorial note.* Part (a) caused students little difficult except in calculating total funds generated from operations. In part (b) students frequently stated that one company's ratios were *higher* or *lower* rather than explaining whether this was *better* or *worse*.

(a)

		Greenwood	Westport
Net profit percentage			
= net profit / turnover × 100	=	(520/4,820) × 100	(620/5,200) × 100
	=	11%	12%
Gross profit margin			
= gross profit / turnover × 100	=	(2,020/4,820) × 100	(2,200/5,200) × 100
	=	42%	42%
Debt:equity ratio			
= long-term liabilities / shareholders' funds × 100	=	(500/2,600) × 100	(800/1,400) × 100
	=	19%	57%
Total funds generated from operations			
= profit before tax and depreciation	=	520 + 250	620 + 100
	=	770	720

(b) Westport's net profit percentage is marginally better than Greenwood's although the two companies' gross profit margins are the same. This implies that Westport has lower overheads. Greenwood, however, has higher depreciation than Westport because its fixed assets are twice as high and so its 'cash profit' (that is, total funds generated from operations) is higher, implying that in fact it has a better cash flow from trading than Westport.

It depends on one's point of view whether one sees low gearing as a good thing. Neither company has imprudently high gearing. Greenwood might benefit from increasing its gearing, depending on interest rates and its expansion plans.

(c) Greenwood seems likely to offer better security than Westport because it has freehold properties in excess of the existing and proposed borrowings. These are easily valued and fairly easy to dispose of in the event that a fixed charge crystallises. This would enable the bank to offer a lower rate of interest in return for the decreased risk attached to the lending. Westport's fixed assets, unless undervalued in the balance sheet, are only just sufficient to cover both borrowings. We do not know what most of its fixed assets are; they could be intangibles or short leaseholds.

Additionally, Greenwood is less highly geared than Westport and so less at risk of running into difficulties if profits fall. Greenwood's 'cash profit' is higher. It therefore seems more capable of repaying the loan and meeting interest payments. Both companies are profitable, at similar levels, and solvent. However, because of Greenwood's lower gearing, stronger balance sheet and better cashflow, it seems the more prudent choice to grant it loan facilities rather than Westport.

SUGGESTED SOLUTIONS

34 THORNVILLE

> *Tutorial note.* Do not be put off by the mention of a price index. There is no need to adjust every figure; turnover alone is sufficient. Similarly, the ratios you are *required* to calculate are the only ones you should calculate, as there is no time or information to calculate others which would add to your analysis. You should have kept your explanations of the adjustments very brief.
>
> The examiner commented that candidates did not tackle this question well, particularly in concentrating on calculations at the expense of analysis, in failing to achieve sufficiently broad coverage of the matters requiring analysis and in failing to use a clear and concise format for the presentation of ratios and calculations.

Workings

1 *Prior year adjustment*

Gross profit in 19X3/X4 must be increased by £21,000 to reflect the true closing stock valuation. Similarly, gross profit in 19X4/X5 is currently overstated by £21,000 because opening stock is understated.

2 *Change in accounting policy*

There are two possible approaches:

(i) add back to profit the amortisation of goodwill in 19X1, 19X2 and 19X3, so that the current accounting policy (of writing goodwill off against reserves) is treated as having been adopted from the outset; or

(ii) deduct £20,000 from profit in 19X4 and 19X5, as if the accounting policy had not been changed.

The former policy is considered preferable here. As well as resulting in a change to profit, it affects shareholders' equity.

3 *Directors' remuneration*

As the company is owned and managed by substantially the same people, it is likely that the decision on how to take money out of the company (the split between dividends and remuneration) is influenced by tax. There is therefore a good case for adding directors' remuneration back to profit to establish the total amount available for distribution. If the owners did not manage the business they would have to employ managers to do it for them. However, as we do not know how much suitable managers would have cost, we shall ignore this expense in our calculations.

FILE NOTE
THORNVILLE LIMITED
FINANCIAL APPRAISAL 19X1 TO 19X5

Introduction

This appraisal is based on:

(a) the company's summarised accounts for 19X1 to 19X5, adjusted to ensure comparability as shown in Appendix 1;

(b) key accounting ratios (shown in Appendix 2);

(c) inflation-adjusted sales figures (shown in Appendix 3).

Gearing

The company's gearing is low and has reduced slightly over the period. In addition, interest cover is satisfactory, although this has almost halved over the five years.

Profitability

The gross profit margin has declined over the last three years, as has the net profit margin. This appears in part to have occurred because in real terms sales have begun to decline (see Appendix 3). In addition, overheads have increased by more than the price index for the cost of goods sold, indicating perhaps that they have gone out of control. The reduction in directors' remuneration may indicate an attempt to compensate for this increase.

The net profit margin is small, even before management costs are taken into account. However, the fall in gross margins appears to be the major reason for the fall in the net margins.

Consequently the return on equity has fallen markedly over the five years.

Conclusion

The directors' claim that turnover and profit have increased substantially in most years is not substantiated. When inflation is allowed for the company is still profitable but its profitability is declining, and the error over stock valuation does not account for it. Since the year end, the overdraft has gone up by 50%, so that gearing will also have increased and interest cover declined. The outlook for the company is doubtful and needs further investigation before a further increase in the overdraft limit can be considered.

APPENDIX 1: ADJUSTED FIGURES

	19X1 £'000	19X2 £'000	19X3 £'000	19X4 £'000	19X5 £'000
Gross profit					
As accounts	775	852	893	949	1,008
Stock	-	-	-	21	(21)
	775	852	893	970	987
Operating profit					
As accounts	40	54	72	60	97
Add back					
Directors' remuneration	100	100	86	86	86
Amortisation of goodwill	20	20	20	-	-
Stock adjustment	-	-	-	21	(21)
As revised	160	174	178	167	162
Shareholders' equity					
Opening balance	150	200	261	335	396
Add adjusted operating profit	160	174	178	167	162
Less tax	(10)	(13)	(18)	(20)	(29)
Less distributions					
Directors' remuneration	(100)	(100)	(86)	(86)	(86)
	200	261	335	396	443

SUGGESTED SOLUTIONS

APPENDIX 2: ACCOUNTING RATIOS

	19X1	19X2	19X3	19X4	19X5
Gross profit margin					
= adjusted gross profit / turnover	775/2,460 = 31.5%	852/2,706 = 31.5%	893/2,977 = 30.0%	970/3,274 = 29.6%	987/3,601 = 27.4%
Net profit margin					
= adjusted operating profit / turnover	160/2,460 = 6.5%	174/2,706 = 6.4%	178/2,977 = 6.0%	167/3,274 = 5.1%	162/3,601 = 4.5%
Return on year end equity					
= adjusted operating profit / adjusted shareholders' equity	160/200 = 80%	174/261 = 66.7%	178/335 = 53.1%	167/396 = 42.2%	162/443 = 36.6%
Interest cover					
= adjusted operating profit / interest	160/12 = 13.3×	174/12 = 14.5×	178/12 = 14.8×	167/16 = 10.4×	162/21 = 7.7×
Debt: equity ratio	100/200 = 0.5:1	100/261 = 0.4:1	100/335 = 0.3:1	130/396 = 0.3:1	160/443 = 0.4:1

APPENDIX 3: INFLATION-ADJUSTED SALES FIGURES

	19X1 £'000	19X2 £'000	19X3 £'000	19X4 £'000	19X5 £'000
At 19X0 prices					
2,460 ÷ 104/100	2,365				
2,706 ÷ 108/100		2,506			
2,977 ÷ 115/100			2,589		
3,274 ÷ 128/100				2,558	
3,601 ÷ 144/100					2,501

35 PINFOLD

> *Tutorial note.* Candidates' main difficulties with this question were in calculating the financial effects of the sales volume growth scheme, allowing for either the volume increase or the price increase, but not both. Many candidates also misunderstood part (b) and tried to prepare cash flow statements. Finally, many candidates did not state the obvious in part (c) and point out that both schemes were profitable and that, as the company sells for cash and not on credit, only *short-term* extra finance was potentially needed.

SUGGESTED SOLUTIONS

(a) PINFOLD LIMITED
BUDGETED PROFIT AND LOSS ACCOUNT
FOR THE YEAR TO 30 JUNE 19X2

	Working	(i) £'000	(i) £'000	(ii) £'000	(ii) £'000
Turnover	1		5,328		6,150
Direct materials	2	1,908		2,290	
Direct labour and variable overhead	3	1,620		2,025	
			3,528		4,315
Contribution			1,800		1,835
Fixed overheads	4		1,320		1,320
Net profit			480		515

(b) PINFOLD LIMITED
INCREASE IN INVESTMENT IN WORKING CAPITAL AS AT 30 JUNE 19X2

	Working	(i) £'000	(ii) £'000
Stocks			
Raw materials	5	159	191
Work in progress	6	453	550
Finished goods	7	294	360
		906	1,101
Cash		52	65
		958	1,166
Trade creditors	8	239	286
Forecast working capital at 30 June 19X2		719	880
Working capital at 30 June 19X1		675	675
Increase required		44	205

(c) *Comparison of alternative sales strategies*

(i) *Operating profit*

Both schemes would, if successful, result in a significant increase in net profit, with the volume growth strategy predicted to be the more profitable. However, because the sales price increase is much lower if volume growth is to be the target, failure to achieve even 20% sales growth would result in net profit lower than that projected if sales volume is unchanged but prices are raised by 11%. Similarly, the directors should consider whether it is realistic to expect that an 11% price increase will result in no loss of sales volume.

Another factor to consider is the availability of increased trade discount if less than 25% growth is achieved. This could also reduce contribution to a level substantially lower than the present forecast. Again it seems questionable that fixed overheads will not increase if production increases by 25%, unless there is currently significant underusage of facilities.

Sensitivity analysis, preferably using a spreadsheet package, would be essential to assess the effect of forecasting errors on the forecast outcome under each strategy. However, there would seem to be less margin for error under scheme (i) because the sales increase of 11% greatly exceeds the expected increases in costs of 6% and 8%.

SUGGESTED SOLUTIONS

(ii) *Funding of working capital increase*

In both cases, since the company appears to sell for cash and not on credit, only a short-term increase in finance is needed to finance extra materials costs.

Since profit is expected to accrue at £40,000 per month under scheme (i), once non-cash expenses such as depreciation are allowed for, the £44,000 increased investment in working capital could probably be financed entirely from profits.

Under scheme (ii), an increased overdraft facility is probably the most appropriate form of finance. If extra capacity (such as new equipment or factory space) is needed, (contrary to the current forecasts) then a medium-term loan or extra equity should be arranged.

(iii) *Conclusion*

A sales volume growth strategy appears to be riskier, as a much larger investment in working capital is required than under the alternative strategy, while the expected increases in operating profit are roughly similar. The extra finance costs of scheme (ii) could wipe out the operating profit advantage forecast, even if all the other forecasts are accurate (as discussed above).

It therefore seems advisable, on the basis of the current forecasts, to adhere to the current strategy. However, both strategies should be analysed further to establish the worst possible outcomes.

Workings

1 *Turnover*

(i) Nil sales volume growth and an 11% price increase: forecast sales for 19X1/2 = 111% × £4.8m = £5,328,000.

(ii) Sales volume growth of 25% and a 2.5% price increase: forecast sales for 19X1/2 = 102.5% × 125% × £4.8m = £6,150,000.

2 *Direct material costs*

(i) *No sales volume increase*
Budgeted costs = £1.8m × 106% = £1,908,000

(ii) *25% sales volume increase*
Budgeted costs = £1.8m × 125% × 106% × 96% = £2,289,600 (round to £2,290,000)

3 *Directed labour and variable overheads*

(i) *No sales volume increase*

Budgeted costs = £1.5m × 108% = £1,620,000

(ii) *25% sales volume increase*

Budgeted costs = £1.5m × 108% × 125% = £2,025,000

SUGGESTED SOLUTIONS

4 *Fixed overheads*

   Under both schemes, budgeted costs = £1,200,000 × 110% = £1,320,000.

5 *Stocks of raw materials*

   (i) $\frac{1}{12}$ × £1,908,000 (W2) = £159,000

   (ii) $\frac{1}{12}$ × £2,289,600 (W2) = £190,800 (round up to £191,000)

6 *Work in progress*

		£'000
(i)	Materials: $\frac{2}{12}$ × £1,908,000 (W2)	318
	Labour and overheads: $\frac{2}{12}$ × 50% * × £1,620,000 (W3)	135
		453

		£
(ii)	Materials: $\frac{2}{12}$ × £2,289,600 (W2)	381,600
	Labour and overheads: $\frac{2}{12}$ × 50%* × £2,025,000	168,750
		550,350

   (round to £550,000)

   * Labour and overheads are incurred at an even rate over two months and so the average element to be included in work in progress is half of two months.

7 *Stocks of finished goods*

   (i) $\frac{1}{12}$ × £3,528,000 (total variable costs) = £294,000

   (ii) $\frac{1}{12}$ × £4,315,000 (total variable costs) = £359,583 (round to £360,000)

8 *Trade creditors*

   Materials only; all other costs paid in the month incurred.

   (i) $\frac{1\frac{1}{2}}{12}$ × £1,908,000 (W2) = £238,500 (rounded to £239,000)

   (ii) $\frac{1\frac{1}{2}}{12}$ × £2,290,000 (W2) = £286,250 (rounded to £286,000)

SUGGESTED SOLUTIONS

36 ALBAN AND LAMB

> *Tutorial note.* If you were preparing partnership accounts for external use, you would not treat Alban's and Lamb's salaries as an expense but as an appropriation of profit. Here, the accounts are being used to assess the performance of the business and in making comparison with a similar company business, you would have to allow for that part of directors' remuneration which represents management costs rather than a return on share capital (paid as a tax efficient alternative to a dividend). Here, therefore, we treat partners' salaries as a business expense and the accounts are not therefore adjusted for this item before calculating ratios. Support for this approach comes from the observation that all salaries appear to have been taken as drawings.
>
> *Capital accounts*
>
> | | Alban £ | Lamb £ |
> |---|---:|---:|
> | Balance at 1 July 19X0 | 5,200 | 3,000 |
> | Revaluations surplus (shared equally: £85,000 - £20,000) | 32,500 | 32,500 |
> | Share of deficit | (1,250) | (1,250) |
> | Balance at 30 June 19X1 | 36,450 | 34,250 |
>
> There is no addition for undrawn salary nor do the partners have current account balances.

(a) **FILE NOTE**
FINANCIAL PROGRESS AND POSITION OF ALBAN LAMB & CO IN 19X1

Prepared by: A Banker
Date: 23 October 19X1

Introduction
This report looks at the financial progress and position of Alban Lamb & Co in the light of the partners' request for an increased overdraft facility from £7,500 to £15,000 for a six month period. Appendix 1 shows key accounting ratios for 19X0 and 19X1. Appendix 2 shows the firm's analysed revenue account for 19X1.

Financial developments
Partners' capital has increased substantially in the period because of the revaluation of the freehold premises. There has, however, been no fresh injection of capital. The effect of the revaluation is to reduce gearing and return on partners' capital very considerably, but the ratios shown in appendix 1 should not be taken at face value as the value of the freehold at 30 June 19X0 is not unknown. Had a current valuation been available, the ratios would have been more readily comparable.

The firm has made a small trading loss this year, in spite of a small increase in turnover, after making a reasonably good profit in 19X0. The reasons for this cannot be ascertained as no detailed revenue account for 19X0 has been provided. Profitability is considered further below.

Liquidity and gearing
As remarked above, gearing calculated on balance sheet figures appears to have improved markedly in 19X1 but this is entirely attributable to the revaluation of the freehold. Had the freehold been shown at a valuation in 19X0, gearing would probably have been low, as now (unless the increase in value is solely attributable to some new development, such as

SUGGESTED SOLUTIONS

a proposal to redevelop the area where the building is located). It has been assumed in calculating gearing (results in Appendix 1) that the bank overdraft will only be temporary.

The loan from the financial institution has not been reduced in the year and its terms of interest and repayment are unknown. However, it seems likely to be long-term and secured on the freehold. The business does not at the moment seem to be capable of generating sufficient cash to repay this loan from trading activity alone without significantly increasing commissions received and reducing overheads. There appears to be no other possible source of repayment (such as investments). Interest cover is now negative, although it was very good last year.

Liquidity is poor and has fallen markedly since last year. The year end figures may be distorted by the inclusion in trade creditors of £2,500 owed to a supplier of fixed assets but even eliminating this item the quick ratio would be less than 1:1. The proposed increase in the overdraft would have a very deleterious effect on liquidity if cash flows are not improved.

Profitability

Overall the business was profitable in 19X0 but made a loss in 19X1. It is apparent from the analysed revenue account in Appendix 2 that although all three areas of activity (commercial property sales, domestic property sales and property management) are profitable when only direct costs are considered, if general and financial costs were allocated to each activity, commercial property sales and property management would be loss-making activities. Insufficient information is available to establish on what basis these costs should be apportioned, but it seems likely from the proportion each represents of staff time and commissions received that about 30% of general and financial costs should be allocated to each one, with 40% going to domestic property sales. In this case, the latter activity would be earning a healthy profit margin of 21%, well above last year's margin for the business as a whole, which suggests that the disparity in profitability between activities is perhaps not a recent development. However, a full analysis of recent years' revenue accounts is needed to establish the trends in profitability of each activity.

The absence of detailed information for previous years makes it impossible to say why the business has made a loss this year. Possibilities include:

(i) setting commissions at too low a level (poor budgeting);
(ii) unusually large bad debts;
(iii) failure to respond to falling commission rates and/or volume by cutting overheads;
(iv) increases in partners' salaries which are not justified by trading performance;
(v) increases in finance costs (although this alone is insufficient to account for much of the fall in profits).

Conclusion

Although firm conclusions cannot be drawn in the absence of more detailed information, it would appear that this business is in trouble. It is operating at a loss and its liquidity is poor. It may well be that management information is of poor quality, causing difficulties in planning ahead and controlling costs. Detailed cash flow and profit forecasts should be prepared to establish the likely performance of each activity in the year ahead. The partners should consider:

(i) whether their commission rates can be increased without losing business;

(ii) what scope they have for reducing overheads, including their own salaries;

SUGGESTED SOLUTIONS

(iii) whether all three existing activities should be retained or whether they should concentrate on those most likely to be successful in the future.

APPENDIX 1: ACCOUNTING RATIOS

	19X1		19X0	
Net profit margin	$\frac{(2,500)}{128,500}$ = -1.9%		$\frac{20,600}{123,000}$ = 16.7%	
Interest cover	$\frac{(2,500)+3,200}{3,200}$ = -0.2 times		$\frac{20,600+2,500}{2,500}$ = 8.2 times	
Return on partners' capital	$\frac{(2,500)}{36,450+34,250}$ = -3.5%		$\frac{20,600}{5,200+3,000}$ = 251.2%	
Quick ratio = (debtors + bank): current liabilities	11,100 : (9,300 + 3,400 + 2,100) = 0.75:1		(6,000 + 24,200) : (5,900 + 1,200) = 1.4:1	
Gearing ratio = long-term debt: equity	20,000:(36,450 + 34,250) = 0.3:1		20,000:(5,200 + 3,000) = 2.4:1	

APPENDIX 2: ANALYSED REVENUE ACCOUNT FOR THE YEAR ENDED 30 JUNE 19X1

	£	£
Commercial properties		
Commissions received (28% of total commission)		36,000
Expenses		
Advertising	14,200	
Salaries		
Alban (50%)	12,000	
Other staff (⅓)	7,500	
		33,700
Profit		2,300
Domestic properties		
Commissions received (49% of total commissions)		63,000
Expenses		
Advertising	15,500	
Salaries		
Alban (50%)	12,000	
Other staff (⅓)	7,500	
		35,000
Profit		28,000

	£	£

Managed properties

Commissions received (23% of total commissions)		29,500
Expenses		
Rent collection costs	4,100	
Clearing	3,700	
Salaries		
Lamb	10,800	
Other staff (⅓)	7,500	
		26,100
Profit		3,400
Total operating profit		33,700
General expenses		
Administration costs		(33,000)
Finance costs		(3,200)
Net deficit		(2,500)

(b) (i) Ratio analysis can only produce meaningful results if data for all years given is comparable. If accounting policies have changed or, as in this example, there has been a revaluation, adjustments should be made so that apparent trends can be relied on.

(ii) Ratio analysis is meaningless unless sufficient information is available to establish trends. There is no absolute standard to which all businesses should conform. If a business has a quick ratio of 0.5:1, this should not be considered a bad sign unless it has previously always had a higher ratio and its performance is deteriorating in other ways now.

(iii) Ratio analysis is sometimes seen as an end in itself so that absolute figures and other significant features of the accounts are not considered in interpreting those accounts.

(iv) Frequently, ratios are calculated from out of date or atypical figures and so do not produce reliable results. So, for example, creditors in the example in the question were unusually high because of the fixed asset purchase.

(v) Ratios based on insufficiently detailed information can be misleading. For example, the absence of information on how partners' salaries are calculated in this example means that we cannot be certain that trading results are as poor as they appear. Similarly, the absence of revenue and expenditure breakdowns for 19X0 make it impossible to establish why the results for 19X1 are so much worse than 19X0.

SUGGESTED SOLUTIONS

37 TUTORIAL QUESTION: CASH FLOW STATEMENTS

(a) ARC LIMITED
CASH FLOW STATEMENT FOR THE YEAR ENDED 31 DECEMBER 19X1

	Notes	£'000	£'000
Net cash inflow from operating activities	1	2,390	
Returns on investments and servicing of finance			
Interest received		40	
Interest paid		(280)	
Dividends paid (W3)		(5,100)	
Net cash inflow from returns on investments and servicing of finance			(5,340)
Taxation			
Corporation tax paid (including advance corporation tax)		(3,200)	
Tax paid			(3,200)
Investing activities			
Payments to acquire tangible fixed assets (W4)		(11,800)	
Receipts from sales of tangible fixed assets		1,000	
Net cash outflow from investing activities			(10,800)
Net cash inflow before financing			(16,950)
Financing			
Repurchase of debenture loan	4	150	
Net cash inflow from financing			150
Increase in cash and cash equivalents	2,3		(16,800)

NOTES TO THE CASH FLOW STATEMENT

1 *Reconciliation of operating profit to net cash inflow from operating activities*

	£'000
Operating profit	20,640
Depreciation charges (W1)	5,050
Loss on sale of tangible fixed assets (W2)	700
(Increase)/decrease in stocks	(10,000)
(Increase)/decrease in debtors	(18,200)
Increase/(decrease) in creditors	4,200
Net cash inflow from operating activities	2,390

2 *Analysis of changes in cash and cash equivalents during the year*

	£'000
Balance at 1 January 19X1	600
Net cash inflow/outflow	(16,800)
Balance at 31 December 19X1	(16,200)

3 *Analysis of the balances of cash and cash equilvalents as shown in the balance sheet*

	19X0 £'000	19X1 £'000	Change in year £'000
Cash at bank and in hand	600	–	(600)
Bank overdrafts	–	(16,200)	(16,200)
	600	(16,200)	(16,800)

SUGGESTED SOLUTIONS

4 Analysis of changes in finance during the year

	Debenture loan £'000
Balance at 1 January 19X1	600
Cash inflow/(outflow) from financing	150
Balance at 31 December 19X1	750

Workings

1 Depreciation

	£'000	£'000
Depreciation at 31 December 19X9		10,750
Depreciation at 31 December 19X8	9,500	
Depreciation on assets sold	3,800	
		5,700
Charge for the year		5,050

2 Loss on sale of fixed assets

	£'000	£'000
Proceeds on sale		1,000
Net book value: cost	5,500	
depreciation	(3,800)	
		1,700
Loss on sale		700

3 Dividends paid

	£'000
Dividends payable at 31 December 19X8	3,000
Declared 19X9: preference	100
ordinary interim	2,000
ordinary final	6,000
	11,100
Less: payable at 31 December 19X9	6,000
∴ Paid in year	5,100

4 Purchase of fixed assets

	£'000	£'000
Balance at 31 December 19X9		23,900
Balance at 31 December 19X8	17,600	
Cost of assets sold	(5,500)	
		12,100
		11,800

(b) The main change introduced by FRS 1 compared to the requirements of SSAP 10 is fairly obvious.

'The FRS requires reporting activities to report cash flows rather than accrual based funds flows'.

The FRS exempts a large number of companies from preparing cash flow statements, namely all those which fall under the definition of a small- or medium-sized company. SSAP 10 required all companies with a turnover or gross income of over £25,000 to prepare a statement of source and application of funds (SSAF). Another onerous duty is thereby removed from smaller companies.

SUGGESTED SOLUTIONS

The FRS is much more prescriptive in terms of the way information is presented. One of the most important examples of this is the way the purchase price or sale consideration of a subsidiary must be shown in one line under 'investing activities'. In a SSAF a 'line-by-line' approach could be used to diffuse the information.

The cash flow statement and the required notes to the statement clearly show the user the relationship between profit and cash flows. This is important as it is a concept that non-accountants often find difficult to grasp. In (a) above note 1 shows the cost to the company of the expansion in trading during the year in terms of the increased burden of working capital and depreciation charges. (Compare the profit of £20.64m with the net cash inflow from operations of £2.39m.) The statement itself shows the costs of expansion in terms of taxation, dividend and interest costs.

The cash flow statement will not only help the shareholders, investors and other users of financial statements. The management of the company may also benefit. In this example, the company will obviously require new funding if its trading expansion is to continue. It should be easier to convince existing and potential investors of the need for finance by showing them the cash flow statement.

38 SCAPENS

Tutorial note. The most efficient way of starting this quesiton is to draw up the statement of funds and calculate the required ratios before launching into the report. This will ensure firstly, that you have a chance to think about the company's finances before you start writing the report, and secondly, that you earn the marks available for these requirements even if you run out of time to complete your report.

The examiner commented as follows on answers to this question: 'Candidates often spent time calculating numerous *additional* ratios, despite the fact that this enabled them to add very little to their analysis and, perhaps as a result, prevented them spending sufficient time - sometimes none at all - on the interpretation of those ratios. This naturally limited considerably the total number of marks that they could earn on the question.'

To: The Manager, Big Bank plc
From: J Smith
Date: 31 May 19X2

Subject: *Financial progress and position of Scapens plc*

(a) *Introduction*

Scapens plc is a public company trading in electrical goods. Its directors have approached Big Bank for finance to enable the company to purchase the freehold of a leasehold property (whose lease expires on 30 September 19X2) at a cost of £200,000. This report considers Scapens plc's current financial position and recent developments shown by its accounts for the years ended 31 March 19X1 and 19X2. The appendixes to this report contain a statement of source and application of funds for the year ended 31 March 19X2 and key ratios for 19X1 and 19X2.

SUGGESTED SOLUTIONS

(b) *Financial developments*

In 19X2 Scapens obtained a loan or issued debentures for £500,000. It used these proceeds in part to purchase additional freehold property and vehicles (£220,000) and the remainder seems to have financed a 42% increase in stocks. There has been an improvement in the cash position but this can only be short-term as most of the year-end balance will be needed to pay the final dividend, which is larger than earnings for the year and is therefore partly a distribution of the extraordinary profit.

(c) *Liquidity and gearing*

The current ratio shows that Scapens' liquidity is now much better than average for its sector but when stock is excluded the quick ratio shows that liquidity is poor (0.4:1). It may be that the high level of stock at the year end is unrepresentative of normal levels and this should be investigated. Certainly, stock turnover, based on year end figures, is poor. Stock now takes nearly three months to sell, whereas last year the turnover period was 63 days. The sector as a whole does much better than this. If stock is overvalued in the balance sheet, because of unrecorded obsolescence or similar problems then gross profit is overstated and the company's liquidity is much less impressive than it now appears.

The company's gearing has increased because of its new borrowings but is still low compared with UK companies generally, although the industry appears to have very low gearing. Existing interest cover is quite high at nearly four times.

It may be that the value of fixed assets is understated since there is no evidence that assets have been revalued. If a surplus arose on revaluation, then gearing would fall. It may be that Scapens' competitors' gearing is reduced by the effects of revaluation.

(d) *Asset turnover*

This ratio measures the effectiveness of a company's capital investment by showing how much turnover can be generated by a given level of fixed assets. Scapens is less efficient than others in its sector at 1.73, down from 1.84. It may be that its new fixed assets have not yet been in place long enough to improve performance. Scapens' large stock balances may also be distorting this ratio if they are unusually high. However, if, as suggested above, other companies in the sector have revalued their assets, then their performance is even better in comparison with Scapens' than it appears.

(e) *Profitability*

Turnover growth of 8% has been enhanced by the smaller percentage increases in cost of sales and distribution costs but exceeded by the 18% increase in administrative expenses. It would be useful to know why there has been such a large increase in the latter and whether these expenses can be curtailed in future. However, overall, trading profit has increased by 10%. It would be helpful to know the changes in the retail price index and industry specific price indexes for the period so that the effects of inflation could be discounted.

Interest costs have risen because of the new borrowings and have resulted in a 14% *reduction* in pre-tax profit from 19X1. As mentioned above, the increase in dividend is not warranted by an equivalent increase in earnings.

Because of the fall in earnings, return on equity has fallen to 4.9%. This compares very unfavourably with the trade association's statistics, although the discrepancy is less marked if pre-tax profit has been used in their calculations.

SUGGESTED SOLUTIONS

(f) Conclusion

Scapens plc is at present less profitable than its competitors' performance suggests it could be. It is more highly geared and its working capital management is less efficient. Since it is not making full use of its existing assets its chances of improving performance by increasing its fixed asset base must be doubtful, especially as it would have to find extra funds for legal costs and refurbishment etc, previously paid for by the freeholder, while also paying extra interest costs.

However, it can offer good security for the loan and its interest cover, assuming that it maintains its current level of trading profits, will still be adequate. Its gearing will continue to be fairly low. With the proviso that ways of improving working capital management should be discussed with the directors, and that a profit and cash flow forecast should be prepared to support the application, the company's financial position seems sufficiently sound to justify making the loan.

APPENDIX 1

SCAPENS PLC
STATEMENT OF SOURCE AND APPLICATION OF FUNDS
FOR THE YEAR ENDED 31 MARCH 19X2

	£'000	£'000
Profit on ordinary activities before tax		185
Extraordinary item		70
		255
Adjustments for items not involving the movement of funds		
Depreciation	118	
Loss on disposal of fixed assets (20-9)	11	
Increase in provisions for future warranty costs (52-50)	2	
		131
Total generated from operations		386
Funds from other sources		
Increase in debentures and loans	500	
Proceeds on disposal of vehicles	9	
		509
		895
Applications of funds		
Payment of tax	60	
Payment of dividends	120	
Purchase of fixed assets	220	
		400
		495
Increase/(decrease) in working capital		
Increase in stocks		289
Increase in debtors		4
Decrease in trade creditors		45
(Increase) in creditors (excluding tax): (76-55) - (77-60)		(4)
Movement in net liquid funds		
Increase in cash balance (98 - 12 + 75)		161
		495

SUGGESTED SOLUTIONS

APPENDIX 2

SCAPENS PLC
KEY RATIOS

			19X2	*19X1*
Working capital (current) ratio	= $\dfrac{\text{current assets}}{\text{current liabilities}}$	=	$\dfrac{1,151}{366}$ = 3.1:1	$\dfrac{772}{457}$ = 1.7:1
Ratio of long-term debt to equity		=	$\dfrac{600}{2,665} \times 100$	$\dfrac{100}{2,615} \times 100$
		=	22.5%	3.8%
Rate of stock turnover	= $\dfrac{\text{stock}}{\text{cost of sales}} \times 365$ days	=	$\dfrac{989}{4,311} \times 365$	$\dfrac{700}{4,070} \times 365$
		=	84 days	63 days
Total asset turnover	= $\dfrac{\text{turnover}}{\text{fixed assets + current assets}}$	=	$\dfrac{6,375}{2,532+1,151}$	$\dfrac{5,920}{2,450+772}$
		=	1.73 times	1.84 times
Rate of return on shareholders' equity	= $\dfrac{\text{earnings*}}{\text{equity}}$	=	$\dfrac{130}{2,665} \times 100$	$\dfrac{150}{2,615} \times 100$
		=	4.9%	5.7%

* Earnings = profit after tax and before extraordinary items.

39 NOTLEY

(a) CASH FORECAST FOR THE YEAR TO 30 JUNE 19X8

	Quarter ending			
	30.9.X7	*31.12.X7*	*31.3.X8*	*30.6.X8*
	£'000	£'000	£'000	£'000
Cash receipts				
From debtors (W1)	50	100	125	150
Loan	-	50	-	-
	50	150	125	150
Cash payments				
To suppliers (W2)	70	60	80	90
Direct labour (W3)	10	10	15	15
Variable expenses (W4)	8	12	16	18
Fixed expenses	6	6	6	6
Directors' remuneration	12	12	12	12
Fixed assets	54	-	-	-
	160	100	129	141
Surplus/(deficit)	(110)	50	(4)	9
Opening balance	60	(50)	-	(4)
Closing balance	(50)	-	(4)	5

SUGGESTED SOLUTIONS

(b) The forecast trading profit for 19X7/X8 is as follows.

	£'000
Per question	9.0
Less loan interest (12% × £50,000 × $\frac{9}{12}$)	4.5
	4.5

The easiest way of reconciling this to the cash movement over the year is to prepare a simplified funds statement.

FUNDS STATEMENT FOR THE YEAR ENDING 30 JUNE 19X8

	£'000	£'000
Profit for the year		4.5
Add back depreciation		9.0
Funds generated from operations		13.5
Funds from other sources		
Loan		50.0
		63.5
Application of funds		
Purchase of fixed assets		54.0
		9.5
Movements in working capital (other than cash)		
Increase in stocks	30	
Increase in debtors (W1)	75	
Increase in creditors (30(W2) + 6(W4) + 4.5)	(40.5)	
		64.5
		55.0
Decrease in cash (60 − 5)		55.0

(c) *Tutorial note.* The assessment in this part of the question is to be made from the viewpoint of the directors. The information in note (iii) gives an indication of the comparison that needs to be made: what the directors can earn from their investment, compared with the market rate elsewhere of the services they can offer.

To begin with, it is necessary to estimate the profit for 19X8/X9.

ESTIMATED PROFIT STATEMENT
FOR THE YEAR ENDING 30 JUNE 19X9

	%	£'000	£'000
Sales (12 × £50,000)	100		600
Cost of sales (60%)	(60)	360	
Direct labour costs	(10)	60	
Variable expenses	(12)	72	
Total variable costs	82		492
Contribution	18		108
Fixed expenses		24	
Directors' remuneration		48	
Depreciation		9	
Loan interest (12% × £50,000)		6	
			87
			21

SUGGESTED SOLUTIONS

The return earned by each director on his investment in the business can now be computed. It consists of a salary and a dividend.

	19X7/X8 £'000	19X8/X9 £'000
Salary	24.00	24.0
Dividend	2.25	10.5
	26.25	34.5
Less market value of services (£1,600 × 12)	19.20	19.2
Surplus	7.05	15.3

In 19X7/X8 the company's performance is not unreasonable. Profits of £52,500 (before allowing for directors' remuneration) are generated from sales of £500,000, a return of 10.5%. In the second year of trading this improves to 11.5% as sales of £600,000 generate profits before directors' remuneration of £69,000. Subject to the inevitable uncertainties that surround financial forecasts, the prospects appear good.

However, the directors must consider whether the return earned by the investment of both their effort and their capital is better than could be achieved elsewhere. We are told that the opportunity cost of their effort is £19,200 each per annum. Anything earned in excess of that (the 'surplus' calculated above) represents the return on their capital. In the first year of trading this amounts to £7,050 on an investment of £30,000; while in 19X8/X9 the return goes up to a very substantial 51% (£15,300 on an investment of £30,000).

The main concern is the high level of variable costs, which amount to 82% of turnover. This means that additional sales contribute only marginally to net profit, while any significant shortfall below the sales target would make it difficult to cover fixed costs.

In addition, the directors must consider whether price inflation would increase costs more quickly than their sales prices. This would leave them very vulnerable.

Workings

1   *Cash receipts from debtors*

Debtors pay on average 1½ months after the date of sale. The pattern of cash receipts is therefore as follows:

Date sales made	Sales value £'000	Date of payment
1.7.X7 - 15.8.X7	50	Quarter 1
16.8.X7 - 30.9.X7	50	Quarter 2
1.10.X7 - 15.11.X7	50	Quarter 2
	100	
16.11.X7 - 31.12.X7	50	Quarter 3
1.1.X8 - 15.2.X8	75	Quarter 3
	125	
16.2.X8 - 31.3.X8	75	Quarter 4
1.4.X8 - 15.5.X8	75	Quarter 4
	150	
16.5.X8 - 30.6.X8	75	Debtor at 30.6.X8

SUGGESTED SOLUTIONS

2 Cash payments to suppliers

Creditors are paid on average one month after the date of purchase. The pattern of cash payments is therefore as follows:

	Purchases £'000	Date of payment
For opening stock	30	Quarter 1
For purchases * in July/Aug 19X7	40	Quarter 1
	70	
For purchases in September 19X7	20	Quarter 2
For purchases in Oct/Nov 19X7	40	Quarter 2
	60	
For purchases in Dec 19X7	20	Quarter 3
For purchases in Jan/Feb 19X8	60	Quarter 3
	80	
For purchases in March/April/May 19X8	90	Quarter 4
For purchases in June 19X8	30	Creditor at 30.6.X8

* Since stocks are maintained at a constant level, purchases are equal to cost of sales, ie to 60% of sales. Purchases per month up to 31 December 19X7 are therefore £200,000 ÷ 6 × 60% = £20,000.

3 Direct labour

Direct labour costs vary with sales turnover. The pattern of turnover across the four quarters of the year to 30 June 19X6 is £100,000:£100,000:£150,000:£150,000, a ratio of 2:2:3:3.

Dividing the £50,000 of labour costs in the same ratio we have £10,000:£10,000:£15,000:£15,000.

4 Variable expenses

As with direct labour, variable expenses will be incurred according to the pattern 2:2:3:3, at the rate of £12,000:£12,000:£18,000:£18,000. However, there is a one month delay in paying such expenses, leading to the following payment pattern:

Expenses paid Expenses incurred	Qtr 1 £'000	Qtr 2 £'000	Qtr 3 £'000	Qtr 4 £'000
£12,000 (2/3; 1/3)	8	4		
£12,000 (2/3; 1/3)		8	4	
£18,000 (2/3; 1/3)			12	6
£18,000 (2/3; 1/3)				12
	8	12	16	18

There will be a creditor of £6,000 remaining at 30 June 19X8.

SUGGESTED SOLUTIONS

40 WHALEY

> *Tutorial note.* This question was well answered in the numerical areas and variances in the calculations were accepted, where they were valid. The analysis of the figures was weak, however. Remember that you cannot gain *all* your marks from calculations, as you will make errors with numbers. You should produce a positive statement about the provision of the finance.

(a) MOVEMENT ON RESERVES FOR THE YEAR ENDED 31 MARCH 19X2

	£'000	£'000
Balance on reserves as at 31 March 19X1		4,570
Retained profit for the year ended 31 March 19X2		1,497
		6,067
Revaluation reserve movements		
Surplus on revaluation	4,170	
Depreciation write back	8,200	
		12,370
		18,437
Bonus issue 1:1		(10,000)
Balance on reserves as at 31 March 19X2		8,437

(b) WHALEY PLC
STATEMENT OF SOURCE AND APPLICATION OF FUNDS
FOR THE YEAR ENDED 31 MARCH 19X2

	£'000	£'000
Profit before taxation		3,620
Adjustment for items not involving the movement of funds		
Depreciation		1,320
		4,940
Funds from other sources		
Sale of investments		1,400
		6,340
Application of funds		
Purchase of fixed assets	4,310	
Dividends paid (800 + 500)	1,300	
Taxation paid (W)	1,200	
		(6,810)
		(470)
Increase/(decrease) in working capital		
Increase in current assets		420
Increase in creditors		(890)
		(470)

Working

	£'000
Tax creditor b/f	1,200
Charge for year	1,243
Extraordinary item	180
	2,623
Tax creditor b/f	(1,423)
Tax paid in year	1,200

SUGGESTED SOLUTIONS

(c) *Ratios*

		Year ended 31 March 19X2	Year ended 31 March 19X1
(i)	Gearing	$\dfrac{10,000}{28,437}$ = 35.2%	$\dfrac{10,000}{14,570}$ = 68.6%
(ii)	Net profit percentage	$\dfrac{3,620}{46,150}$ = 7.8%	$\dfrac{3,150}{44,090}$ = 7.1%
(iii)	Gross profit margin	$\dfrac{8,840}{46,150}$ = 19.2%	$\dfrac{7,880}{44,090}$ = 17.9%
(iv)	Total asset turnover	$\dfrac{46,150}{36,460 + 6,700}$ = 1.07	$\dfrac{44,090}{21,900 + 6,280}$ = 1.56
(v)	Return (pre-tax) on shareholders' equity	$\dfrac{3,620}{28,437}$ = 12.7%	$\dfrac{3,150}{14,570}$ = 21.6%
(vi)	Working capital ratio	$\dfrac{6,700}{4,723}$ = 1.42:1	$\dfrac{6,280}{3,610}$ = 1.74:1

(d) The main points (from the bank's point of view) which arise form the examination of the accounts of Whaley plc are as follows.

(i) The value of the freehold land and the buildings has risen considerably, the net book value having been increased on valuations by over 70%. This provides an adequate value for security for any loan. Even if the long-term creditors already hold security over these assets, there is still excess equity value in the assets after deduction of the £10m long term creditors.

(ii) The directors of Whaley plc have taken the opportunity of greatly increased reserves to make a bonus issue. This is because the nominal value of the bonus shares is permitted to be written off the revaluation reserve under the Companies Act 1985 rules. In view of the need for further finance, it would perhaps have been wiser to make a rights issue, although perhaps at a substantial discount (say 50p), to raise the £5m required. This would have avoided the need to approach the bank and the associated interest costs and arrangement fees.

(iii) The company has sold some investments during the year, but not all of them. The value of the remaining investments should be established, and it should be determined whether they should be sold to help with the medium term funding. The proceeds of the sale of investments during 19X2 has obviously aided the purchase of assets.

(iv) The shortfall shown in the statement of source and application of funds would seem to indicate the need for additional funding. This assumes that any future reduction in the level of dividend would be considered imprudent or impolitic (a reduction in future dividends would produce extra internal funding).

(v) The company has made fairly significant investments in new fixed assets this year. Further purchases may be under consideration which would require further funding.

(vi) The company has reduced its gearing ratio quite substantially during the year, but only in a cosmetic way. There has been no actual reduction in borrowings and the shareholders' funds were only increased through the revaluation of the freehold land and buildings. The date of redemption of the current £10m long term debt should be examined, to determined whether it would interfere with the repayment of a medium term loan of £5m.

(vii) There has been a small improvement in both net and gross profit margins on only a small rise in turnover (less than 5%). This indicates that costs are being kept under control, but the lack of growth in sales is slightly worrying. The banks needs to look at the company's growth projections for the future. (Net profit has not increased as much as gross profit due to a rise in administrative expenses, and this should be investigated).

(viii) The asset revaluation has affected asset turnover and return on shareholder's equity. The decline in these figures should be examined in the light of the effect of the revaluation on both assets (total increase £14.98m) and the reserves and share capital (total increase £13.867m). Had no revaluation or bonus issue taken place in 19X2, then the figures for asset turnover and return on shareholders' equity would have been much more stable and might even have increased.

(ix) The working capital ratio has improved since 19X1, although the rise in creditors has been substantial (47%).

Overall, some figures need to be investigated further, but the company seems to be in a stable position with sufficient security. The £5m should therefore be advanced.

41 TUTORIAL QUESTION: GEORGE

(a) Breakeven occurs where contribution equals fixed costs.

In 19X0, fixed costs are:

		£
Production	20,000 × £5	100,000
Selling	20,000 × £1	20,000
		120,000

Contribution per unit is £15.

Breakeven point is $\frac{£120,000}{£15}$ = 8,000 units

SUGGESTED SOLUTIONS

(b)
	£
Fixed costs per (a)	120,000
Additional premises	210,000
Total fixed costs	330,000

$$\frac{£330,000}{£15} = 22,000 \text{ units}$$

George will be manufacturing and selling 40,000 units. The additional rent is a fixed cost. Fixed costs can change in the *long run*.

42 NEWELL

Tutorial note. There are a number of tricky little points to remember in tackling this question.

(a) *Re-allocated costs* are fixed costs of head office only and are presumably unaffected by the closure of the Oxford factory as we are not told to the contrary. They will therefore still have to be covered by the profits made on operations at Glasgow and Wokingham and so are irrelevant to the calculations of revised profit.

(b) Capacity available at Wokingham is insufficient to take on all of Oxford's production. However, Wokingham must be assumed to increase production to its maximum before Newell takes on agency sales to supply former Oxford customers.

(c) Although Oxford's *contribution per widget* is lower than that achieved at Wokingham and Glasgow, once transport costs are deducted from Wokingham's contribution per widget, sales to Oxford customers are *less* profitable form Wokingham (before taking fixed costs into account).

(a) NEWELL LIMITED

Financial effects of Oxford factory closure

Prepared by: A Chap, Financial Controller   July 19X0
Circulation: A Bloggs, Managing Director
               G Bloke, Financial Director

The Oxford factory's operations are currently insufficiently profitable. Four possible alternatives have been identified, which would enable the company to close the Oxford factory. These are as follows.

(i)   Close the factory but make no attempt to increase production elsewhere or to find an alternative source of supply.

(ii) Close the factory and increase production at Wokingham to maximum capacity.

(iii) Close the factory and become UK agents for Leyton SA, which would enable us to supply all former Oxford customers but earning commission rather than selling in our own name.

SUGGESTED SOLUTIONS

(iv) Close the factory, supply as many former Oxford customers as possible from increased production at Wokingham and supply the remainder with Leyton widgets, thus earning commission on these sales.

Each of these options will now be considered in turn. Detailed calculations are shown in the attached appendix.

Option (i)

The loss of contribution on Oxford sales would outweigh the savings in fixed costs. An overall reduction in forecast profit of £45,000 would result.

Option (ii)

This option would result in a £30,000 increase in forecast profit because the saving on fixed costs at Oxford exceeds the extra fixed costs at Wokingham and lost/reduced contribution on Oxford sales.

Option (iii)

Adoption of this policy would increase forecast profit by £51,000 because the loss of contribution on Oxford sales is outweighed by fixed cost savings and commission earned from Leyton.

Option (iv)

This option produces the greatest increase in forecast profit (£90,000) because as well as the overall increase in profit on our own production we would earn £60,000 commission on sales of Leyton widgets.

APPENDIX

	(i) £'000	(ii) £'000	(iii) £'000	(iv) £'000
Net profit as previously forecast	720	720	720	720
Add saving on fixed costs of Oxford factory	515	515	515	515
Less extra fixed costs of Wokingham factory	-	(105)	-	(105)
Less lost contribution on Oxford widgets (W1)				
32,000	(560)	-	(560)	-
20,000	-	(350)	-	(350)
Less reduction in contribution on production at Wokingham for Oxford customers	-	(30)	-	(30)
Add commission earned from sales of Leyton widgets (W3)	-	-	96	60
Net profit as forecast under policy options	675	750	771	810

(b) On purely financial grounds, option (iv) is the most profitable and has the advantage of ensuring that all Oxford customers are supplied, albeit with Leyton widgets where necessary. Since, however, Leyton's name will be on the widgets, Newell would be taking a risk in introducing its customers to Leyton. In the long term, Leyton might set up a UK

SUGGESTED SOLUTIONS

subsidiary or branch to compete directly with Newell, thus removing the need to pay commission to Newell and also threatening Newell's customer base. It might be best, therefore, taking a long-term view, to go for option (ii) in 19X1 and to expand capacity at Wokingham and Glasgow as quickly as possible so that production can return to previous levels.

An option well worth investigation before any of those considered above would be to find out whether Oxford's contribution could be increased to at least that achieved at the Glasgow and Wokingham factories and whether any of its fixed costs could be cut.

Workings

1 *Contributions per widget at Oxford factory*

	£
Sales price	50.00
Variable costs (1,040 ÷ 32)	32.50
Contribution	17.50

If Oxford's production is not made up by Wokingham as far as possible, then 32,000 units contribution is lost (£560,000).

If Oxford's production is partly taken over by Wokingham, then contribution is lost on 20,000 units (£350,000). Wokingham only has spare capacity for 12,000 widgets (60,000 - 48,000).

2 *Contribution per widget at Wokingham factory*

	£
Sales price	50.00
Variable costs (1,440 ÷ 48)	30.00
Contribution on sales to Wokingham customers	20.00
Transport costs	5.00
Contribution on sales to Oxford customers	15.00

The loss in contribution from transferring part of Oxford production to Wokingham is therefore 12,000 × (£17.50 - £15.00) = £30,000.

3 *Commission from Leyton SA*

On 20,000 widgets (Wokingham produces an extra 12,000 widgets) = £60,000.

On 32,000 widgets (Wokingham produces no extra widgets) = 96,000.

43 HELMORE

(a) (i) *Budgeted profit*

	£
Sales (50,000 × £20)	1,000,000
Variable costs (50,000 × £12)	600,000
Contribution (£8 per unit)	400,000
Fixed costs	300,000
	100,000

SUGGESTED SOLUTIONS

(ii) *Break-even point*

$$\frac{\text{Fixed costs}}{\text{Contribution per unit}} = \frac{£300,000}{£8} = 37,500 \text{ units}$$

(iii) *Margin of safety*

	Units	%
Budgeted sales volume	50,000	100
Break-even volume of sales	37,500	75
Margin of safety	12,500	25

(*Tutorial note.* This shows how far sales could fall before the company will make a loss.)

(b) *Expected results for 19X1*

Range of activity units	Contribution £'000	Fixed costs £'000	Budgeted profit/(loss) £'000
0	-	300	(300)
10,000	80	300	(220)
20,000	160	300	(140)
30,000	240	300	(60)
40,000	320	300	20
50,000	400	300	100
60,000	450	450	-
70,000	500	450	50
80,000	550	450	100

Contribution on south-west sales is £8 (as calculated above). 10,000 units therefore produce £80,000 contribution. Contribution on north of England sales is £5 (£18 - £13). 10,000 units therefore produce £50,000 contribution. If production is 50,000 units then breakeven point is 37,500 units but at 80,000 units breakeven point is 60,000 units.

Tutorial note. Whereas most students got full marks on part (a), answers to part (b) were not so strong. Many prepared breakeven or profit/volume charts rather than the table required.

(c) The margin of safety on Helmore Ltd's budgeted results for its existing operations is adequate and its budgeted results have been calculated with the benefit of experience from earlier years' sales. However, in forecasting sales in the new market, the company's estimates vary between 5,000 (which is below the breakeven point) and 40,000. Assuming production for the new market of 30,000, the margin of safety is 66⅔%, which seems high. However, budgeted profit shows no increase over production of 50,000 units. Given the risk that fixed costs may increase by more than the estimated increase and the uncertainty of sales demand, there must be a considerable risk that extra production may result in a reduced overall profit in 19X1.

Taking a longer view, however, Helmore may foresee a decline in demand in the south-west or pressure on contribution from increased competition there. It may also be possible to improve contribution on the northern sales by price increases or cost cutting and/or to increase demand once market share is established. If demand is poor in the north, then the increased production capacity could be used to increase sales in the south-west or to expand into another new market.

SUGGESTED SOLUTIONS

Currently Helmore's profit margins are fairly low (although without further information on its activities no meaningful assessment can be made). Its net profit margin on 19X1 budgeted figures without expansion is 10%. If it undertook the expansion, its net profit margin would fall (£100,000 ÷ total sales of £1,540,000: 6.5%).

Without further more reliable market research it would seem inadvisable to make the expansion, especially if the costs of increasing capacity must be funded by borrowing. However, if further research indicates that longer term prospects in the new market are good, then the expansion may be worthwhile.

44 HENLEY

> Tutorial note. This is the only time limiting factor analysis has been examined in recent years. If you know the topic, this is a very straightforward question.

(a) HENLEY LIMITED
FORECAST OPERATING STATEMENT FOR 19X2

	Product A £	Product B £
Forecast sales price per unit	45.00	40.00
Cost per unit		
Direct materials	11.00	14.00
Direct labour	15.00	10.00
Variable overheads	4.00	3.00
Sales commission (5% of sales price)	2.25	2.00
	32.25	29.00
Forecast contribution per unit	12.75	11.00
Forecast sales volume	12,000	10,000
Forecast total contribution	£153,000	£110,000

	£
Forecast total contribution	
Product A	153,000
Product B	110,000
	263,000
Forecast fixed costs	150,000
Forecast net profit	113,000

(b) One of the more common decision-making problems is a budgeting decision in a situation where there are not enough resources to meet the potential sales demand, (that is, there is a limiting factor) and so a decision has to be made about using what resources there are as effectively as possible.

Examples of limiting factors are:

(i) *sales:* there is a limit to sales demand;

(ii) *labour* (either of total quantity or of particular skills): there is insufficient labour to produce enough to satisfy sales demand;

(iii) *manufacturing capacity:* (usually) there is not sufficient machine capacity to produce enough;

(iv) *financial resources:* (usually) there is not enough cash to pay for enough production.

(c) To produce 12,000 units of product A, 36,000 hours of labour would be needed (£15 per unit at £5 per hour).

To produce 10,000 units of product B, 20,000 hours of labour would be needed (£10 per unit at £5 per hour).

Therefore, production could not proceed as planned, since only 26,000 hours of labour are available. Limiting factor analysis suggests that production should be planned so as to maximise contribution per unit of scarce resource.

	Product A	Product B
Contribution per unit	£12.75	£11.00
Labour hours per unit	3	2
	= £4.25	£5.50

∴ Profit will be maximised if as much product B as possible is produced, and the balance of labour hours available is used to make product A.

	Available hours	Production volume	Forecast total contribution £
Product B	20,000	10,000	110,000
Product A	6,000	2,000	25,500
	26,000		135,500

45 CARBURTON

Tutorial note. You must split the fixed and variable elements of the production overhead to answer this question. Remember, do *not* include sunk costs. Make sure you read the requirements thoroughly - it is easy to miss the point in this question.

(a) (i) *Contribution per unit of XL*

	£	£
Sale price		70
Costs		
Direct materials (£480,000/16,000)	30	
Direct labour (£80,000/16,000)	5	
Variable production overhead (£160,000(W)/16,000)	10	
		45
Contribution per unit		25

Working

The rise in production overheads of £40,000 to £300,000 represents a 20% increase in variable production overheads, therefore variable production overheads at 80% capacity are:

SUGGESTED SOLUTIONS

$$£40,000 \times \frac{80}{20} = £160,000$$

Note. Variable overheads at 100% capacity = £160,000 × $\frac{100}{80}$ = £200,000.

(ii) OPERATING STATEMENT: 60% CAPACITY

	Units	£'000	£'000
Sales (16,000 × $\frac{60}{80}$)	12,000		840
Costs			
Direct materials (£600,000 × 60%)		360	
Direct labour (£100,000 × 60%)		60	
Variable production overhead (£200,000 × 60%)		120	
			540
Contribution			300
Fixed production overhead		100	
Administration costs		220	
			320
Loss			(20)

OPERATING STATEMENT: 80% CAPACITY

	Units	£'000	£'000
Sales	16,000		1,120
Costs			
Direct materials		480	
Direct labour		80	
Variable production overhead		160	
			720
Contribution			400
Fixed production overhead		100	
Administration costs		220	
			320
Profit			80

(iii) *Breakeven point*

$$\text{Breakeven point} = \frac{\text{Fixed costs}}{\text{Contribution per unit}}$$

$$= \frac{£320,000}{£25} = 12,800 \text{ units}$$

(iv) *Relevant costs and revenues*

	Scheme		
	1	2	3
	£	£	£
Proceeds	40,000	56,000	54,000
Costs			
Materials		(7,000)	(6,000)
Labour		(4,000)	(1,500)
Advertising			(1,000)
	40,000	45,000	45,500

(b) *Advice to Carburton's management*

(i) *XL production*

The forecast for sales (and therefore production) is that the number of units of XL sold will fall to 12,000 during next year. This will place the company in a position whereby fixed costs are not being covered by total contribution (the difference between total sales and total variable costs).

In order to cover fixed costs as they stand at present, it will be necessary to produce and sell at least 12,800 units. This is the 'breakeven point', producing neither a gain nor a loss.

Alternatively, the company could aim to reduce fixed costs. This might be difficult with production costs as the factory is of a fixed size. It might be possible to rent out some of the factory space to offset fixed production costs. Administration costs might be reduced by cutting staff and imposing other economies.

Cutting fixed costs is a longer term solution, but in the short run the company should continue production even if annual sales fall to well below 12,000 units, as a contribution will still be made to fixed costs.

(ii) *SM machine*

In making the decision about which course of action to take with regard to the SM machine, the cost of production to date of £42,000 should be ignored. This is because it is a sunk cost: it has been incurred and no decision made now can change that cost.

The revenues and costs which have been taken into consideration are those which might be incurred in the future, depending on which scheme is chosen.

Scheme 3 produces the highest incremental revenue of £45,500 and this will in fact produce a profit of £45,500 - £42,000 = £3,500. However, the concept of risk has not been considered, particularly in the case of Scheme 3, where further costs are to be incurred with no definite buyer or guaranteed price. Scheme 1 has the advantage of immediate sale and receipt of cash.

If Scheme 2 can be undertaken with a guaranteed sale, then it may be the most prudent course of action.

46 FELL

Tutorial note. Many candidates failed to take account of interest payable in each scheme; some produced monthly cash flow statements (totally unnecessary); and further matters to take into account, apart from the calculations in (a), were not discussed in (b). *Think* before you start to answer the question.

SUGGESTED SOLUTIONS

(a) *Scheme 1*

	£	£
Computer rental		
£800 × 6		4,800
Interest on rental		
1.5% × £800	12	
1.5% × £1,600	24	
1.5% × £2,400	36	
1.5% × £3,200	48	
1.5% × £4,000	60	
1.5% × £4,800	72	
		252
		5,052

Scheme 2

	£
Interest (20% × £30,000 × 6/12)	3,000
Arrangement fee	1,000
Interest an arrangement fee (£1,000 × 1.5% × 6)	90
	4,090

Scheme 3

	£
Discount cost (£160,000 × 25% × 2.5% × 6)	6,000
Less reduction in interest (W)	(585)
	5,415

Working

	£			£
Cash received	40,000			
Less cost of computer	30,000			
	10,000			
Less July discount (£160,000 × 25% × 2.5%)	1,000	× 1.5%	=	135
	9,000			
Less August discount	1,000	× 1.5%	=	120
	8,000			
Less September discount	1,000	× 1.5%	=	105
	7,000			
Less October discount	1,000	× 1.5%	=	90
	6,000			
Less November discount	1,000	× 1.5%	=	75
	5,000			
Less December discount	1,000	× 1.5%	=	60
	4,000			585

SUGGESTED SOLUTIONS

(b) *Evaluation of the schemes*

The following points are relevant.

(i) In terms of cost, Scheme 2 appears to be the best option.

(ii) It may be difficult to meet monthly rental payments under Scheme 1 as the company runs so close to its overdraft limit all the time.

(iii) It is likely that the customers who took advantage of the cash discounts in Scheme 3 would expect it to continue after the six month period in question. This would be costly, but a great deal of goodwill may be lost by halting the discounts.

(iv) The computer system hired in Scheme 1, even if it was identical to the system eventually purchased, would need to be programmed, loaded with all the relevant information and tested. This process (which involves quite a lot of work) would have to be repeated when the new computer arrived.

(v) If the timing of the purchase was delayed, the interim finance would have to be extended. This might not be possible or it might be too expensive. In addition, the computer might not then be available at the same price, or it might not be available at all.

(vi) Is security available for a loan? It may be that the land which is being sold could be used as security.

47 LANDORE

> *Tutorial note.* The examiner commented as follows on the answers to this question. '[The accounting rate of return] is a well known measure, specifically identified in the syllabus, which expresses the average forecast annual profit as a percentage of the average investment. It is clear that the vast majority of candidates were totally unfamiliar with this method and instead calculated payback or the internal rate of return. These are both perfectly valid methods of appraisal in certain circumstances, *but were not asked for in this case*. Turning to requirement (b), candidates were asked to discuss the relative merits of the two methods of *capital project appraisal*. Many candidates instead focused entirely on an examination of the relative merits of the two projects.' The moral is clear: cover the *whole* syllabus and read the question carefully!

(a) (i) *Accounting rate of return*

Net *cash* inflows on the project exclude depreciation of fixed assets and include the return of working capital at the end of projects.

Year	Project 1	£'000	Project 2	£'000
1	80 - 48	32	60 - 48	12
2	80 - 48	32	200 - 48	152
3	90 - 48	42	90 - 48	42
4	100 - 48	52	10 - 48	(38)
5	50 - 48 - 10	(8)	15 - 48 - 10	(43)
	Total profit	150	Total profit	125

SUGGESTED SOLUTIONS

Average profit = 150 ÷ 5 = £3,000   Average profit = 125 ÷ 5 = £25,000

Note. This calculation has been set out in full for tutorial purposes but in this case could have been bypassed simply by deducting the initial investment from the total net inflows. Check this for yourself.

Average investment for both projects

	£'000
Plant: 240,000 ÷ 2	120
Working capital (constant)	10
	130

	Project 1	Project 2
ARR	$\frac{30}{130} \times 100 = 23.1\%$	$\frac{25}{130} \times 100 = 19.2\%$

(ii) *Net present value*

Year	Discount factor	Flow £'000	Present value £'000	Flow £'000	Present value £'000
0	1.000	(250)	(250)	(250)	(250)
1	0.870	80	70	60	52
2	0.756	80	60	200	151
3	0.658	90	59	90	59
4	0.572	100	57	10	6
5	0.497	50	25	15	7
			21		25

Tutorial note. These are the common errors noted by the examiner.

NPV: omission of working capital from initial investment.

ARR: (1) failure to deduct initial investment from net cash inflows to arrive at profit;

(2) failure to average profit;

(3) failure to realise that the plant has no value at the end of the project and so the value of the investment falls over the period, reducing the average investment;

(4) omission of working capital from investment.

(b) *Accounting rate of return*

This method gives a measure of relative project profitability by comparing the average accounting profit per annum to come from the project with the average capital employed in it. Its advantages are that it is relatively easy to understand, it does measure profitability of returns compared with outlay, and it gives an indication as to whether the firm's target return on capital employed is exceeded.

Its main weaknesses are as follows.

(i) It pays no attention to the timing of project returns. Cash received at an early stage is more valuable than the same cash received in a few years time because it can be reinvested to earn interest.

(ii) It is a relative rate of return, rather than an absolute measure of gain in wealth. All rate of return methods ignore the size of the project.

(iii) Because it is a percentage measure, there is a tendency to compare the ARR with interest rates and investment yields, which is invalid.

Discounted cash flow methods

Both of the traditional methods (ARR and payback) are surpassed by discounted cash flow methods. The basic arguments are:

(i) it is better to consider cash rather than profits because cash is how investors will eventually see their rewards (dividends, sale of shares, interest);

(ii) the timing of the cash flows is important because early cash can be reinvested to earn interest.

The technique of discounting reduces all future cash flows to equivalent values now (present values) by allowing for the interest which could have been earned if the cash had been received immediately.

There are two possible techniques, net present value and internal rate of return.

Net present value is simply the cost of the present value of the project cash flows, discounted at the company's 'cost of capital' (the average required return for the company's operations).

48 BUCKNALL

> *Tutorial note.* This is a very straightforward question if you have revised this topic thoroughly. There are no complications such as tax or inflation.

(a)

Year	Discount factor @ 15%	Project Y Cash flow £	Present value £	Project Z Cash flow £	Present value £
0	1	(10,000)	(10,000)	(16,000)	(16,000)
1 - 3	2.284	4,897	11,185	7,596	17,349
			NPV 1,185		NPV 1,349

(b)

Year	Discount factor @ 22%	Project Y Cash flow £	Present value £	Project Z Cash flow £	Present value £
0	1	(10,000)	(10,000)	(16,000)	(16,000)
1 - 3	2.042	4,897	10,000	7,596	15,511
			NPV -		NPV (489)

SUGGESTED SOLUTIONS

The IRR of project Y is 22%
The IRR of project Z can be found as follows:

$$15\% + \left[\frac{1,349}{1,349 + 489} \times (22 - 15)\% \right] = 20.1\%$$

(c) Project Y has a higher internal rate of return than project Z, but project Y has a slightly lower NPV than project Z. This reflects the fact that project Y requires a smaller original investment and generates a higher return on that investment than project Z, which nevertheless produces a larger absolute return. A larger absolute return should always be preferred and so project Z should be undertaken, if capital is not scarce.

49 KAPLAN

> *Tutorial note.* An appropriation account shows where the profit or loss for the year goes. It includes the charge or credit for corporation and deferred tax for the year, any amount proposed or already paid as dividend and transfers to reserves other than the profit and loss account (also known as retained profits). To reconstruct it you must compare the two balance sheets given and identify which changes would be reflected in the appropriation account. Here no dividends payable at the year end are shown in the balance sheet and no information is given to suggest that a dividend was paid during the year. However, there is a creditor for corporation tax, which from the wording of the balance sheet caption must be equivalent to the charge in the profit and loss account. The only source of the increase in the plant replacement reserve is a transfer from the profit and loss account. The reconstruction of the appropriation account is simply an arithmetical exercise once its components have been identified.

(a) KAPLAN LIMITED
PROFIT AND LOSS APPROPRIATION ACCOUNT
FOR THE YEAR ENDED 31 DECEMBER 19X9

	£'000
Profit before tax	140
Tax	35
Profit after tax	105
Transfer to plant replacement reserve (200 - 150)	50
Retained profit for the year	55
Retained profit brought forward	86
Retained profit carried forward	141

SUGGESTED SOLUTIONS

(b) **CONSERVATORY SALES**
CASH FLOW FORECAST FOR THE SIX MONTHS ENDED 31 DECEMBER 19X9

	July £'000	August £'000	Sept £'000	Oct £'000	Nov £'000	Dec £'000
Cash receipts (W1)						
Sales: installation instalments	24	24	24	36	36	36
Sales: final instalments	–	6	6	6	9	9
	24	30	30	42	45	45
Cash payments						
Advertising costs	10	1	1	1	1	1
Purchase of conservatories	20	20	20	30	30	30
Installation expenses (W2)	2	2	2	3	3	3
General administration expenses	6	6	6	6	6	6
	38	29	29	40	40	40
Surplus/deficit for month	(14)	1	1	2	5	5
Cumulative surplus/(deficit)						
Brought forward	(60)	(74)	(73)	(72)	(70)	(65)
Carried forward	(74)	(73)	(72)	(70)	(65)	(60)

(c)

	£'000
Cash at bank at 31 December 19X8	56
Less corporation tax paid 30 September 19X9	35
	21
Add profit before tax on existing activities (as (a))	140
Add depreciation charge for the year*	50
	211
Less cash deficit on conservatory sales (as (b))	60
Forecast bank balance at 31 December 19X9	151

*In the absence of further information it must be assumed that the increase in accumulated depreciation from 19X7 to 19X8 of £50,000 represents the charge for the year and that this will be the same in 19X9.

(d) **PROFIT FORECAST FOR CONSERVATORY SALES FOR THE SIX MONTHS ENDED 31 DECEMBER 19X9**

	£'000	£'000
Sales		225
Cost of sales		
Purchases (W3)	150	
Installation costs	15	
		165
Gross profit		60
Expenses		
Advertising costs	16	
General expenses	36	
		52
Profit before tax		8
Tax @ 25%		2
Net profit		6

SUGGESTED SOLUTIONS

(e) KAPLAN LIMITED
FINANCIAL IMPLICATIONS OF EXPANSION INTO CONSERVATORY MARKET

REPORT FOR DOGGER BANK PLC

Prepared by B N Kerr

Date: 15 May 19X9

The company's proposed new project is profitable ignoring interest costs but, because of the high level of stock to be held and the absence of credit from the suppliers, its cash balance will be reduced by £60,000 by the year end (maximum deficit in the period £74,000 in July). Depending on the timing of other cash flows this may result in the creation of an overdraft for part of the year and the resultant interest costs could considerably reduce the profit on the project.

However, profits for the first six months are lowered by initial heavy advertising costs and reduced sales in the first three months. In the future, if sales and expenses continue at the same level profit will accrue at £3,750 per month after tax on conservatory sales. The deficit should therefore be more or less eliminated after eighteen months of sales.

Workings

1   Cash receipts

    July to September
    Customers pay 80% of £30,000 on installation: £24,000.

    One month later they pay the balance: £6,000.

    October to December
    Customers pay 80% of £45,000 on installation: £36,000.

    One month later they pay the balance: £9,000.

2   *Purchases of conservatories*

    Sales price = 150% × purchase price.

    ∴ Conservatories sold for £30,000 cost £20,000 to purchase; conservatories sold for £45,000 cost £30,000 to purchase.

    ∴ Purchases = £20,000 per month (July to September) and £30,000 per month (October to December).

3   *Cost of sales*

    Closing stock = opening stock (purchased June 19X9) = £60,000.

    There is no increase in stock in the period since each month's sales are exactly matched by purchases of fresh stocks.

50 ROWAN

> *Tutorial note.* This is a straightforward question (resulting in high marks when set) simply requiring you to readjust the information given in the question and to keep an eye open for the relevant dates and periods.

(a) FORECAST PROFIT FOR SIX MONTHS TO 31 MARCH 19X1

	£'000	£'000
Sales (52 + 60 + 60 + 52 + 55 + 48)		327
Cost of sales		
Materials (21 + 24 + 24 + 21 + 22 + 19)	131	
Direct factory wages (11 + 12 + 12 + 10 + 11 + 10)	66	
Factory expenses: fixed (6 × 1)	6	
variable (4 + 4 + 4 + 3 + 4 + 3)	22	
		225
Gross profit		102
Expenses		
General expenses (4 + 5 + 4 + 5 + 5 + 5)	28	
Salesmen's salaries (6 × 5)	30	
Salesmen's commission (3 + 3 + 3 + 3 + 3 + 2)	17	
Loss on disposal of plant (12 - 10)	2	
Depreciation	12	
		89
Net profit		13

(b) REVISED MONTHLY CASH FORECAST FOR THE FOUR MONTHS COMMENCING 1 NOVEMBER 19X8

	Nov £'000	Dec £'000	Jan £'000	Feb £'000
Receipts				
Sales of stock	50	52	-	60
Plant sold	10	-	-	-
	60	52	-	60
Payments				
Materials	20	21	-	24
Direct factory wages	-	12	10	11
Other factory expenses				
Fixed	1	1	1	1
Variable	-	4	3	4
General expenses	4	5	4	5
Salesmen's salaries	5	5	5	5
Salesmen's commission	3	-	3	3
	33	48	26	53
Monthly surplus/(deficit)	27	4	(26)	7
Brought forward	2	29	33	7
Carried forward	29	33	7	14

SUGGESTED SOLUTIONS

(c) *Effect of strike on forecast profit for six months to 31 March 19X9*

	£'000
Net profit as forecast	13
Less November sales lost	(60)
Add expenses not incurred	
Material costs for November	24
Direct wages for November	12
Factory variable expenses for November	4
Salesmen's commission on November deliveries	3
Forecast loss if strike goes ahead	(4)

Tutorial note. You can prove that this is correct by calculating the decrease in the forecast cash balance as at 31 March 19X9. Since all the effects of the strike affect cash the decrease in profit and the decrease in cash should be the same.

	£'000
Original forecast (profit)	13
Revised forecast loss	4
Reduction in profit	17
Original forecast cash as at 28 February 19X9	31
Revised forecast cash as at 28 February 19X9	14
Reduction in cash	17

(d) ROWAN LIMITED
REPORT ON EFFECT OF THREATENED STRIKE

   To: Board of directors
   From: B N Kerr
   Date: 15 October 19X8

From the attached calculations, you will see that the financial implications of the proposed strike are that, if it lasts for a month, as you predict, then forecast profit for the six months to 31 March 19X9 will fall by £17,000 to produce a forecast loss of £4,000. The cash balance forecast for 31 March 19X9 will be £18,000 instead of £35,000.

However, the company will not require overdraft facilities as a result of the strike unless it continues for over a month. If you were to lose December's sales as well as November's then you would by the end of February need an overdraft of £3,000; this would increase to £18,000 by the end of March if you lost January's production and sales. The longer term effects on customer goodwill are, of course, unquantifiable.

If you could find an alternative source of supply of finished goods for your November deliveries, although you would make a reduced profit (or even a loss) on these orders, then you would have a much better chance of retaining customers who would otherwise find alternative suppliers, thus creating a risk that you will lose their custom permanently. It would be wise to reassess the budgeted sales figures for December onwards to assess how much custom might be lost.

You should also consider the effect on the morale of sales staff if they have to go without commission (averaging nearly 40% of their earnings) even for one month. Since it will not be their fault if November sales are lost it will seem unjust that they should suffer in this way as well as facing the loss of their future commission if customers go elsewhere. This might be an inducement to leave which could further damage your customer relations.

SUGGESTED SOLUTIONS

There seems to be little scope for recovering profit by cutting overheads as these are already low in comparison with direct costs. You should consider whether there are any short-term assets which could be realised at a profit during the strike period (for example, short-term investments or surplus stocks). At the cost of a discount, if it seemed that the company was about to go into overdraft you could factor some of your debts through the bank to improve cash flow at a lower cost than overdraft interest.

51 HOBHOUSE

> *Tutorial note.* The first thing to establish in tackling this question is the *timing* and accounting treatment of receipts and payments.
>
> Since deposits paid by customers are shown as creditors on the balance sheet, sales must be recorded only on completion and so the 19X1/X2 profit forecast should include the profit on jobs commenced in September 19X1 but completed in October 19X2. Similarly, expected profit on jobs started in September 19X2 should not be reflected in the profit forecast for 19X1/X2. However, the cash flow forecast *should* reflect the cash receipts and payments as they occur.
>
> The sequence is as follows.
>
> | | |
> |---|---|
> | Month 1, order placed: | 20% deposit received
materials transferred to job
purchases of replacement materials made
half total wages cost per job incurred
sales commission paid
general expenses paid |
> | End of month 1: | WIP valued at 100% materials and 50% of wages cost |
> | Month 2, job completed: | balance of sales price paid
remaining 50% of wages cost incurred
suppliers paid for previous month's purchases |

(a) (i) See following page

(ii) HOBHOUSE LIMITED
PROFIT FORECAST FOR THE YEAR ENDING 30 SEPTEMBER 19X2

	£	£
Sales (W2)		337,500
Opening stock	8,000	
Purchases (total of purchases in note 1)	154,000	
Closing stock (September purchases)	(12,000)	
Change in value of WIP (W3)	(5,000)	
Wages (total of wages paid in note 1)	76,000	
		221,000
Gross profit		116,500
Expenses		
Sales commission (W1)	41,580	
Depreciation	3,000	
General expenses (£5,500 × 12)	66,000	
		110,580
Forecast operating profit		5,920

183

SUGGESTED SOLUTIONS

(a) (i) **HOBHOUSE LIMITED**
CASH FLOW FORECAST FOR THE YEAR ENDING 30 SEPTEMBER 19X2

	Oct £	Nov £	Dec £	Jan £	Feb £	Mar £	Apr £	May £	June £	Jul £	Aug £	Sept £
Receipts												
Deposits (W1)	4,500	4,500	4,500	3,600	3,600	5,400	9,000	9,000	9,000	5,400	5,400	5,400
Balance (W1)	14,400	18,000	18,000	18,000	14,400	14,400	21,600	36,000	36,000	36,000	21,600	21,600
	18,900	22,500	22,500	21,600	18,000	19,800	30,600	45,000	45,000	41,400	27,000	27,000
Payments												
Trade creditors (= previous month's purchases)	8,000	10,000	10,000	10,000	8,000	8,000	12,000	20,000	20,000	20,000	12,000	12,000
Wages	4,500	5,000	5,000	4,500	4,000	5,000	8,000	10,000	10,000	8,000	6,000	6,000
Sales commission (W1)	2,700	2,700	2,700	2,160	2,160	3,240	5,400	5,400	5,400	3,240	3,240	3,240
General expenses	5,500	5,500	5,500	5,500	5,500	5,500	5,500	5,500	5,500	5,500	5,500	5,500
	20,700	23,200	23,200	22,160	19,660	21,740	30,900	40,900	40,900	36,740	26,740	26,740
Surplus/(deficit)	(1,800)	(700)	(700)	(560)	(1,660)	(1,940)	(300)	4,100	4,100	4,660	260	260
Opening balance	(7,500)	(9,300)	(10,000)	(10,700)	(11,260)	(12,920)	(14,860)	(15,160)	(11,060)	(6,960)	(2,300)	(2,040)
Closing balance	(9,300)	(10,000)	(10,700)	(11,260)	(12,920)	(14,860)	(15,160)	(11,060)	(6,960)	(2,300)	(2,040)	(1,780)

(iii) HOBHOUSE LIMITED
FORECAST CURRENT RATIOS FOR THE YEAR ENDING 30 SEPTEMBER 19X2

	End of Qtr 1	End of Qtr 2	End of Qtr 3	End of Qtr 4
Current assets				
Stock of double glazing units	10,000	12,000	20,000	12,000
Work in progress (W3)	12,500	15,000	25,000	15,000
	22,500	27,000	45,000	27,000
Current liabilities				
Deposits from customers (W1)	4,500	5,400	9,000	5,400
Trade creditors	10,000	12,000	20,000	12,000
Bank overdraft (as (i))	10,700	14,860	6,960	1,780
	25,200	32,260	35,960	19,180
Current ratio	0.89:1	0.84:1	1.25:1	1.41:1

(b) The forecast current ratios for 19X1 exceed 0.8:1 for each quarter end but in the first two quarters the margin is very narrow, because of low sales (the business is seasonal). The bank should check the sales and cost forecasts very carefully, comparing them with the equivalents for the current year, to ensure that they are not too optimistic. The valuation of stocks and work in progress should also be considered, as no allowance has been made for the possibility of cancelled orders. Finally, prices are unlikely to be stable over the whole year, because of inflation. Has this been fully allowed for in calculating sales, purchase costs, wages and general expenses? Changes in the forecasts for each of these will affect the company's liquidity.

Workings

1 *Deposits and sales commission*

	Value of jobs commenced £	Deposits (20%) £	Balance (80%) £	Commission (12%) £
October	22,500	4,500	18,000	2,700
November	22,500	4,500	18,000	2,700
December	22,500	4,500	18,000	2,700
January	18,000	3,600	14,400	2,160
February	18,000	3,600	14,400	2,160
March	27,000	5,400	21,600	3,240
April	45,000	9,000	36,000	5,400
May	45,000	9,000	36,000	5,400
June	45,000	9,000	36,000	5,400
July	27,000	5,400	21,600	3,240
August	27,000	5,400	21,600	3,240
September	27,000	5,400	21,600	3,240
				41,580

The balance payable in October 1991 will be 80% × £18,000 (orders placed in September 19X1, note (b)) = £14,400.

SUGGESTED SOLUTIONS

2 *Sales*

	£
Value of jobs commenced in previous month	
October	18,000
November	22,500
December	22,500
January	22,500
February	18,000
March	18,000
April	27,000
May	45,000
June	45,000
July	45,000
August	27,000
September	27,000
	337,500

3 *Work in progress*

(a)

	£	£
Opening WIP		10,000
Closing WIP		
Materials transferred to jobs commenced in September (= purchases)	12,000	
Wages paid re jobs commenced in September	3,000	
		15,000
Increase in WIP over years		5,000

(b) *WIP at quarter ends*

	End of Qtr 1 £	End of Qtr 2 £	End of Qtr 3 £	End of Qtr 4 £
Materials transferred to jobs commenced in month (= purchases)	10,000	12,000	20,000	12,000
Wages paid re jobs commenced in month (as question)	2,500	3,000	5,000	3,000
	12,500	15,000	25,000	15,000

Test paper

(CIB examination set 21 October 1992)

ACCOUNTANCY

1. Answer FOUR questions:
   SECTION A: ONE COMPULSORY question (30 marks)
   SECTION B: ONE question (30 marks)
   SECTION C: TWO questions (20 marks each)

2. The number in brackets after each question, or part of a question, shows the marks allotted.

3. Silent non-programmable electronic calculators may be used in this examination. Whether or not candidates use them, it is in their interest to show the basic figures from which their calculations are made.

4. No other aids such as books, dictionaries, papers, mathematical tables or slide-rules are permitted in this examination.

5. Time allowed: three hours.

6. An additional 15 minutes' reading time is allowed at the beginning of an examination when candidates may write on this paper but NOT in the answer book.

DO NOT TURN THIS PAGE UNTIL YOU ARE READY TO START

UNDER EXAMINATION CONDITIONS

TEST PAPER: OCTOBER 1992 EXAMINATION

SECTION A

Question 1 is compulsory

1. Shelton plc is a trading company which was formed on 1 October 1991 to acquire business assets from the liquidators of Pochin Ltd. Shelton's accountant is in the course of preparing the final accounts for the year to 30 September 1992, and he has been told by the board of directors that he 'should do his best to ensure that the published accounts will create a good impression of the company's performance when examined by the bank, creditors and shareholders'. He has produced three drafts (A, B and C) of the accounts and their contents are summarised below.

Profit and loss account, year to 30 September 1992

	A £'000	B £'000	C £'000
Sales	20,000	20,000	20,000
Net profit before depreciation	1,500	1,500	1,500
Depreciation charged	500	800	500
Operating profit	1,000	700	1,000
Interest	450	450	450
Net profit	550	250	550
Proposed dividend	500	200	500
Retained profits	50	50	50

Movement on reserves, year to 30 September 1992

	A	B		C	
	Retained profit £'000	Retained profit £'000	Revaluation reserve £'000	Retained profit £'000	Revaluation reserve £'000
Balance brought forward	-	-	-	-	-
Additions during year	50	50	3,000	50	3,000
Further depreciation	-	-	-	(300)	-
Balance carried forward	50	50	3,000	(250)	3,000

TEST PAPER: OCTOBER 1992 EXAMINATION

Balance Sheet as at 30 September 1992

	A £'000	B £'000	C £'000
Fixed assets: at cost	5,000	-	-
at revaluation	-	8,000	8,000
Less accumulated depreciation	500	800	800
	4,500	7,200	7,200
Net current assets	550	850	550
Total assets less current liabilities	5,050	8,050	7,750
15% debentures 2001	3,000	3,000	3,000
	2,050	5,050	4,750
Capital and Reserves			
Share capital	2,000	2,000	2,000
Reserves	50	50	(250)
Revaluation surplus	-	3,000	3,000
	2,050	5,050	4,750

The fixed assets were acquired from Pochin at a highly favourable price, and it is the directors' policy to maintain them in first class condition. The firm of surveyors called in to revalue the fixed assets at 30 September 1992, pronounced them 'as good as new'.

Required:

A report for the board of directors to accompany the three draft sets of accounts prepared by the accountant (shown above). Your report should cover the following five areas:

(a) An identification of the differences between the accounting methods used for the purpose of preparing the three draft sets of accounts. **(4 marks)**

(b) An examination of the proposed level of dividends under each of the three accounting methods. Your examination should include a calculation of the amount legally available for distribution as a dividend and an indication of the impact of the proposed distributions on the company's financial position. **(4 marks)**

(c) Calculations of the percentages and ratios, listed below, based on each of the three draft sets of accounts set out above. You should present the calculations, made to one decimal place, in the following format:

	A	B	C
Interest cover	....	....	....
Net profit percentage	....	....	....
Fixed asset turnover	....	....	....
Return on shareholders' equity	....	....	....
Debt: equity ratio	....	....	....

(10 marks)

(d) An analysis and comparison of the financial implications of the calculations made under part (c) above. **(6 marks)**

TEST PAPER: OCTOBER 1992 EXAMINATION

(e) An assessment of the relative merits of the three draft sets of accounts for the purpose of publication, including an indication of any alternative method of accounting for fixed assets which might be considered (the actual calculation is not required). **(6 marks)**

(30 marks)

Note. Ignore taxation

SECTION B

Answer ONE question from this section

2 Wigan Ltd is a well established company owned and run by three cousins. The company traded successfully up until the late 1980's, but has suffered badly during the recession. Sales have fallen significantly and two of its main customers have gone into liquidation. The directors are confident that the company remains viable, provided that certain actions are taken, and that a high level of profitability will be restored once the recession ends.

The directors have prepared the following estimate of the company's financial position, as at 21 October 1992, at which date a meeting of creditors is to be held to consider the company's financial difficulties.

Estimated Balance Sheet as at 21 October 1992

	£'000	£'000
Fixed assets at cost less depreciation		125
Current assets		
Stock and work in progress at cost	293	
Debtors and prepayments	167	
	460	
Current liabilities		
Creditors and accruals	124	
VAT, corporation tax and income tax owing	136	
Bank overdraft	90	
Loan from Dorning plc	100	
	450	
Net current assets		10
		135
Financed by		
Share capital (£1 shares)		100
Retained profit		35
		135

Discussions between the bank and Wigan's directors have indicated that debts amounting to £50,000 are likely to prove 'bad' and, assuming that the company continues as a going concern, the saleable value of certain items of stock is £30,000 below their book value. The bank's overdraft and the loan from Dorning plc (a supplier) are each unsecured. The preferential creditors comprise (a) taxation owing and (b) £14,000 of the figure for creditors and accruals.

TEST PAPER: OCTOBER 1992 EXAMINATION

The following three proposals are to be considered at the creditors' meeting.

1   **Immediate liquidation of the company**

    In these circumstances the fixed assets would realise £30,000 and the stock and work in progress £203,000. Liquidation expenses are estimated at £20,000.

2   **Reconstruction scheme A**

    This would involve the following.

    -   The directors to subscribe for a further 200,000 ordinary shares of £1 each at par.

    -   The preferential creditors to be repaid immediately.

    -   All non-preferential creditors to agree to reduce their claims by 20%, postpone repayment for one year, and waive their right to interest during that period.

3   **Reconstruction scheme B**

    This would involve the following:

    -   Dorning plc to convert its loan into 100,000 shares of £1 each, at par, and agree to subscribe for a further 160,000 shares of £1 each at par.

    -   The preferential creditors to be repaid immediately.

    -   All non-preferential creditors to agree to reduce their claims by 30%, postpone repayment for six months, and waive their right to interest during that period.

    -   Dorning plc to guarantee to advance Wigan Ltd a further £150,000 at the end of six months, if this proves necessary to repay the non-preferential creditors (who have agreed to postpone repayment and reduce their claims by 30%).

Wigan Ltd's bank charges 16% per annum on overdrafts. Dorning plc earns 12% per annum on monies deposited with the bank.

Required:

(a) A calculation of the amounts the bank and Dorning plc will receive if Wigan Ltd is liquidated. **(6 marks)**

(b) The revised balance sheet of Wigan Ltd if reconstruction scheme A is adopted. **(6 marks)**

(c) The revised balance sheet of Wigan Ltd if reconstruction scheme B is adopted. **(6 marks)**

(d) An examination of the relative merits of the three proposals from the viewpoint of (i) Dorning and (ii) the bank. **(12 marks)**

(30 marks)

TEST PAPER: OCTOBER 1992 EXAMINATION

Notes

1 Assume that the calculations are being made on 21 October 1992 and that any of the three proposals can be put into effect immediately.

2 Under each of the reconstruction schemes, the present bank overdraft would be frozen (at the appropriately adjusted level) and a new bank account opened for subsequent transactions.

3 Knowles Ltd was incorporated in 1980 and the company's existing activities have remained at a steady level for the last few years despite the recession. The demand for the company's existing product lines is steady, and it is expected that trading results for the year to 30 June 1993 will repeat those of the previous year. The accounts for the year to 30 June 1992 showed a post-tax profit of £420,000, of which £200,000 was paid out in dividends.

The directors are keen to expand the level of activity and consideration is being given to the introduction of an additional product line, designated XZ, to be separately located in rented accommodation. The following plans and financial forecasts have been prepared.

1 The annual rent will be £30,000 and will be paid in advance on 1 November 1992. In the same month plant will be purchased for £211,500 cash (ie a net cost of £180,000 plus £31,500 VAT - value added tax). The plant is expected to have a six-year life and zero residual value at the end of that time.

2 Raw materials, sufficient to manufacture 150 units of XZ, will be purchased for £56,400 (net cost £48,000 plus £8,400 VAT). They will be both purchased and paid for in November 1992. Monthly purchases, on one month's credit terms, will subsequently be made, sufficient to replace raw materials issued to production each month.

3 Production will commence on 1 December 1992 at the rate of 200 units of XZ per month. Raw materials will be purchased for £376 per unit (net cost £320 plus £56 VAT). All materials issues to production will be converted into finished goods during the same month, ie there will be no work-in-progress at the end of the month.

4 Direct labour costs are estimated at £250 per unit of XZ and will be paid in the month the work is done.

5 Sales will commence on 1 January 1993 at the rate of 200 units of XZ per month. The selling price is to be fixed at £940 per unit (net selling price £800 plus £140 VAT). Sales will be for cash.

6 Overheads, other than depreciation and rent, are expected to amount to £30,000 per month, commencing in December 1992, and will be paid during the month they are incurred.

7 Finished stock is to be valued at direct cost (raw materials plus direct labour).

8 The company will receive a repayment of VAT in April 1993 amounting to £700 (the excess of VAT suffered on purchase of raw materials and plant over and above VAT due in respect of sales) and will owe £50,400 in respect of VAT at the end of June 1993.

9 Assume a corporation tax charge of 30% on the forecast net profit.

TEST PAPER: OCTOBER 1992 EXAMINATION

Required:

(a) A forecast of the receipts and payments in respect of the new project for each of the eight months from 1 November 1992 to 30 June 1993. **(6 marks)**

(b) A forecast profit statement for the new project in respect of the eight-month period to 30 June 1993. (Monthly figures are not required.) **(9 marks)**

(c) A forecast balance sheet for the new project as at 30 June 1993. **(7 marks)**

(d) A brief report on the profitability and cash implications of the new project, for which your bank has been asked to provide overdraft facilities if required. **(8 marks)**

(30 marks)

Notes

1. Ignore bank interest, if any.
2. It has been assumed that the company pays VAT to its suppliers only on purchases of plant and raw materials.

SECTION C

Answer TWO questions from this section

4. The following information is provided relating to stock and work-in-progress belonging to a trading and manufacturing company called Markham Ltd.

   1. The company stocks three entirely different types of raw material, in respect of which the following data is provided as at 31 December 1991.

Stock	Cost £	Net Realisable Value (NRV) £
A	7,000	10,000
B	12,000	13,200
C	3,000	1,600

   2. The company trades in product MN, for which the following data is made available in respect of 1991.

      Opening stock (300 units)
         Last in first out (LIFO) cost per unit   £10.00
         First in first out (FIFO) cost per unit   £12.00
      Purchases - 2,000 units at £13.50 each
      Sales - 1,920 units at £20,000 each.

   3. The company began to manufacture product YZ on 1 January 1991. All raw materials required to produce the product are introduced immediately manufacture commences.

	£
Raw materials issues to production (250)	30,000
Direct labour costs (£10 per hour)	13,500
Overhead costs: Production	9,000
Administration	7,000
Distribution	3,000

TEST PAPER: OCTOBER 1992 EXAMINATION

One unit of raw material and six labour hours are required to produce one unit of YZ. The company manufactured 200 units of YZ during 1991, which was the planned level of production. Items of work-in-progress had incurred 50% of the total costs for direct labour and relevant overheads. The company sold 180 units of YZ during 1991.

Required:

(a) Outline the main rules to be followed when valuing stock and work-in-progress for the purposes of the published accounts. **(8 marks)**

(b) Calculate the values to be placed on the closing stock and work-in-progress of Markham Ltd, so far as the above information permits. The calculations should be made in accordance with the Companies Acts and SSAP 9. Where more than one treatment is permissible, you should calculate the alternatives. **(12 marks)**

(20 marks)

5 The directors of Keeper Ltd plan to expand operations by adding a new product to the existing range. The following forecasts have been prepared by the planning department for producing two alternative products.

	Product A £	Product B £
Initial investment: Plant	50,000	200,000
Working capital	25,000	60,000
Fixed costs per annum (other than depreciation)	35,000	80,000
Variable costs per unit	15	25
Sales price per unit	30	50

The sales department estimates demand at 4,500 units per annum for Product A and 10,000 units per annum for Product B, but points out that it is difficult to forecast accurately demand for any new product.

The plant required to produce either product will last for five years and will have zero residual value at the end of that time.

The company applies a target rate of return of 20% on the *initial* investment when assessing the viability of all new products.

Required:

(a) For each new product calculate:

  (i) the number of units which must be produced and sold each year to break even;
  (ii) the number of units which must be produced and sold each year to achieve the target rate of return. **(10 marks)**

(b) A discussion of the relative merits of the two proposed products based on your calculations in (a) above, and any other calculations you consider appropriate. **(10 marks)**

(20 marks)

Note. Ignore the time value of money.

TEST PAPER: OCTOBER 1992 EXAMINATION

6 The following financial information is provided for Walker Ltd, which makes up its accounts on the calendar year basis.

Year to 31 December	1990 £'000	1990 £'000	1991 £'000	1991 £'000
Sales		3,150		4,560
Purchases	2,032		3,410	
Increase in stock level	(23)		(230)	
Cost of goods sold		2,009		3,180
		1,141		1,380

Balance at 31 December

	1990	1991
Trade debtors	394	651
Trade creditors	226	341
Taxation and social security payments	165	201
Stock	530	760
Bank balance (overdraft)	72	(56)

All purchases and sales were made on credit and occurred at an even rate throughout each year. The directors have approached the bank to requires an extension of their existing overdraft facility.

Required:

A report for the bank which explains, so far as the information permits, the likely reasons for the decline in the cash balance of Walker Ltd. Your report should include calculations, in respect of each year, of:

- the gross profit percentage;
- the working capital ratio;
- the cash operating cycle.

(20 marks)

Notes

1 Assume a 360 day year for the purpose of your calculations.
2 All calculations should be made to one decimal place.

TEST PAPER
SUGGESTED SOLUTIONS

DO NOT TURN THIS PAGE UNTIL YOU

HAVE COMPLETED THE TEST PAPER

TEST PAPER: OCTOBER 1992 EXAMINATION SUGGESTED SOLUTIONS

1

> *Tutorial note.* The calculations in this question are very straightforward and give a large number of marks. The discussion is more complicated, requiring a knowledge of distributable profits and the revaluation and subsequent depreciation of fixed assets. If you read the *Signpost* article in the March 1992 edition of *Banking World* on the treatment of fixed assets, you should already have a clear insight into some of the problems this question raises. Comparisons between different treatments in sets of accounts is very important and you should make sure you understand the implications of the answer.

REPORT TO THE BOARD OF DIRECTORS OF
SHELTON PLC: RESULTS TO 30 SEPTEMBER 1992

The following report discusses the results for the year ended 30 September 1992 and considers the methods used in the preparation of certain items, the impact of proposed dividends and an analysis of the results which might be obtained for each draft set of accounts.

(a) *Accounting methods*

The main differences in accounting methods used in the three drafts are those used in the valuation of fixed assets and the related depreciation charges.

Draft A shows fixed assets valued at the cost to Shelton plc (the purchase price from Pochin Ltd). Depreciation is charged in the profit and loss account at 10% on a straight line basis, the assets being deemed to have a 10 year life.

Draft B shows fixed assets in the balance sheet at revaluation, which has substantially increased the balance sheet figure compared to Draft A. The difference between the cost and the revalued figure has been transferred to a revaluation reserve. Depreciation has been charged at 10% of the revalued amount on a straight line basis, as with Draft A, but obviously producing a higher charge (£800,000 rather than £500,000). The depreciation has been charged in full to the profit and loss account.

In Draft C the fixed assets are again shown at their revalued amount with the excess transferred to a revaluation reserve. Depreciation has also been calculated at 10% of the revalued amount. However, only the depreciation relating to the original cost (£500,000) has been charged to the profit and loss account. The remainder (£300,000) has been passed through revenue reserves, producing a debit on the profit and loss account in the balance sheet.

(b) *Proposed level of dividends*

The amount legally available for distribution as a dividend can be calculated as follows.

	Draft A £'000	Draft B £'000	Draft C £'000
Net profit	550	250	550
Excess depreciation (s 263)	–	300	–
	550	550	550

These profits are realisable and therefore available for distribution, subject to the limitation for public limited companies (s 264).

TEST PAPER: OCTOBER 1992 EXAMINATION SUGGESTED SOLUTIONS

	Draft A £'000	Draft B £'000	Draft C £'000
Before proposed distribution			
Net assets (net assets as shown plus proposed dividend)	2,550	5,250	5,250
Capital plus undistributable reserves	2,000	5,000	5,000
Maximum distribution	550	250	250

The restrictions relating to public limited companies in distributing profits means that the proposed dividend under Draft C is actually illegal. The maximum distribution permitted by the Companies Act 1985 is £250,000. The difference between the maximum allowed in Draft A and that allowed in Drafts B and C reflects the increase in depreciation due to the revaluation.

The proposed dividends for the year for all three drafts are very high, leaving only a small proportion of retained profits to be carried forward. If the company fails to make a net profit of over £450,000 in the following year, then there will be no profits left to pay dividends as it will all be used up in paying the interest on the 15% debentures.

The debentures are also due to be redeemed in less than ten years' time. Unless a definite scheme has been formulated to replace them with a new issue of debentures of some other form of funds, the company needs to build up its cash reserves in order to redeem the debt.

It would seem likely that such large dividends would leave the company with few cash resources in the short term, as well as the long term. This might cause problems with trading cash flow, and further investment in fixed assets might be hampered.

(c) *Ratios*

	Working	Draft A	Draft B	Draft C
Interest cover	1	2.2	1.6	2.2
Net profit percentage	2	2.8%	1.3%	2.8%
Fixed asset turnover	3	4.4	2.8	2.8
Return on shareholders' equity	4	26.8%	5.0%	11.6%
Debt: equity ratio	5	1.5:1	0.5:1	0.6:1

Workings

1 *Interest cover*

$$= \frac{\text{Profit before interest and tax}}{\text{Interest paid in the year}}$$

A $= \dfrac{1,000}{450}$ B $= \dfrac{700}{450}$ C $= \dfrac{1,000}{450}$

$ = 2.2$ times $ = 1.6$ times $ = 2.2$ times

2 *Net profit percentage*

$$= \frac{\text{Net profit}}{\text{Sales}} \times 100\%$$

A $= \dfrac{550}{20,000}$ B $= \dfrac{250}{20,000}$ C $= \dfrac{550}{20,000}$

$ = 2.75\%$ $ = 1.25\%$ $ = 2.75\%$

TEST PAPER: OCTOBER 1992 EXAMINATION SUGGESTED SOLUTIONS

3   *Fixed asset turnover*

$$= \frac{\text{Sales}}{\text{Fixed assets (NBV)}}$$

A $= \dfrac{20,000}{4,500}$ B $= \dfrac{20,000}{7,200}$ C $= \dfrac{20,000}{7,200}$

= 4.44 times = 2.78 times = 2.78 times

4   *Return on shareholders' equity*

$$\frac{\text{Profits after interest and tax}}{\text{Ordinary share capital and reserves}} \times 100\%$$

A $= \dfrac{550}{2,050} \times 100\%$ B $= \dfrac{250}{5,050} \times 100\%$ C $= \dfrac{550}{4,750} \times 100\%$

= 26.8% = 5.0% = 11.6%

5   *Debt: equity ratio*

$$= \frac{\text{Long term debt}}{\text{Ordinary share capital plus reserves}}$$

A $= \dfrac{3,000}{2,050}$ B $= \dfrac{3,000}{5,050}$ C $= \dfrac{3,000}{4,750}$

= 1.46:1 = 0.59:1 = 0.63:1

(d) *Ratio analysis*

It can be seen from the ratios in (c) above that the method used in each draft has advantages and disadvantages.

Draft B gives a much lower interest cover than Drafts A and C, as well as a lower net profit percentage, because of the effect of the extra £300,000 of depreciation passing through the profit and loss account. This highlights the danger that there will not be sufficient distributable profits for both interest and dividends on this scale in future years.

Draft A has a much higher fixed asset turnover than B or C, but this is largely cosmetic, as it is recognised that the real value of the assets is much higher than their purchase costs. The creation of the revaluation reserve has also reduced the return on shareholders' equity in Drafts B and C, and B's return is again affected by the fall in profits due to extra depreciation.

The debt/equity ratio is much worse in Draft A than in B and C because there is no revaluation reserve to boost the equity ownership.

(e) *Merits of each draft*

As stated in (d) above, the method used in each draft has advantages and disadvantages. When deciding which draft would be the best to present, the following factors should be taken into consideration.

TEST PAPER: OCTOBER 1992 EXAMINATION SUGGESTED SOLUTIONS

(i) *The bank*

The bank will be most concerned with security and ability to repay and service debt. The revaluation of fixed assets will show the security of the company in a better light and so Drafts B and C would be favoured.

The bank would also wish to see good interest cover, which is better in Draft C.

(ii) *Creditors*

Creditors are also interested in security and in liquidity, so that debts will be repaid as they fall due. Creditors would therefore prefer to see higher assets and lower distributions, as shown in Draft B.

(iii) *Shareholders*

Shareholders are primarily concerned with dividends and therefore, by inference, with distributable profits. The level of dividends in Drafts A and C might meet with their approval, but the distribution in Draft C is illegal (see (iv) below). The shareholders might be concerned that such a level of dividend could not be sustained in future years.

(iv) *Legality and the treatment of fixed assets*

The distribution in Draft C is illegal, as has already been shown. In addition, SSAP 12 does not permit the split of the depreciation charge between the profit and loss account and reserves. The adjustment to write off the excess depreciation against the revaluation reserve can *only* be made through reserves *after* the full depreciation charge has been made in the profit and loss account.

If this transfer were to be made, then the proposed dividend in Draft C would become legal, because the undistributable reserves would fall to £4,700,000.

	£'000
Net assets	5,250
Undistributable reserves	4,700
Maximum distribution	550

The transfer is not compulsory, but it advisable because otherwise the revaluation reserve remains static and it can only be reduced by making a bonus issue.

---

2 *Tutorial note.* Once again, the calculations are quite straightforward in the different balance sheets. The reserves can be shown as a balancing figure, although it is a good check to work them out. When considering the viability of the schemes, you should bear in mind time, uncertainty and security.

TEST PAPER: OCTOBER 1992 EXAMINATION SUGGESTED SOLUTIONS

(a) *Liquidation*

	£'000	£'000
Amounts received		
Fixed assets		30
Stock and work in progress		203
Debtors (167-50)		117
		350
Payments		
Secured creditors	14	
Liquidation expenses	20	
Taxation	136	
		170
		180
Available to		
Unsecured creditors (124-14)		110
Bank		90
Dorning plc		100
		300

These creditors would receive 60p in the pound (180 ÷ 300)

(b) *Reconstruction Scheme A*

	£'000	£'000
Fixed assets		125
Current assets		
Stock and work in progress (293 - 30)	263	
Debtors and prepayments (167-50)	117	
Bank account (W1)	50	
	430	
Current liabilities (note)		
Creditors and accruals (124-14) × 80%	88	
Bank overdraft (90 × 80%)	72	
Loan from Dorning plc (100 × 80%)	80	
	240	
Net current assets		190
		315
Financed by		
Share capital (£1 shares)		300
Retained profit (W2)		15
		315

Note. These amounts may be due after one year, but the situation is precarious and this treatment is probably more prudent.

Workings

1   Bank balance

	£'000
Cash received from directors	20
Paid to: secured creditors	(14)
tax authorities	(136)
	50

TEST PAPER: OCTOBER 1992 EXAMINATION SUGGESTED SOLUTIONS

    2   *Retained profit*

		£'000
Balance before reconstruction		35
Write back: unsecured creditors (124−14) × 20%		22
bank (90 × 20%)		18
Dorning (100 × 20%)		20
		95
Write off: debtors which are bad		(50)
overvalued stock		(30)
		15

(c) *Reconstruction Scheme B*

	£'000	£'000
Fixed assets		125
Current assets		
Stock (293 − 30)	263	
Debtors and prepayments (167−50)	117	
Bank balance (W1)	10	
		390
Current liabilities		
Creditors and accruals		
(124−14) × 70%	77	
Bank overdraft (90 × 70%)	63	
		140
Net current assets		250
		375
Share capital (£1 shares)		360
Retained profit (W2)		15
		375

Workings

1   *Bank balance*

	£'000
Dorning plc for shares	160
Paid to: secured creditors	(14)
tax authorities	(136)
	10

2   *Retained profit*

	£'000
Balance before reconstruction	35
Write back: unsecured creditors (124−14) × 30%	33
bank (90 × 30%)	27
	95
Write off: debtors which are bad	(50)
overvalued stock	(30)
	15

TEST PAPER: OCTOBER 1992 EXAMINATION SUGGESTED SOLUTIONS

(d) *Relative merits of the three proposals*

(i) *Dorning plc*
Dorning plc has already made a substantial commitment to Wigan Ltd by offering such a large unsecured loan. The management of Dorning will have to decide whether it is in their best interests to support Wigan further. If it is not, then a liquidation would involve writing off £40,000 of the loan, with the certainty of receiving £60,000 immediately.

If Scheme A were undertaken, Dorning would have to lose at least the following amounts.

	£
Immediate write off on loan	20,000
Loss of interest for one year (£80,000 × 12%)	9,600
	29,600

If Scheme B were undertaken, then the loss per annum in interest would be:

£260,000 × 12% = £31,200

The first problem with both of Schemes A and B is that there is a risk that, if trading does not improve at Wigan Ltd, then Dorning could lose more than the £40,000 envisaged in a liquidation. At least with Scheme A the maximum loss is the £100,000 invested (plus any interest) although the period of uncertainty is a year, rather than six months with Scheme B. In Scheme B the Dorning plc would be committed to Wigan as a new subsidiary, with a 72% equity investment.

As a subsidiary, it is assumed that Wigan would have to produce a return which at least compensated Dorning for the loss of interest, not only on the amount invested in equity, but also on the possible future loan of £150,000 (a further £150,000 × 12% = £18,000). Presumably, Dorning would have to be convinced that Wigan could return to an acceptable level of profitability in the near future to undertake such an investment.

(ii) *The bank*
As with Dorning plc, the bank must consider that it is certain to receive £54,000, and therefore lose £36,000, if liquidation took place immediately.

In Scheme A, the bank would make the following losses.

	£
Immediate write off	18,000
Loss in interest (£72,000 × 16%)	11,520
	29,520

This is less than the £36,000 write off on liquidation, but it is gambling that trading at Wigan Ltd does not deteriorate further, even after the directors of the company have subscribed £200,000 for shares. This will increase the assets available for distribution to unsecured creditors by £50,000 (after paying the secured creditors). Again, this injected capital would have to remain intact, and indeed be increased by trading to produce enough money to refund unsecured creditors at the end of a year.

TEST PAPER: OCTOBER 1992 EXAMINATION SUGGESTED SOLUTIONS

Scheme B will involve the following losses for the bank.

	£
Immediate write off	27,000
Loss in interest (£63,000 × 16%)	10,080
	37,080

This is much closer to the figure which would be lost in a liquidation, but here Dorning plc is guaranteeing the debts of Wigan Ltd and so there is no risk of losing further amounts (the £150,000 promised by Dorning would cover the reduced claims of unsecured creditors - see the Scheme B balance sheet). The bank would therefore probably find Scheme B acceptable as long as Dorning's financial situation was acceptable.

3

> *Tutorial note.* Once you have laid out the cash flow forecast, the profit and loss account and balance sheet should be straightforward. As there is no 'investment' in the product (just an overdraft availability), the only 'reserve' in the balance sheet will be the profit.

(a) KNOWLES LIMITED: NEW PROJECT
CASH FLOW FORECAST
1 NOVEMBER 1992 TO 30 JUNE 1993

	Nov £	Dec £	Jan £	Feb £	March £	April £	May £	June £
Receipts								
Sales			188,000	188,000	188,000	188,000	188,000	188,000
VAT repayment						700		
Total receipts			188,000	188,000	188,000	188,700	188,000	188,000
Payments								
Rent	30,000							
Plant	211,500							
Purchases	56,400		75,200	75,200	75,200	75,200	75,200	75,200
Direct labour		50,000	50,000	50,000	50,000	50,000	50,000	50,000
Overheads		30,000	30,000	30,000	30,000	30,000	30,000	30,000
Total payments	297,900	80,000	155,200	155,200	155,200	155,200	155,200	155,200
Net inflow/(outflow)	(297,900)	(80,000)	32,800	32,800	32,800	35,000	32,800	32,800
Balance b/f	-	(297,900)	(377,900)	(345,100)	(312,300)	(279,500)	(246,000)	(213,200)
Balance c/f	(297,900)	(377,900)	(345,100)	(312,300)	(279,500)	(246,000)	(213,200)	(180,400)

TEST PAPER: OCTOBER 1992 EXAMINATION SUGGESTED SOLUTIONS

(b) KNOWLES LIMITED: NEW PROJECT
PROFIT AND LOSS ACCOUNT
FOR THE EIGHT MONTHS ENDING 30 JUNE 1993

	£	£
Sales (W1)		960,000
Cost of sales		
Opening stock	-	
Purchases (W2)	496,000	
Direct labour (£50,000 × 7)	350,000	
	846,000	
Closing stock (W3)	(162,000)	
		684,000
Gross profit		276,000
Expenses		
Rent (£30,000 × 8/12)	20,000	
Depreciation (W4)	20,000	
Overheads (£30,000 × 7)	210,000	
		250,000
		26,000
Corporation tax at 30%		7,800
Net profit		18,200

Workings

1 *Sales*

200 units × £800 × 6 months = £960,000

2 *Purchases*

	£
'Opening stock'	48,000
Purchases 200 units × £320 × 7 months	448,000
	496,000

3 *Closing stock*

	£
Raw materials	
150 units @ £320 per unit	48,000
Finished goods	
200 units @ £320 cost	64,000
200 units @ £250 labour	50,000
	162,000

4 *Depreciation*

Cost of plant = £180,000

Annual depreciation = $\frac{£180,000}{6}$ = £30,000

∴ 8 months' depreciation = £30,000 × 8/12 = £20,000

Note. It would not necessarily be wrong to charge only 7 months' depreciation as production only started in December.

TEST PAPER: OCTOBER 1992 EXAMINATION SUGGESTED SOLUTIONS

(c) KNOWLES LIMITED: NEW PROJECT
BALANCE SHEET AS AT 30 JUNE 1993

	£	£
Fixed assets		
Cost		180,000
Depreciation		20,000
		160,000
Current assets		
Stock	162,000	
Prepayment – rent ($\frac{4}{12} \times £30,000$)	10,000	
	172,000	
Current assets		
Bank	180,400	
Taxation	7,800	
VAT	50,400	
Trade creditors (£376 × 200)	75,200	
	313,800	
Net current liabilities		(141,800)
		18,200
Profit and loss account		18,200

(d) REPORT ON NEW PROJECT: KNOWLES LIMITED

This report discusses the profitability and cash flow of Knowles Ltd's intended new project: the introduction of a new product, the XZ. The report uses the forecast cash flow statement, profit and loss account and balance sheet attached (see (a) to (c)).

(i) *Profitability*

The project is expected to achieve a profit of £18,200 after tax in the first eight months. Assuming that no further capital expenditure is required for the first six years (the life of the plant) the *annual* profit after tax will be approximately as follows.

	£'000
Sales (200 × £800 × 12)	1,920
Cost of sales: materials (20 × £320 × 12)	768
labour (200 × £250 × 12)	600
Gross profit	552
Expenses	
Rent	30
Overheads (£30,000 × 12)	360
Depreciation	30
Net profit	132
Corporation tax at 30%	40
Retained profit	92

This figure compares favourably with Knowles Ltd's current profit after tax. The addition of the profit from the XZ would increase post tax profit by 22%. At the current level of dividend payments, however, the shareholders would probably expect nearly half the increase in profits to be paid out as a dividend.

TEST PAPER: OCTOBER 1992 EXAMINATION SUGGESTED SOLUTIONS

It should also be remembered that bank interest and charges have not been included in the calculation. The current state of Knowles Ltd's bank balance is not shown here, but were it necessary to provide an overdraft for anywhere approaching this level of borrowing, the interest charges are likely to be quite high. This could have a severe impact on the profitability of the project, as well as the cash flows.

It might be suggested to the directors of Knowles Ltd that they reduce the dividend payments for the next few years in order to finance the project. The reward for shareholders would be increased dividends in future years.

(ii) *Cash flow*

The initial investment in plant and payment for rent create quite a high negative cash flow at the beginning of this project. Even when sales are established, the 'overdrawn' balance is only being paid very slowly. The situation will be made worse in July 1993 when the VAT of £50,400 has to be paid to Customs & Excise. The same level of payment will be necessary throughout the project. The same applies to corporation tax payments. This means that the 'overdrawn' position will exist for approximately the first two years of the project (interest payments will also make the 'overdrawn' position worse).

It may be that this level of overdraft will not be required because of the company's current cash position, but the viability of the cash flows from the bank's point of view must be judged in the context of the company as a whole.

It may be feasible to offer a loan for the purchase of the required plant, at a lower rate of interest than the overdraft rate. A lease or hire purchase may be possible.

---

4 | *Tutorial note.* The SSAP 9 rules on stock valuation are clear and straightforward. The calculations in this question should give few problems.

(a) The rules on valuation of stock and work-in-progress are given in SSAP 9 *Stocks and long-term contracts*.

The first rule of stock valuation is that stocks should be stated at cost, or, if lower, at net realisable value. The comparison of cost and net realisable value (NRV) needs to be made in respect of each item separately. Hence, with raw materials A, B and C, the individual costs and NRVs of each line must be compared in isolation.

The method used to determine the cost of stocks should be chosen so that the fairest possible approximation to the expenditure incurred is obtained. Various methods for allocating cost of materials are available, including first in first out (FIFO), average cost, standard cost and last in first out (LIFO) and so on. SSAP 9 discourages the use of LIFO (and some other more unusual methods) as it tends to anticipate profits.

The definition of cost provided by SSAP 9 is 'that expenditure which has been incurred in the normal course of business is bringing the product or service to its present location and condition.' As such, the cost will not only include the purchase price of raw materials, but also 'costs of conversion', including direct labour and expenses, production overheads and any other overheads attributable in the particular circumstances of the business in bringing the product or service to its present location and condition.

TEST PAPER: OCTOBER 1992 EXAMINATION SUGGESTED SOLUTIONS

Work in progress should be valued on the same basis as raw materials and finished goods, to reflect the value of the resources used to bring it to whatever stage of completion it has reached.

(b) (i) *Raw materials* £

Value at the lower of cost and NRV on an individual basis
A	7,000
B	12,000
C	1,600
	20,000

(ii) *Product MN* Units

Opening stock	300
Purchases	2,000
Sales	(1,920)
	380

Valuation using FIFO
 380 units @ £13.50 = £5,130

Valuation using LIFO

	£
300 units at £10.00	3,000
80 units at £13.50	1,080
	4,080

FIFO is an acceptable method of calculating cost under SSAP 9 but LIFO is not. The figure used in the accounts would therefore be £5,130.

(iii) *Product YZ*

	Work in progress	Finished goods
Opening stock	-	-
Raw materials issued	250	
Produced	(200)	200
Sold		(180)
Finished goods stock		20
Work in progress	50	

Stock valuation

Finished goods £

Raw materials (£30,000 ÷ 250) × 20	2,400
Labour £10 × 6 × 20	1,200
Direct cost valuation	3,600
Production overheads absorbed (£49,000 ÷ 200) × 20	900
Production cost valuation	4,500
Other overheads	
$\dfrac{7,000 + £3,000}{200} \times 50$	1,000
Total cost valuation	5,500

TEST PAPER: OCTOBER 1992 EXAMINATION SUGGESTED SOLUTIONS

Work in progress

Raw materials (£30,000 ÷ 250) × 50	6,000
Labour £10 × 6 × 50 × 50%	1,500
	7,500
Production cost valuation (£9,000 ÷ 200) × 50 × 50%	1,125
Production cost valuation	8,625
Other overheads $\frac{£7,000 + £3,000}{200} \times 50 \times 50\%$	1,250
Total cost valuation	9,875

It would be unusual to absorb the administration and distribution costs into stock. SSAP 9 states that '"costs" of stock should comprise that expenditure which has been incurred in the normal course of business in bringing the product or service to its present location and condition'. This is normally taken to mean production overheads and perhaps carriage inwards and such costs involved in obtaining raw materials. However, other overheads could be allocated to the cost of stock if it could be shown that the costs directly affected the production function.

5 | *Tutorial note.* You should have no problems with the calculations in this question, as long as you can remember the basic relationship between contribution, fixed costs and profit.

(a) (i) *Breakeven point*

	Product A	Product B
	£	£
Sales per unit	30	50
Variable cost per unit	15	25
Contribution per unit	15	25

Breakeven point = $\frac{\text{fixed costs}}{\text{contribution per unit}}$

Product A = $\frac{£35,000}{£15}$ = 2,334 units

Product B = $\frac{£80,000}{£25}$ = 3,200 units

(ii) *On 20% of the initial investment*

Return required

Product A = (£50,000 + £25,000) × 20% = £15,000 pa

Product B = (£200,000 + £60,000) × 20% = £52,000 pa

TEST PAPER: OCTOBER 1992 EXAMINATION SUGGESTED SOLUTIONS

∴ Number of units required

$$\text{Product A} = \frac{£15{,}000 + £35{,}000}{£15} = 3{,}334 \text{ units}$$

$$\text{Product B} = \frac{£52{,}000 + £80{,}000}{£25} = 5{,}280 \text{ units}$$

(b) *Further calculations*

Profitability

Product A

	At 20% return £	At expected demand £	At break-even point £
Sales	100,020	135,000	70,020
Cost of sales	50,010	67,500	35,010
	50,010	67,500	35,010
Fixed costs	35,000	35,000	35,000
Depreciation (£25,000 ÷ 5)	5,000	5,000	5,000
Profit (loss)	10,010	27,500	(4,900)

Product B

	At 20% return £	At expected demand £	At break-even point £
Sales	264,000	500,000	160,000
Cost of sales	132,000	250,000	80,000
	132,000	250,000	80,000
Fixed costs	80,000	80,000	80,000
Depreciation (£60,000 ÷ 5)	12,000	12,000	12,000
Profit (loss)	40,000	158,000	(12,000)

The overall profitability of Product B is greater than that of Product A. At expected demand, Product A achieves a net profit percentage of 20% on sales compared to 32% for Product B. Product B, however, requires a greater level of resources than Product A, just because of the relative size of the projects. It may be necessary to look at the opportunity cost of using the initial investment capital elsewhere. In this context, any interest payable (or cost of capital) should be brought into the calculations.

Other factors to be considered include the effect of each product on market share and the expected variability of demand for each product.

In this context, it is useful to note that demand for Product B would have to fall 68% from the expected demand to reach the breakeven point, whereas a drop of 48% in demand for Product A would reach breakeven point. Product B is thus less exposed to variability in demand than Product A.

It might be worth carrying out market research to give more certainty to the expected demand figures, and discover how variable demand might be. The cost of the market research must be justified by comparing it with the likely loss, or return below the expected minimum, which might occur if demand was less than predicted.

TEST PAPER: OCTOBER 1992 EXAMINATION SUGGESTED SOLUTIONS

6
> *Tutorial note.* It is neater to show your ratio calculations in an appendix to the report, although this is not strictly necessary. Make sure that you note any limitations to your calculations.

REPORT ON DECLINE IN CASH BALANCE OF WALKER LIMITED

This report studies the results of Walker Ltd for the calendar years of 1990 and 1991 and makes use of the ratios and calculations in the Appendix attached. In general, the 1991 results show an expansion on 1990, with sales rising by 44.8%, although the rise in gross profit was only 20.9%. The discrepancy here shows the marked deterioration in gross profit between 1990 and 1991, from 36.2% to 30.3%.

This reduction in margins may have been deliberate: new products or new markets may give lower returns; prices may have been cut to increase market share. Alternatively, profit margins may have deteriorated due to a failure to control costs and working capital in a period of expansion.

It is possible that the expansion occurred through an acquisition at the beginning of 1991, as the information given states that purchases and sales occurred at an even rate throughout the year. In this case, failure to rationalise the new business, or integrate it into the existing structure, may be causing costs to rise. The capital cost of any such purchase would, of course, affect the cash balance of the business.

The rise in cost of sales (58.3%) is certainly greater than the rise in sales, even when the cost of increasing stock levels has been taken into account. The increase might be explained in a number of ways, some of which have been discussed above. Clearly an increase in costs, with the resulting decrease in profit margins, will have a direct impact on cash flow.

The working capital ratio has remained relatively consistent, although this disguises the changes in the actual figures. The rise in creditors and the existence of an overdraft rather than a bank balance have been offset by the rise in debtor's and stock. The quick ratio (or acid test ratio), which removes stock from the equation, would show the following.

$$1990 = \frac{394 + 72}{226 + 165} = 1.2$$

$$1991 = \frac{651}{341 + 201 + 56} = 1.1$$

These figures indicate that the overdraft has arisen in order to finance the larger increases in debtors and stock. It may be necessary to consider the reliability of these figures, by investigating the recoverability of debtors and stock.

With reference to the cash operating cycle, debtors give the greatest cause for concern as the average length of credit has risen considerably from 45.0 to 51.4 days. This indicates that the rise in debtors (65.2%) is not entirely due to increased sales (only up 44.8%). This contrasts with a small fall in days credit taken from suppliers, from 40.0 to 36.0 days. Again, by giving more credit to debtors, but taking less from suppliers, the company is adversely affecting cash flow.

TEST PAPER: OCTOBER 1992 EXAMINATION SUGGESTED SOLUTIONS

The stock turnover figures show a marked improvement in the relationship between cost of sales and stock held. However, although the stock levels in relation to the total cost of stock has fallen, the average cost of stock in relation to sales has risen, increasing the cost of sales, and decreasing the margin.

The company is still perfectly viable, and many of the working capital ratios show improvement. There are worrying aspects, however, which must be tackled if increased funding (via the overdraft) is to be arranged. The main areas for concern are control of costs and control of debtors.

APPENDIX

The following calculations have been used in this report.

1 *Gross profit percentage*

	1990	1991
$\dfrac{\text{Gross profit}}{\text{Sales}} \times 100\% =$	$\dfrac{1{,}141}{3{,}150}$	$\dfrac{1{,}380}{4{,}560}$
	= 36.2%	= 30.3%

2 *Working capital ratio*

$$\frac{\text{Current assets}}{\text{Current liabilities}} = \frac{394 + 530 + 72}{226 + 165} \qquad \frac{651 + 760}{341 + 201 + 56}$$

$$= 2.5:1 \qquad = 2.4:1$$

3 *Cash operating cycle*

(a) Stock turnover period = $\dfrac{\text{Average stock held}}{\text{Cost of sales}} \times 360$

1990 = $\dfrac{(530 + (530 - 23)) \div 2}{2{,}009} \times 360$ = 92.9 days

1991 = $\dfrac{(760 + 530) \div 2}{3{,}180} \times 360$ = 73.0 days

(b) Debtors' turnover period = $\dfrac{\text{Debtors}*}{\text{Sales}} \times 360$

1990 = $\dfrac{394}{3{,}150} \times 360$ = 45.0 days

1991 = $\dfrac{651}{4{,}560} \times 360$ = 51.4 days

(c) Creditors' turnover period = $\dfrac{\text{Trade creditors}*}{\text{Purchases}} \times 360$

1990 = $\dfrac{226}{2{,}032} \times 360$ = 40.0 days

TEST PAPER: OCTOBER 1992 EXAMINATION SUGGESTED SOLUTIONS

$$1991 = \frac{341}{3,410} \times 360 = 36.0 \text{ days}$$

* Average not available for 1990: therefore use year end figures for both years.

(d) *Cash operating cycle*

	1990 Days	1991 Days
Stock turnover period	92.9	73.0
Less creditors' turnover period	(40.0)	(36.0)
Add debtors' turnover period	45.0	51.4
Cash operating cycle	97.9	88.4

CIB - ACCOUNTANCY (1/93)

FURTHER READING

BPP publish a companion Study Text on Accountancy. The new edition will be published in February/March 1993 and is priced at £15.95.

You may also wish to test your grasp of the subject by tackling short questions in multiple choice format. BPP publish the Password series of books, each of which incorporates a large collection of multiple choice questions with solutions, comments and marking guides. The Password title relevant to Accountancy is *Basic Accounting* (for revision). This is priced at £6.95 and contains about 300 questions.

To order your Study Text and Password books, ring our credit card hotline on 081-740 6808. Alternatively, send this page to our Freepost address or fax it to us on 081-740 1184.

To: BPP Publishing Ltd, FREEPOST, London W12 8BR   Tel: 081-740 6808
   Fax: 081-740 1184

Forenames (Mr / Ms): _____

Surname: _____

Address: _____

_____

Post code: _____

Please send me the following books:	Quantity	Price	Total
CIB Accountancy Text		£15.95	
Password *Basic Accounting*		£6.95	

Please include postage:

Study text:
UK: £2.50 for first plus £1.00 for each extra book
Overseas: £6.00 for first plus £5.00 for each extra book
Password:
UK: £1.50 for first plus £0.50 for each extra book
Overseas: £3.00 for first plus £1.50 for each extra book

I enclose a cheque for £_____ or charge to Access/Visa

Card number [ ][ ][ ][ ][ ][ ][ ][ ][ ][ ][ ][ ][ ][ ][ ][ ]

Expiry date _____   Signature _____

> On the reverse of this page there is a Review Form, which you can send in to us (at the Freepost address above) with comments and suggestions on the Kit you have just finished. Your feedback really does make a difference: it helps us to make the next edition that bit better.

CIB - ACCOUNTANCY (1/93)

Name: _____

How have you used this Kit?

Home study (book only)	☐	With 'correspondence' package	☐
On a course: college _____	☐	Other _____	

How did you obtain this Kit?

From us by mail order	☐	From us by phone	☐
From a bookshop	☐	From your college	☐

Where did you hear about BPP Kits?

At bookshop	☐	Recommended by lecturer	☐
Recommended by friend	☐	Mailshot from BPP	☐
Advertisement in _____	☐	Other _____	

Have you used the companion Text for this subject?   Yes/No

Your comments and suggestions would be appreciated on the following areas.

Study notes and quiz

Content of solutions

Errors (please specify, and refer to a page number)

Presentation

Other